DeBord

Family Life Education

AN INTRODUCTION

Lane H. Powell
Texas Tech University

Dawn Cassidy
National Council on Family Relations

MAYFIELD PUBLISHING COMPANY
Mountain View, California
London • Toronto

Library of Congress Cataloging-in-Publication Data

Powell, Lane H.
    Family life education : an introduction / Lane H. Powell, Dawn Cassidy.
        p. cm.
    Includes bibliographical references and index.
    ISBN 0-7674-0570-6
    1. Family life education—United States. 2. Family life education—Canada. I. Cassidy, Dawn. II. Title.

    HQ10.5.U6 P69 2000
    306.85′071′173—dc21

                                                                            00-038687

Manufactured in the United States of America
10   9   8   7   6   5   4   3   2   1

Mayfield Publishing Company
1280 Villa Street
Mountain View, California 94041

Sponsoring editor, Franklin C. Graham; production, Penmarin Books; manuscript editor, Elaine Kehoe; design manager, Susan Breitbard; text and cover designer, Joan Greenfield; cover art, Hans Hofman, *Morning Mist* © Estate of Hans Hofmann/Licensed by VAGA, New York, NY (University of California, Berkeley, Art Museum; gift of the artist. Photographed by Benjamin Blackwell); print buyer, Danielle Javier. The text was set in 9.5/12 Stone Serif by Carlisle Communications and printed on 50# Finch Opaque by R. R. Donnelley and Sons Company.

Pages 152–153, with permission from Sara M. Rohar; page 191, from N. Carter, 1996, "See How We Grow." A Report on the Status of Parenting Education in the U.S. Philadelphia: The Pew Charitable Trusts. Used with permission; pages 214–215, with permission from Laura Pinsoneault; pages 217–218, reprinted with publisher's permission from the Family Support America vision statement, 2000.

CONTENTS

CHAPTER 6

Evaluation of Family Programs   *112*

CHAPTER 10

Parenting Education   185

PREFACE

This book is written primarily for undergraduate majors in human development and family studies. It can also be useful to persons in related fields of study who have had little exposure to education principles and practices, particularly in a nontraditional teaching format with adolescent or adult learners. Because these students are preparing for careers that will necessitate the preparation, presentation, and evaluation of educational programs and workshops, it is imperative that they have a working knowledge of how to accomplish these tasks effectively. The text is a realistic blend of theory and praxis (action with reflection) designed to encourage the type of hands-on experience students need in order to interact comfortably with diverse groups and a variety of topics.

Our goal in writing this text was to present family life education (FLE) as a profession with a history and an exciting future. Persons seeking certification as family life educators through the certification program of the National Council on Family Relations are required to have a course that addresses family life education issues. A textbook for such a course has been hard, if not impossible, to find, and this fact was a major motivator in our decision to write this book. We hope your students will find it to be readable, interesting, and helpful in their future careers. Although FLE is applicable worldwide, we chose not to expand our focus beyond the United States and Canada. However, cultural diversity within the United States is addressed throughout the book at points at which it interacts with program designs and effectiveness. We trust that as an instructor you will teach and model respect and appreciation for diverse points of view, stages in life, and cultural norms.

Major foci of the book include the application of theory and program models to program designs and teaching effectiveness. Students will have the opportunity to evaluate their competencies and comfort in areas of professional development, group leadership, evaluation, and program design. Each chapter includes a series of questions for class discussion, as well as research problems and activities for independent or auxiliary study and a case-study suggestion. The case studies are indicative of a problem-based learning focus, which many educational specialists are now recommending as preferable to a lecture course based on a body of content. Certainly it is preferable for a class that emphasizes praxis. When students are challenged to figure things out for themselves, they tend to retain information and strengthen their personal skills.

In Part III we address the three areas that are most highly developed in the field of FLE and that have received some evaluation and certification attention: sexuality education, marriage education, and parent education. The final chapter suggests ways to adapt these programs (and others) to religious, work, and school settings and considers future trends.

We wish to express our deep appreciation to several persons who have contributed to the success of this endeavor: Genie and Preston Dyer of Baylor University for their assistance on the marriage education chapter; Christa Treichel of Cooperative Ventures for her input on the evaluation chapter; our sponsoring editor, Franklin Graham; and of course our patient and encouraging spouses, Bob Powell and Tom Cassidy. We are also indebted to Margaret Arcus, Jay D. Schvaneveldt, and Joel Moss, editors of a seminal book in our field, the *Handbook of Family Life Education*, volumes 1 and 2. Their foundational work provided a starting point for our efforts, and we are eternally grateful.

PART I

The Field of Family Life Education

CHAPTER 1

Why and What Is Family Life Education?

IN A CITY ANYWHERE IN AMERICA. . . . The Liberty High School young mothers' class, composed of ten very pregnant teenagers, watch their teacher bathe and change a real baby. Giggles about the little boy's anatomy and questions underscore their nervousness and fear about their impending role as young mothers. In the next period they will be discussing infant development both before and after birth. In the afternoons, they work in the nursery with the young children of other teen mothers, under the close attention of the nursery director or lab teacher, who models, instructs, and guides their participation.

Down the street, a grandparents' support group is meeting at the New Hope Community Church. A nursery is provided, because some of these elders are raising a second generation of children: a task that has its own unique set of stressors. Others are there because of the recent loss of a spouse—or a child or grandchild—or just as a way to deal with loneliness. The sharing often centers around ways of coping with the life crises for which they have no prior experience. Their leader, a grandmother herself, is a family resource coordinator at a church association office in the area. She hopes to develop and train support group leaders for many neighborhoods around the city. Every week she meets with the group. Although she brings some handouts and suggestions of available resources, she is also learning from her group. She opens the floor for sharing, then listens with a practiced ear, responding to every person's concerns and opinions with empathy and appreciation. She takes mental notes and transfers them to paper after the meetings. This will be helpful in training other group leaders and perhaps in writing a manual or a book that would help others to cope.

Not far away, another group meets for study and support, sponsored by the family case managers of Family and Child Services. These are foster parent applicants who responded to a plea for more temporary placement homes for children and teens. They are meeting with the case manager–group leader for the first time. Their faces register their anxiety: What if the child doesn't warm up to us? How do you keep them from running away? What if a teen turns violent?

The group leader has anticipated their questions. He has brought some seasoned foster parents to share their own experiences. "It's not an easy job," they all seem to say, "but the agency will help you, and it's amazing what persistent caring can accomplish." The group leader has planned a six-session orientation for the potential new caregivers. He outlines the plan tonight. The anxiety visibly lessens. He knows that the couples will form a support group of their own by the time the six sessions end. This process will involve some minilectures, but the bulk of the time will involve doing exercises, sharing case studies, and role playing. They will enter the process with low-level sharing and involvement and gradually increase the interaction level. It will keep them busy, awake, and growing in confidence.

Family . . . life . . . education . . . three words that encompass a multitude of images and expectations. The situations described previously list only a few. All call for a combination of skills and expectations of the leader-educator and of the group. How do we define family life education in a way that encompasses its multifaceted contexts? How do we even define "family"? And what value does family life education have in supporting and educating individuals for family living? How do you, as a professional or future professional who will be working with families, develop the skills to respond effectively to so many demands?

This book was written to address the many issues involved in the educational preparation of family life educators, using an approach that promotes the interactive teaching style that is typical of the family life education model. Chapter 1 provides an overview of the definitions, history, and future directions of family life education, setting the context and developing an understanding and appreciation for the profession. Chapter 2 continues the discussion of the family life educator as a professional: what it means and how one gains certification and recognition. Chapters 3 through 6 address the practice of family life education, from theory models and types of methodology to assessing the needs of the audience, understanding group dynamics, and the actual design, implementation, and evaluation of programs. Chapters 7 through 10 become more specific and address three areas of family life education that are the most developed and the most often presented within the profession: sexuality education, premarital and marriage education, and parent education. Chapter 11 discusses how to adapt programs for the workplace, religious settings, and schools. This is truly designed to be a practitioner's handbook. So when you get that call: "Will you help us start a group for . . . ?", you'll be ready!

THE DEFINITION DEBATE

The problem of coming to general agreement on a definition of family life education is fully examined in the *Handbook of Family Life Education,* volume 1 (Arcus, Schvaneveldt & Moss, 1993). Lee (1963) and Kerckhoff (1964) observed that because family life educators differed on what they meant by family life education, there was general confusion and a retarding of growth in the field. Prominent family specialists in the 1970s and 1980s (e.g., Arcus, 1986; Darling, 1987; Fisher & Kerckhoff, 1981; Somerville, 1971) agreed. Yet a definition that is broad enough to gain consensus is also criticized as "too vague, ambiguous, and idealistic" (Arcus et al., 1993, p. 2). For example, in 1964, 90 family specialists representing public education and community and national agencies were asked to comment on the following definition by Avery and Lee (1964):

> Family life education involves any and all school experiences deliberately and consciously used by teachers in helping to develop the personalities of students to their fullest capacities as present and future family members—those capacities which equip the individual to solve most constructively the problems unique to his family role. (p. 27)

Although response to the definition was largely positive—some 75% of the specialists accepted this as a working definition—the reader may have some immediate questions: Is the definition too broad and too vague? Is it too limited in its assumption about families or where family life education takes place? Is it too complex? Arcus et al. (1993) concluded that "In spite of the general agreement among these early family life educators on a working definition, little real consensus was apparently achieved, as family life educators continued their efforts to refine and redefine the term" (p. 4). Box 1.1 summarizes the attempts at further definition.

More success at consensus has been achieved by moving beyond a concise definition to a descriptive discussion of the aims and concepts (i.e., "analytical inquiry") that comprise family life education. Arcus et al. (1993) reduced the aims, or rationale, for family life education to three primary ones: (1) dealing with problems that impinge upon families, (2) preventing problems, and (3) developing potentials for individuals and families. In other words, family life education is a process designed to "strengthen and enrich individual and family well-being" (p. 12). Such a process can incorporate a broad range of topics, from child development and parenting skills to adjusting to divorce or retirement or learning communication and time, money, or conflict management skills.

To develop an "operational definition" of family life education, Thomas and Arcus (1992) posed the question, What features must something have in order to be called family life education? After extensive review of the literature and of program designs, Arcus et al. (1993) concluded that family life education generally:

- Is relevant to individuals and families across the life span
- Is based on the needs of individuals and families
- Is multidisciplinary in area of study and multiprofessional in its practice
- Is offered in many different settings

BOX 1.1	Date	Definition and Author
Emerging Definitions of Family Life Education, 1962–1989	1962, 1963, and 1964	"Family life education involves any and all school experiences deliberately and consciously used by teachers in helping to develop the personalities of students to their fullest capacities as present and future family members—those capacities which equip the individual to solve most constructively the problems unique to his family role" (Avery, 1962, p. 28; Avery & Lee, 1964, p. 27; Lee, 1963, p. 106).
	1964	"Family life education included facts, attitudes, and skills related to dating, marriage, and parenthood....Throughout the concept of family life education is woven the idea of relationships—parent-child, husband-wife, boy-girl, and so on" (Kerckhoff, 1964, p. 883).
	1967	"Family life education is the study of the behavior of people as family members ... to broaden the student's understanding of the alternatives from which he can choose in his functioning as a family member in a changing society which brings new responsibilities and opportunities in spousal, parental, filial, sibling, and grandparental roles" (Somerville, 1967, p. 375).
	1968	"It is a program of learning experiences planned and guided to develop the potentials of individuals in their present and future roles as family members. Its central concept is that of relationships through which personality develops, about which individuals make decisions, to which they are committed, and in which they gain convictions of self worth" (Smith, 1968, p. 55).
	1968	"To help individuals and families learn what is known about human growth, development, and behavior throughout the life cycle is the main purpose of family life education. Learning experiences are provided to develop the potentials of individuals in their present and future family roles. The central concept is that of relationships through which personality develops, about which individuals make decisions, to which they are committed, and in which they develop self-esteem" (National Commission on Family Life Education, 1968, p. 211).
	1969	"Family life education ... deals with people in groups primarily on a cognitive and information exchange level, around issues and problems of family life ... [and] the cognitive components of behavioral and emotional functioning. Its techniques involve discussions and didactic teaching around ideas, values, and behavioral patterns of the family as a social system and the consequences of these on individual functioning, as well as more behavioristic material concerning interpersonal functioning within the family unit" (Stern, 1969, p. 40).
	1971	"...any activity by any group aimed at imparting information concerning family relationships and providing the opportunity for people to approach their present and future family relationships with greater understanding" (The Vanier Institute of the Family, 1971, p. i).

Date	Definition and Author
1973	"Programs of family-life education that will help individuals to prove [*sic*] their understanding of and capacity for forming and maintaining effective human interrelationships … [it] has come to center about the many interactions between individuals and within the family, and the characteristics in individuals that influence the quality of interpersonal relationships" (Kirkendall, 1973, p. 696).
1973	"… human education in the broadest sense, the essence being human relations … concerned with one's total being: physical, mental, and emotional" (Whatley, 1973, p. 193).
1974	"Family life education is the study of individual roles and interpersonal relationships, family patterns and alternative life styles, emotional needs of individuals at all ages, and the physiological, psychological and sociological aspects of sexuality" (Herold, Kopf, & deCarlo, 1974, p. 365).
1975	"… an educational program geared to enrich family life and help the individual better understand himself in relation to others" (Levin, 1975, p. 344).
1976	"Family life education promotes the development, coordination and integration of family development resources to individual family units in order to improve family life" (Cromwell & Thomas, 1976, p. 15).
1984	"… instruction to develop an understanding of physical, mental, emotional, social, economic, and psychological aspects of interpersonal relationships … between persons of varying ages" (Sheek, 1984, p. 1).
1985	"Family life education … builds on the strengths of individuals to extend their knowledge of personality development, interpersonal relations, and the influence of environmental factors on behaviors" (Barozzi & Engel, 1985, p. 6).
1985	"… as the professional process by which information is offered to individuals of all ages, about various life issues, through the use of the small group setting" (Gross, 1985, p. 6).
1987	"… concerned with preserving and improving the quality of human life by the study of individuals and families as they interact with the resources in their multi-faceted environments" (Darling, 1987, p. 818).
1989	"Family life education … is devoted to enabling adults to increase the effectiveness of their skills in daily living, that is, in relating to others, in coping with life events, and in realizing personal potential" (Tennant, 1989, p. 127).

- Is an educational rather than a therapeutic approach
- Presents and respects differing family values
- Requires qualified educators who are cognizant of the goals of family life education

Although all of these principles have not been fully analyzed or examined from a theoretical perspective, they do provide a foundation for the family life education discipline that supports the framework for life span family life education that was developed by the National Council on Family Relations in 1984 and revised in 1997. The framework looks at three major dimensions of family life education: age (broadly defined as childhood, adolescence, adulthood, and later adulthood) topic area (families in society, internal dynamics of families, human growth and development, human sexuality, interpersonal relationships, family resource management, parent education, family law and public policy, and ethics), and content (areas of individual and family development to be addressed through education). For example, within the "childhood" age category, the topic area of human sexuality includes content that addresses physical and sexual development, body privacy and protection against sexual abuse, uniqueness of each person, similarities and differences in individual sexual development, aspects of human reproduction (prenatal development, birth, puberty), children's perceptions about sexuality, and social and environmental conditions affecting sexuality. It is easy to see how personal values could also affect content and receptivity to family life education. Certainly the field is not without its points of controversy! Appendix A presents the whole framework by age category. The National Council on Family Relations has developed the framework in tabular poster form and has transparencies for use in the classroom. Also illustrated in the framework poster is the inclusive perspective of the educator, which should be multicultural, gender fair, and aware of special needs. This further underscores the need for educators to be carefully chosen, well trained, and informed about the history and future directions of family life education.

THE HISTORY OF FAMILY LIFE EDUCATION

The task of passing on education in family living to the next generation has been part of the human experience since life began. But how and by whom it is done have varied among family groups, tribes, and cultures. It has also changed drastically over time and is still evolving. But at the beginning of the twenty-first century, one thing is agreed upon by all: The family—in all its different forms and circumstances—needs support and education. This also is not such a new idea.

Early Concerns

As early as the fourth century B.C., the Greek philosopher Aristotle listed among his educational purposes "the education of parents for raising their children" (Dickinson, 1950, p. 5). The famous educator Horace Mann (1796–1859) echoed that observation, calling for "such education as qualifies for the fulfillment of parental duties" (Dickinson, 1950, p. 5). Philosopher Herbert Spencer (1820–1903) listed among his five types of activities that constitute human life those activities involved in the rearing and discipline of children. Spencer urged educators to include courses in public school curricula that would "develop efficiency" in these activities. Yet he observed that formal education was largely ignoring this universal task (Dickinson, 1950). Why was this so?

It is easy to understand how formal education for family living was bypassed in the early years of U.S. history. Pioneer life was hard, and children's lives were often short and tragic. At a survival level, the tasks needed for daily living have always taken precedence over the finer subtleties of excellence in parenting and family life. Youcha (1995) reports that during the seventeenth century, 1 child in 10 died before his or her first birthday. Today, the infant mortality ratio is less than 1 in 100 overall (although it is still drastically higher among disadvantaged groups and developing nations). Recollections from early settlers and Native Americans illustrate the fragility and harsh demands of family life, as well as the enmity that existed between groups who saw their ways of life threatened by one another. The Reverend John Williams (1707) described an Indian attack on a settlement in Deerfield, Massachusetts:

> On the twenty-ninth of February, 1703, not long before the break of day, the enemy came in like a flood upon us. . . . They came to my house in the beginning of the onset, and by their violent endeavors to break open door and windows, with axes and hatchets, awaked me out of sleep. . . . I cannot relate the distressing care I had for my dear wife, who had lain-in but a few weeks before, and for my poor children, family, and Christian neighbors. . . . Some (of the attackers) were so cruel and barbarous as to take and carry to the door two of my children and murder them, as also a Negro woman. (p. 9)

During the forced march of the captive settlers, some persons who could not keep up were killed by the attackers, including Williams's wife. Yet apparently many settlers were spared and eventually returned to their homes.

Life among Indian tribes and settlers on the western frontier also left little time to ponder parenting and life management skills. Pretty Shield, a Crow Indian, recalled the expectations of the women in her tribe during the late 1800s:

> We women had our children to care for, meat to cook and to dry, robes to dress, skins to tan, clothes, lodges and moccasins to make. Besides these things we not only pitched the lodges, but took them down and packed the horses and the travois when we moved camp, yes, and we gathered the wood for our fires too. We

were busy, especially when we were going to move. (Pretty Shield, oral account, 1932, as cited in Bartley & Loxton, 1991, p. 7)

The pioneer settler also had her hands full. Mathilda Wagner, Texas pioneer, recounted a typical day:

> This was a little of my day: When you first get up in the morning, before daybreak, you start your fire . . . and put your coffee on. Then, just as it is getting light over the hills, you go after the calves. When you bring back the calves, you milk the cows; then bring the calves to their mother cows. Leaving them for a while, you fix breakfast, which is a big meal. After breakfast, at a time when people are getting up in the cities nowadays, you skim the milk and make the butter, feed the dogs, cats and the hogs . . . and turn the calves in their pasture and the cows in theirs. When the butter is made and the dishes washed, the house spic and span, you go to help in the fields. The woman leaves the little baby at the edge of the field with a quilt put above it so the sun won't harm it. When the baby cries the woman leaves the hoe or the plow and goes to tend it or nurse it. Then she goes back to the plow or her work in the field. There was usually a little baby or several small children at a time. When the sun is in the middle of the sky it is time for dinner. The woman leaves for the house and prepares the food. After eating, the men might lay down for a little while to rest, but there is no rest for the women. There is always work to be done. In the afternoon there may be more work in the fields, or baking, candle making, soap-making, sewing, mending, any of the hundred pressing tasks, and then the calves must again be rounded up and brought home, as the shadows fall the cows milked, the chickens fed, always something, early and late. (As cited in Bartley & Loxton, 1991, p. 24)

Large families were the norm in the days when working the farm called for many hands and before birth control devices were available and legal. Rebecca Felton (1919) recalled life for her grandmother in rural Georgia:

> When my grandmother's brood of eleven circled around the big open fireplace in the evening, knitting work in hand, she understood without doubt, that she must rise early and work late, start before daylight and endure until after dark to put clothes on them and keep them with changes and well-fed for their health's sake. (p. 41)

The inhumane conditions endured by slave families of the eighteenth and nineteenth centuries are recorded in detail by Youcha (1995). Although conditions varied widely for slave families, depending on the size of the plantation and the temperament of the owners, parenting was always an exhausting extra task for the mother who spent all her daylight hours working in the fields. One mother recalled:

> My master would make me leave my child before day to go to the canefield; and he would not allow me to come back till ten o'clock in the morning to nurse my child. When I did go I could hear my poor child crying long before I got to it. And

la, me! My poor child would be so hungry! Sometimes I would have to walk more than a mile to get my child, and when I did get there I would be so tired I'd fall asleep while my baby was sucking. (Sterling, 1984, as cited in Youcha, 1995, p. 52)

Children past infancy were usually cared for in large groups, "watched over" by elderly slaves and older children who were not big enough to use a hoe or pick crops. Some spent their entire young lives in this communal living setting, rarely seeing their parents. While no account is typical, Jennie Webb's story of her childhood has elements that appear again and again:

"De fus things I recollect is living in a slave cabin back of o'marse's big house along wid forty or fifty other slaves. All my childhood life I can never remember seeing my pa or ma gwine to wuk or coming in from wuk in de day light as dey went to de fiel's fo'day an' wuked 'till after dark." Jennie was born someplace between the fields and the cabin as her mother returned from a regular workday. When she was old enough to help, Jennie looked after the younger children, keeping them quiet and getting them to go to sleep. She also helped feed them from the large wooden bowls that held all the food. She and the other bigger children scooped the food out with their hands. The bowls were never washed, and "after we got through eatin' in 'em de flys swarmed over 'em and de dogs licked 'um an' day sho' did smell bad." Finally, the big children virtually stopped eating and "we began to git skinny." One day the master stopped by, saw Jennie hand-feeding a toddler, and asked why she wasn't eating herself. She told him. He scolded the cook (who was Jennie's aunt) with "Adeline, how do you think I can raise de little niggers an' you feedin 'em lak dis?" And after that "we wuz fed right." (Rawick, 1972, as cited in Youcha, 1995, p. 51)

Needless to say, many women and babies died under such harsh conditions. Such intolerable conditions were made somewhat bearable because of a strong *fictive kin* support network of other slave families on larger plantations. This was especially important because many fathers were sold and permanently separated from their families.

Family Education in Nineteenth-Century America

Not all white families of the nineteenth century were wealthy slave owners with servants to help in the house and with the children. Actually, only a very few were. Many more families lived backbreaking existences of demanding work and poverty. It was concern for the physical and mental health of the many women who were not able to bear up under the demands of large families and unending tasks that caused Miss Catherine Beecher to write *A Treatise on Domestic Economy* in 1842. In the preface to the third edition (1858), she states her concern:

The number of young women whose health is crushed, ere the first few years of married life are past, would seem incredible to one who has not investigated this subject, and it would be vain to attempt to depict the sorrow, discouragement, and distress experienced in most families where the wife and mother is a perpetual invalid. (p. 5)

The nineteenth century also saw a wave of immigrants arriving in the "promised land," who supplied factories with cheap labor. Youcha (1995) described the life of women living in tenements in the cities:

> Women in the tenements who tried to maintain any semblance of order and cleanliness often had to cart water five flights up. Privies were in the backyards. There was no "outside" as there had been in the small European villages from which most of them had come. Here, all life—birth, eating, sleeping, dying—took place in three rooms into which were crammed families and boarders and relatives. The only "outside" was the street, or the air space between buildings over which laboriously hand-washed clothes could be hung on lines like flags of defiance against the dehumanizing conditions. (p. 122)

While the poor struggled with basic survival for their families, middle- and upper-class families lived an existence in stark contrast. The new and popular ladies' magazines pictured the ideal home as a refuge for the family. Here the tired husband relaxed from the struggles of the wage-earning day and happy children played under the benevolent eye of a loving mother. Home was no longer the center of work for the whole family, as it had been in colonial days, and motherhood was considered the purpose of life for women. "Of course, some women were beginning to question their confinement to a golden cage and to stand up for women's rights. A small number entered the professions and were economically independent" (Youcha, 1995, p. 123).

Jane Addams (1860–1935) was such a young woman. Born to affluence, she struggled with physical and emotional distress until she discovered a valuable purpose for her life: bettering the lives of poor families by living among them and offering parent education and child-care services. Centered around what was to be known as the settlement house model, Addams's Hull House in Chicago, Illinois, developed a model of family intervention and education that was—and is—one of the most successful to be found:

> Addams envisioned the settlement as serving two purposes: It would help the poor "Germans and Bohemians and Italians and Poles and Russians and Greeks in Chicago, vainly trying to adjust their peasant habits to the life of a large city," while at the same time giving privileged young women a purpose and a place. (Youcha, 1995, p. 138)

As the women of Hull House cared for the children of desperate mothers who were widowed or abandoned by their husbands and had to work 10- to 12-hour days for pennies, they did parent education as well. Using the child as the "bridge" for education, they introduced new habits of hygiene and medical care, new foods and activities. The children then demonstrated to their parents the advisability of the education by their improved health and spirits. The parents asked for recipes and explanations of what the teachers did. The teachers asked for daily reports on each child's activities at home, including diet, bedtime, and bowel movements. This interchange called attention to the importance of such factors and routines in children's lives, and the parents made adjustments to carry them out. Weekly mothers' meetings that included instruction on making children's clothes and preparing American foods were also held. Often the meetings were the mothers' only social outlet in a life of burdened toil. They were eagerly attended. Addams noted, "Through this medicine, the faces of the mothers have been noticeably softened" (as cited in Youcha, p. 145).

Ironically, Addams's highly successful model of family life education, which included home visits, interactive learning, and individualized group learning goals, has been a victim of what Youcha (1995) calls "national amnesia." Addams's programs and her life have been "relegated to the historical dustbin in which this country stores its forgotten past" (p. 140).

Another issue that has been addressed, then ignored, then addressed again for more than 150 years is whether family life education is worthy or appropriate for academic study. Quoting a well-known educator of the day, George B. Emmerson, Catherine Beecher (1858) wrote in her nineteenth-century text:

> It may be objected that such things cannot be taught by books. Why not? Why may not the structure of the human body and the laws of health deduced there-from, be as well taught as the laws of natural philosophy? Why are not the application of these laws to the management of infants and young children as important . . . as the application of the rules of arithmetic to the extraction of the cube root? (p. 7)

In 1872, the Massachusetts legislature responded affirmatively to that question and became the first state to recognize and support family life education in a public school setting by passing a statute to legalize domestic science for educating young women (Quigley, 1974). Other states soon followed suit, and between 1875 and 1890, domestic science and industrial education courses in public schools proliferated nationwide. In 1884, the first college program to meld subject matter and teaching methodology was offered at Columbia University. By 1895, 16 colleges were offering courses in home economics (East, 1980). Their subject matter and focus varied widely, but recognition of the importance of training for family living skills was certainly increasing. Male as well as female scholars promoted the concern for home and family education as the home economics movement gained credibility. When the New York Board of Regents decided to include household science on college entrance exams, Ellen Richards was invited to construct the questions (Quigley, 1974). Richards, who held degrees in chemistry from Vassar and the Massachusetts Institute of Technology, was interested in household management and the quality of family life

(Quigley, 1974). In 1898, Richards was invited to speak at a conference in Lake Placid, New York, on the topic of applying scientific principles to management of the home.

Nine annual conferences at Lake Placid were instrumental in making the last years of the nineteenth century a time of clarification on expanded views of education for family, home, and household management orientations. "Home economics" was given formal recognition as the title of education for home and family life in the public school system (McConnell, 1970).

The Rise of Professional Organizations

Another outgrowth of the conferences was the official formation of the American Home Economics Association (AHEA) on January 1, 1909, with 830 charter members: 765 women and 65 men. Its stated purpose was "the improvement of life conditions in the home, the institutional household, and the community" (Baldwin, 1949, p. 2). The group started a journal publication the same year, with Benjamin Andrews of Columbia's Teachers College as editor (Parker, 1980). The first White House Conference on Child Welfare was also held in 1909 and resulted in a 1914 publication on infant care for parents (Bridgeman, 1930).

The two decades that followed (1910–1930) were a time of great support and study of the American family. In 1914, the Cooperative Extension Service was established at land-grant universities in each state. Included in their responsibilities was the charge to "aid in diffusing . . . useful and practical information in subjects relating to . . . home" (Rasmussen, 1989, p. 153). In the first year, it was reported that home economists visited 5,500 homes and trained 6,000 women to lead in educating others (Rasmussen, 1989).

Research on child development and family organization became a strong interest of sociologists and social psychologists. The first Child Welfare Research Center was established at the University of Iowa in 1917, and other centers, including the Merrill Palmer Institute, rapidly followed at several major universities (Frank, 1962). Parent education became a national interest during the 1920s. The National Congress of Parents and Teachers, organized during this decade, boasted more than 500 study groups comprising both fathers and mothers by 1929. All told, more than 75 major organizations were conducting parent education programs at this time. Many were supported with government grants, which then were seriously curtailed in the 1930s. The reason? The increasing instability of marriages made some professionals question if money spent on parent education was worth the effort when families appeared to be crumbling (Brim, 1959). A curious logic, but perhaps understandable in the years of a depressed economy and the resulting stress on families. Ernest Burgess, who developed the first documented course on the family at the University of Chicago in 1917, described the crisis in contemporary families in a 1926 journal article:

In a stable, homogeneous society, ideas of family life and the roles of its different members are relatively fixed and constant. In a changing society composed of heterogeneous elements, familiar attitudes are almost inevitably in a state of flux. Instead of a common pattern of family life entrenched in tradition and crushing out all impulse to variation by the sheer weight of universal conformity, our American society presents what at first sight seems to be a chaotic conglomeration of every conceivable pattern of family organization and disorganization, from the patriarchal kinship groups of our Southern Mountain highlands to the free unions of our Greenwich Villages. Hardly a day passes but the public is shocked and outraged by some new form of wild and reckless behavior, particularly of youth in revolt no longer regulated by customary controls. (p. 5)

Burgess was not a pessimist, however, and he challenged the gloomy prediction that the family was disintegrating into chaotic ruin:

But these random and aimless variations away from the basic pattern of family life are not, as some believe, an indication of the future of family life and sexual relationships. They are only the symptoms in the present, as in similar times in the past, that society is undergoing change. When an equilibrium is re-established a new pattern of family life will emerge, better adapted to the new situation, but only a different variety of the old familiar pattern of personal relationships in the family. (p. 6)

One professional response to the growing family crisis brought together representatives from the American Home Economics Association, the American Social Hygiene Association, the Teachers College of Columbia, and other professionals from fields of sociology and psychology for the Conference on Education for Marriage and Family Social Relations in 1934. Their concern for collaboration among professionals who study the family resulted in the organization of the National Conference on Family Relations, renamed in 1938 the National Council on Family Relations (NCFR; Kerckhoff, 1964). A combined interest in theory, research, and practice has allowed NCFR to develop a membership base among academicians and practitioners in several disciplines related to family studies—primarily human development, marriage and family therapy, family sociology, and developmental psychology. NCFR has also spearheaded the development of standards and certification for family life educators. The Certified Family Life Educator (CFLE) approval process reviews a practitioner's academic preparation, work experience, and continuing education. Most recently, NCFR has established a program certification process that will allow graduates of approved academic programs to participate in an expedited review for provisional CFLE approval.

Canada has also seen great activity in the area of family life education in the last 40 years. In 1964, the first Canadian Conference on the Family brought together leaders in the family area (Gross, 1993). Out of the conference was born a permanent organization, the Vanier Institute of the Family, in order to "encourage research and study in family life as well as serve as a clearing house for information" (Gross, 1993, p. 10). The Vanier Institute also recognized the importance of high qualifications and standards for educators. In 1970, they issued a statement regarding qualifications of family life educators, emphasizing that more than academic training is needed. The "quality of mind and spirit" was seen as equally important. This concept was further defined as depth of perception, personal integrity, flexibility in teaching methods, sensitive awareness to the human condition, and commitment to growth, both intellectually and emotionally, as a person and a professional (Gross, 1993).

Despite getting a later start than the United States in developing the profession, Canada has moved rapidly to incorporate family studies in a number of Canadian colleges and universities and to develop a professional certification program. In 1993, the Canadian Certified Family Educator (CCFE) was established. The National Committee of Family Service of Canada is working to further consolidate family life educators in the country by publishing a newsletter, *Putting Families First,* particularly for the educator. Canadian family life educator Pauline Gross observes:

> Clearly the significance of Family Life Education and its role in prevention have gained acceptance and recognition. More and more families turn to our programs for help in addressing their current needs and interests, solving their problems, supporting their aspirations, and enriching the quality of their lives. (p. 15)

Increased Interest in Family Life Education

Ninety percent of all research and publication about family sociology and related issues has been written since 1940 (Mogey, as cited in Howard, 1981, pp. viii–ix). The first textbook for use in high school and college family living courses was written in 1945 by Evelyn Mills Duvall, executive secretary of NCFR, and Reuben Hill, a family sociologist at the University of Minnesota. Entitled *When You Marry,* the book had a very readable style, with many examples and cartoon illustrations. Because it was written at the end of World War II, it particularly addressed the problems of war brides' adjustment to couple living after the war (Duvall & Hill, 1945). The book was expanded in 1950 to respond to some 25,000 questions asked by student readers of the first text and was published as *Family Living* (Duvall, 1950).

> Because of home economics' ties to public education delivery systems, Duvall's book helped set the stage for home economics to replace sociology as the preponderant discipline in family life education. Home economics' position of dominance was enhanced nationally through the publication of specific materials related to family life education and enhanced internationally as home economists, supported by such government programs as the Marshall Plan, established family life education programs nationwide. (Lewis-Rowley, Brasher, Moss, Duncan, & Stiles, 1993, p. 39)

The American Home Economics Association has remained a strong force in public school education for family life skills. However, as family roles and responsibilities have changed drastically during the last half of the twentieth century, public concern and undergraduate student interest have shifted away from a generalist approach that taught traditional homemaking skills (clothing construction, food preparation), as well as family living (Schultz, 1994). In 1994, members of the national organization voted to change their name to the American Association of Family and Consumer Sciences (AAFCS) in order to more accurately reflect the new emphases. Many public schools, under state legislature mandates to add more "academic" course requirements for their graduates, have squeezed out vocational education programs, which often included the home economics curriculum. Many college and university home economics programs have also been phased out because of low enrollment of majors in the traditional home economics education area. At the same time, interest in the area of human development and family studies (HDFS) has expanded rapidly. Students see the HDFS major as a good foundation from which to launch careers in marriage and family counseling, family ministry, social work, and child life and early childhood education. All of these careers would carry an expectation of expertise in conducting family life education classes in a variety of community settings and for diverse audiences.

Resources and interest in parent education have also greatly increased in the past four decades, with a number of programs being developed that include leader training and a complete package of promotional and training materials. In the 1980s, some employee assistance programs and health maintenance organizations (HMOs) began to appreciate the value of education and preventive programs as appropriate billable therapeutic services. The number of clinically trained faculty in university departments that prepare family life educators has concurrently increased, and marriage and family enrichment programs with research and therapeutic foundations are emerging in clinics and community centers (Lewis-Rowley et al., 1993).

THE MANY FACES OF TODAY'S FAMILIES

Burgess's 1929 assessment of family trends toward diversity and change not only has continued to prove true but also has accelerated. Within the United States, racial and ethnic culture groups now represent a larger percentage of the total population than ever before. According to Census Bureau updates (U.S. Bureau of the Census, 1999), all 50 states are increasing in minority populations. Sixteen states recorded a rise of 25–50% between 1990 and 1998, and three showed an increase of more than 50%. Taylor (1994), referring to the work of Simpson and Yinger (1985), defines minority families as "those families that have historically experienced social, economic, and political subordination vis-à-vis families of the dominant majority, as a consequence of their race, ancestry, and/or other characteristics the latter holds in low esteem" (p. 1). In other words, from a sociological standpoint, *minority* and *majority* are not referring necessarily to the size of the population but rather to a status designation. In that sense women (who are actually the gender majority) are often seen as a minority group. Taylor (1994) also stresses the diversity within the major culture groups. Customs and cultural values can vary widely within the general cultural classification. The African American designation, for example, includes people of color from Haiti, Jamaica, Trinidad, and many countries in Latin America. African Americans are currently the largest minority group in the United States. In 1998, they numbered more than 34.4 million, or 12.7% of the total population (U.S. Bureau of the Census, 1999). This internal ethnic diversity is true of the Hispanic and Asian American minority groups as well. Hispanics include an amalgamation of persons from Spanish-speaking countries, including Mexican Americans, or Chicanos (the largest single group in the Hispanic category), but also Cubans, Puerto Ricans, and other persons from Central and South America, as well as Spain (Taylor, 1994). Hispanics are the fastest growing minority group, making up 11% of the population in 1998, a growth of nearly 20% in 8 years. By 2050, the Hispanic population is projected to become the largest minority group in the country, making up 25% of the population (*Kiplinger Washington Letter,* 1998). The Asian American category encompasses more than a dozen distinct subgroups and cultures (Taylor, 1994). Among the largest are Chinese, Japanese, Korean, Filipino, and Vietnamese. Together they compose some 3% of the resident population in the United States. By 2020, all minority groups combined will represent 36% of the total population.

Marital status, family composition, and economic conditions of families are also changing. Zimmerman (1995) gives a thorough review of trends, citing 1990 U.S. Census statistics. Although three fourths of all U.S. citizens currently live in family groups defined by the Census Bureau as "a group of two or more persons related by birth, marriage, or adoption, residing together in a household," the percentage of married-couple households continues to decline (from 82% in 1970 to 69% in 1990). Cohabitation of unmarried couples reached 3 million in 1990, an increase of 80% over the previous decade; however, it still does not represent a major change in family trends, as about half of all women who cohabit later marry (Zimmerman, 1995).

The percentage of divorced persons doubled during the same time period, but divorced persons still make up less than 11% of the total population. An all-time high divorce rate of 5.3 per 1,000 persons was reached in 1979, having doubled in only 9 years. The divorce rate has declined somewhat and has remained at about 4.7 per 1,000 since 1981 (Zimmerman, 1995). The number of divorced persons aged 50 to 54 expanded the most rapidly during this time: from 1.5 million in 1970 to over 6 million in 1990, accounting for one third of all divorced women and one fourth of all divorced men.

TABLE 1.1 Change in Single Adult Population
Primary racial group comparisons, 1970–1990

Racial Group	Percentage of Change
African American	up 66%
White	up 29%
Hispanic	down 8%

SOURCE: Zimmerman, 1995, p. 23.

SINGLE ADULTS   With the number of remarriages declining more than 44% between 1970 and 1988 and with males and females marrying much later than they did 4 decades ago (now around age 26.8 for males and 25 for females), the result is a burgeoning population of single adults. Unmarried males now compose about one fourth of the male population; unmarried females, about one fifth of the female population (Zimmerman, 1995). When this statistic is broken into primary racial group comparisons, a picture of even greater change in some families emerges (see Table 1.1).

SINGLE PARENTS   About one in every eight families in the United States is headed by a single parent, most of whom are women (Ahlburg & De Vita, 1992). Other major changes that have brought the family to the attention of researchers and government officials are the increasing number of births to unmarried women and the rising number of mothers of young children in the workplace. Between 1983 and 1993, births to unmarried women increased by 70% (Saluter, 1994). Birth rates to unmarried teens aged 18–19 reached an unprecedented high of 65.7 per 1,000 in 1991. Birth rates to unmarried teens aged 15–17 increased by more than 50% during the 1980s. Births to older unmarried women, aged 20–44, also rose rapidly during this time. Coupled with the rising number of divorces among families with children, these statistics show that the single mother (15–44) is a major constituent in the population of parents today (Zimmerman, 1995).

STEPFAMILIES   According to demographer Paul Glick, at least one of every three Americans is part of a stepfamily: either a stepparent, a stepchild, a stepsibling, or some other relation (Ahlburg & DeVita, 1992). The difficulty and complexity involved in blending two or more families is considered to be one of the reasons that there is such a high rate of divorce among remarrieds. Some 44% of White children and 66% of African American children in stepfamily households will also experience the breakup of the second marriage (Ahlburg & DeVita, 1992).

MOTHERS IN THE WORKFORCE   Married or single mothers with young children now make up 60% of the workforce, another significant change since the 1970s, when only 30% of married women and 52% of single women with children under six were in the workplace. At every level, women continue to earn less than men with equivalent schooling or experience, representing an average difference of $4,000 in earnings per year (Zimmerman, 1995). Because more than 95% of custodial parents are women, the discrepancy represents increasing stress and economic distress for many single mothers and their children.

OLDER AMERICANS   By the year 2030, the elderly population in the United States (those aged 65 or older) is expected to climb to 20% of the total population. By age 75, 60% of women are predicted to be living alone, many on a fixed income with declining buying power and increasing medical costs (Zimmerman, 1995). Older Americans are increasingly finding themselves raising a second generation of children. The U.S. Bureau of the Census (1999) reports that over 3½ million children under 18 are currently living in their grandparents' household.

ECONOMIC DISTRESS   The general economy experienced a significant upheaval during the last years of the twentieth century. Since 1990, median incomes for minority wage earners have increased significantly. Asians now report a higher median income ($45,250) than non-Hispanic White workers ($38,975), Hispanics ($26,630), or African Americans ($25,050) (*The Kiplinger Washington Letter,* 1998). Although an unprecedented economic boom has moved some segments of the population into higher income brackets and pushed the unemployment rate to an all-time low, wages and job security have declined for many others and brought added pressure to bear on families of all types. The Personal Responsibility and Work Opportunity Reconciliation Act of 1996 (PRWORA), commonly referred to as welfare reform, has nudged persons—many of them single mothers—into the workforce and phased out subsidies for cash assistance. Some new workers have received training and education that have positively influenced their self-esteem and their income level. But many more have moved into low-paying entry-level jobs with few benefits. A recent Associated Press release citing Department of Agriculture data estimates that 1 in 10 American households is unable to afford the food it needs (Briscoe, 2000). Unfortunately, a proposed raise in the minimum wage by $1 per hour will not significantly enhance the ability of many families to cover the basic costs of food, housing, child care, health care, and other necessary expenses. For example, a person working full-time at a minimum-wage job (currently $5.15 per hour) cannot provide enough income to lift a family of two or more above the poverty threshold, which now stands at $11,060 for a family of two and $16,700 for a family of four (HHS Poverty Guidelines, 1999). A raise of $1 per hour would bring minimum wage yearly earnings for a full-time job to $12,792, still significantly below the poverty threshold for a family of four. Homelessness is another fear that becomes reality for an estimated 2 million people a year in the United States as housing costs continue to rise and subsidized housing becomes more scarce (Franklin, 2000). Increasingly the homeless include families and women and children who may be escaping abusive situations.

FUTURE DIRECTIONS OF FAMILY LIFE EDUCATION

"We must think of families differently than scholars have in the past," note family scientists Wesley Burr, Randal Day, and Kathleen Bahr (1993). They propose a new terminology and way of perceiving "the family." Rather than the narrow definition of the traditional family that has been considered the normative standard, that is, "a cultural unit which contains a husband and wife who are the mother and father of their child or children" (Schneider, 1980, p. 33), Burr et al. suggest viewing the family as a sphere of one's life similar to the way one views the spiritual, occupational, or educational aspects of one's life. The *family realm* addresses aspects of the human experience that are uniquely tied to procreation and the generational connections that are created by birth or adoption of children and committed unions of adults. The family realm also includes the spatial and emotional relationships that persons develop with those they call "family," the ability to manage crises together and to show affection and loyalty, and the shared family traditions, rituals, values, and routines that form strong connections.

The scholars (Burr et al., 1993) also strongly caution against imposing one's own cultural and class standards on those we are teaching. An example is the assumption that higher income and social status are automatically "improvements" in family function and are sought after by all family groups:

> It is noteworthy that the educators and social workers [through the years] represented the middle and upper classes, while the families who needed to be taught "proper" principles of family economics tended to be poor or ethnic. Their poverty and their adherence to "foreign" or "primitive" values were evidence that they managed inefficiently. The possibility that they cherished values other than income maximization or economic advantage seems to have been entirely lost on the specialists grounded in the economic perspective who, over much of the twentieth century, devoted their professional lives to fostering family choices based on economic maximization. (p. 10)

The purposes and goals for engaging in family life education with diverse families need to be reevaluated in light of this growing understanding of the unique and varied ways that cultures and ethnic groups "do family." Moreover, the study of diverse families should include more attention to the unique strengths, and not just comparative deficits, of various culture groups. Identifying and affirming a culture's ways of coping and connecting can enhance the lives of "enlightened" middle- and upper-class families and educators. If members of a particular culture group are utilized as the primary resources for designing relevant family life education programs, program effectiveness and design will be strengthened.

In predicting future directions for the field, Lewis-Rowley et al. (1993) foresee four major trends:

1. Collaborative approaches to family life education will increase between generalists and specialists who value each other's contributions and realize that issues are too complex to be solved by one single organization or professional group.

2. More refinement of theory and research will strengthen understanding and practice of educational intervention and support. The research is expanding and becoming more discriminating as it is driven by the full force of computer-age technology. A challenge continues to be the communication of findings to practitioners, legislators, and the general public.

3. Intervention in private and public spheres will focus more on prevention and education, appreciating the involvement of the total family as part of the teaching/learning team.

4. Global information gathering and policy making will increase, as technology allows information to flow across oceans and continents and as cross-cultural studies and diversity in families is recognized and appreciated.

SUMMARY

David Mace was a strong champion of preventive education programs for couples and families for many years until his death in 1990. He often told the story of a little town planted deep in a valley at the end of a twisty and treacherous mountain road. The road was dark and narrow, with no caution signs or reflectors to mark the most dangerous curves. Over the years, many cars plunged over the cliff. Scores of people were seriously injured or killed. Finally, the town council decided to do something about the problem. After several weeks of study, the council issued a report. An ambulance would be purchased to park at the bottom of the cliff. Then, when a crash occurred, survivors could be rushed to the hospital, and hopefully a few lives would be saved. The illogical reasoning is obvious: Why wait to do something until after an accident occurs? Why not invest in caution signs and reflectors? Then many accidents would be prevented and it would cost so much less, in terms of money and human misery!

We continue to ask the same questions regarding the value of family life education. Why wait until children and families have suffered great emotional anguish when education could prevent many tragedies from occurring, greatly enhance the quality of family interaction, or both? Such solutions have always been an emphasis of visionary educators and social reformers. Unfortunately, society and the government are still more likely to respond to crisis than to preventive correction. In past centuries, family life education also lacked definition. That is changing. In the recent past (the last 50 years) more attention has been focused on collaboration, definition, academic research and theory, and leader training and certification. Family life education is moving to a new level of appreciation among behavioral scientists and program developers.

Furthermore, the crisis in families that Burgess and others observed in the 1930s has come to the forefront of attention in the 1990s. Skeletons long hidden in closets of abuse, exploitation, and violence have seen the light of celebrity confession and high media coverage. Divorce and single parenthood are no longer squelched by social stigma. The sexual revolution has "outed" us all. Courts are mandating anger control and parent education programs. Technology is taking us to new levels of involvement with one another, offering new opportunities for distance education and resources. Around the world, we are interacting with diverse cultures and discovering new ways of being family. And families, struggling to survive and to thrive, are more willing to ask for help. It is time to bring knowledge and families together, and it can best be done face-to-face with person-centered, trained professionals and effective programs. Chapter 2 addresses what it means to be a profession and a professional.

QUESTIONS/PROBLEMS FOR DISCUSSION AND REVIEW

Class Discussion

1. From the list of definitions in Box 1.1, choose the definition you think best describes the range of tasks and settings for family life education described by Thomas and Arcus (1992) and explain why you chose this particular one. In reviewing all the definitions, what do you see that has endured over time? What elements have expanded or contracted?

2. Do you agree with Herbert Spencer that public school curricula should include parenting courses? Why or why not? Spencer observes that formal education has largely ignored this aspect of education. Is this still the case? What do you think is the reason?

3. How do the demands and stresses of family life today differ from those in the past? Consider particularly the dual-career family; single-parent low-income family; immigrant family.

Research Problems

1. What makes prevention and education programs hard to document in terms of effectiveness? Find examples of research that document the effectiveness of prevention strategies.

2. What do you see as the value of prevention/education programs, in comparison to crisis intervention and remediation programs?

Case Study Design

Using the three examples at the beginning of this chapter and the three other examples in Chapter 11 as cases for study, complete the following tasks through the use of reasoning, research, and interview. (Over a period of several weeks, as you study the succeeding chapters, you will add to your "found" knowledge.)

1. After reading the example, what basic information do you have about
   a. The target population
   b. The training and task of the family life educator
2. What additional information would you need in order to design an effective family life education program?
3. What programs have been developed and assessed for this population? Find some examples.
4. Design a short-term and a long-term program for this population.
   a. How can you determine what the learning goals should be for each program?
   b. What format and teaching methodologies will you use?
5. Develop an assessment design to measure program effectiveness.

CHAPTER 2

The Developing Profession/Professional

THE DEVELOPING PROFESSION/PROFESSIONAL

Carl has a baccalaureate degree in art history. He has worked for the past 9 years as a youth coordinator for the YMCA and organizes activities and classes for neighborhood kids identified as high risk. He is a member of the National Association for the Education of Young Children and has served on their board of directors.

Gretchen has a degree in child development. She organizes a parent group in her neighborhood for other stay-at-home moms and dads with kids under 2 years old. The group meets regularly and discusses a predetermined topic each time. Members rotate responsibility for researching the topic and presenting information. Much of the meeting is spent in casual conversation and support.

Kathleen is the executive director of a neighborhood family resource center. She has a degree in human development and family studies and is a Certified Family Life Educator. Her responsibilities include overseeing the development and implementation of family activities, well baby classes, parent support groups, and a home visiting program. She has worked in the field of family life education for more than 12 years.

Which of these people would you consider to be professional family life educators? What makes someone a professional? What makes something a profession? Is family life education a profession?

Chapter 1 recounted the history of family life education and the gradual appreciation of its importance and role in strengthening society. With this evolution has come recognition of the importance of the individual's role in effective family life education programs and offerings—a recognition of the value of professionalism (see, e.g., Fohlin, 1971; National Commission on Family Life Education [NCFLE], 1968).

This chapter looks at issues of professionalism. How do we define a profession? What is involved in becoming a competent professional? What skills and knowledge are needed to provide quality family life education experiences and to develop effective materials? Are there certain personal characteristics or traits that make someone a more effective family life educator? What ethical practices are necessary underpinnings of the profession?

DEFINING THE PROFESSION

Let us begin by looking at the concept of professionalism. Numerous individuals and organizations have studied professionalism. Some identify certain attributes commonly acquired in the process of professionalization (Weigley, 1976), whereas others focus on the political and sociological aspects of identifying professions (Torstendahl & Burrage, 1990). One approach developed by East (1980) contends that the development of a profession involves eight criteria. According to East's framework, certain criteria must be in place in order for a field or occupation to be considered a profession. Application of these criteria to the field of family life education shows that many criteria have been met, with progress being made toward meeting others.

THE ACTIVITY BECOMES A FULL-TIME PAID OCCUPATION   Although the title "family life educator" is not always used specifically, family life education is practiced by professionals in various settings throughout the world, including junior and senior high schools; education extension programs; community education, health care, and religious settings; and higher education. Family life education is carried out under such titles as parent education, sex education, health education, marriage enrichment, youth advocacy, and so forth.

TRAINING SCHOOLS AND CURRICULA ARE ESTABLISHED   Universities and colleges have been offering family degree programs since the 1960s. However, recognition of the training requirements needed for family life education has come more recently. In 1984 the National Council on Family Relations established standards and criteria for the certification of family life educators, college/ university curriculum guidelines, and content guidelines for family life education, including a framework for planning programs over the life span (NCFR, 1984). In 1996, NCFR introduced the Academic Program Review and began to review university and college family degree programs for adherence to the standards and criteria needed for the Certified Family Life Educator program. Numerous programs have sought this "industry" approval, which recognizes a defined and accepted curriculum content for the field.

THOSE WHO ARE TRAINED ESTABLISH A PROFESSIONAL ASSOCIATION   A number of related professional organizations exist, including the American Association of Family and Consumer Sciences (formerly the American Home Economics Association, established in 1909), Family Service International (established in 1911), the NCFR (established in 1938), and Family Support America (formerly the Family Resource Coalition of America, established in 1980). NCFR is most widely recognized as the professional association for family life educators because of its sponsorship of the Certified Family Life Educator (CFLE) program. Related groups include the American Association of Sexuality Educators, Counselors, and Therapists (AASECT) and Educational Training Resources (ETR). The focus of these organizations is more specifically sexuality, however, which is only one aspect of family life education.

Development of a professional association recognizes a shared body of knowledge and common interests among a select group of professionals. Professional family associations offer membership at several levels of involvement and provide opportunities for continuing education and networking with others practicing in the family field.

A NAME, STANDARDS OF ADMISSION, A CORE BODY OF KNOWLEDGE, AND COMPETENCIES FOR PRACTICE ARE DEVELOPED   Through a series of task forces and committees beginning in 1968, the National Council on Family Relations developed its college and university curriculum guidelines (NCFR, 1984). Published in 1984, they provided content guidelines for university and college programs. The same committee developed standards and criteria for the certification of family life educators (NCFR, 1984), which provided minimum standards and criteria for professional practice. The first Certified Family Life Educators were approved in 1985.

The CFLE Standards and Criteria originally included nine family life substance areas considered to represent the core of family life education. They were families in society, internal dynamics of families, human growth and development, human sexuality, interpersonal relationships, family resource management, parent education and guidance, family law and public policy, and ethics (see Appendix B, this volume). Family life education methodology was added as a 10th substance area in 1991. Professionals seeking certification provide documentation of academic preparation, professional development, and work experience in each of these 10 areas as part of the application process. In 1996, the National Council on Family Relations began approving university and college family degree programs for adherence to the criteria needed for the Certified Family Life Educator designation. The NCFR academic program recognizes the preceding as a defined and accepted curriculum content for the field.

INTERNAL CONFLICT WITHIN THE GROUP AND EXTERNAL CONFLICT FROM OTHER PROFESSIONS WITH SIMILAR CONCERNS LEAD TO A UNIQUE ROLE DEFINITION   There is ongoing debate among many organizations regarding the nature of the field and the appropriate "home" for family life educators. The National Council on Family Relations has been active in defining and developing family life education curriculum and certification criteria since the early 1960s. The American Home Economics Association (AHEA) identified competencies and criteria for home economics in 1974 and established the Certified Home Economist (CHE) designation in 1987. In 1995, the American Home Economics Association changed its name to the American Association of Family and Consumer Sciences (AAFCS), reflecting increased emphasis on the family. Certified Home Economists are now called Certified Family and Consumer Scientists (CFCS). There are some similarities between the NCFR and AAFCS certification programs. Both require a minimum level of education and knowledge in the areas of human growth and development, family systems, and family resource management. However, the Certified Family Life Educator designation requires additional knowledge in more specialized topics, such as sexuality, parenting, family policy, and family law. The CFCS designation requires knowledge in food and nutrition, apparel and textiles, and design and technology in the environment (Ponzetti, 1995).

Numerous other organizations exist with interests relevant to family life education. For example, professionals involved directly in sex education might join AASECT or ETR, and parent educators might be members of the Center for the Improvement of Child Caring (CICC) or the National Parenting Educators Network (NPEN). Couples or educators active in couples and marriage education may wish to join the Association for Couples in Marriage Education (ACME) or the Coalition for Marriage, Family and Couples Education (CMFCE). These organizations have formed to provide a professional forum for discussion of the many issues inherent in family life education. This proliferation of related organizations reflects the multidisciplinary nature of family life education. The debate over role definition may temper as more widespread agreement evolves over the content of family life education.

THE PUBLIC SERVED EXPRESSES SOME ACCEPTANCE OF THE EXPERTISE OF THOSE PRACTICING THE OCCUPATION   As society increasingly faces crises and challenges related to family (e.g., divorce, single parenting, blended families, delinquency, youth violence), the interest in prevention and education for families is growing. There has been an increased recognition of the value of prevention and education in the past decade. Health maintenance organizations are more frequently offering classes dealing with parenting, stress management, and balancing work and family because they recognize the relationship between stress and health. More businesses are recognizing that personal and family problems account for decreased productivity and attendance. More companies are offering lunchtime brown-bag seminars and other educational opportunities to employees in the hope of increasing employee productivity.

When groups or organizations decide to offer a family life education program, they tend to seek someone to lead the experience who has expertise in an academic discipline or profession related to families. Certification and experience can enhance one's credibility as an expert in the area of family relationships.

The marriage enrichment movement has for more than 40 years offered opportunities for enhancing couple-relationship skills and intentional-growth activities (Mace, 1982). Acceptance and recognition from therapists and academicians, as well as from couples who have participated in the weekend or ongoing experiences over the years, is growing. The well-attended national conferences of the CMFCE, which was formed in 1996, attest to this burgeoning interest. The value of trained leadership has always been emphasized by such international marriage enrichment organizations as the Association of Couples for Marriage Enrichment, founded by David and Vera Mace in 1973, and Marriage Encounter, founded by Father Gavriel Calvo in 1962. Both groups offer rigorous and well-developed leader-training programs, which require leader couples to have experience as well as academic preparation. Leaders in training must also work under the supervision of an experienced leader couple and receive positive evaluations of their skills by participants before receiving full certification.

Family life education professionals, as well as program participants, recognize that it takes more than being a "good parent" or a "happy couple" to facilitate effective learning experiences and the skill building that enhance interpersonal relationships. Adequate training and experience are imperative.

CERTIFICATION AND LICENSURE ARE THE LEGAL SIGNS THAT A GROUP IS SANCTIONED FOR A PARTICULAR SERVICE TO SOCIETY AND THAT IT IS SELF-REGULATED The CFLE program was developed by the NCFR for the purpose of regulating the qualifications of family life education providers and, indirectly, the quality of the materials presented. States are beginning to require licensure and certification in order to practice family life education within government-sanctioned settings. Minnesota has required early childhood and parent educators to be licensed since 1989. The NCFR is currently working to incorporate the CFLE designation criteria into state licensing qualifications for relevant positions.

A CODE OF ETHICS IS DEVELOPED TO ELIMINATE UNETHICAL PRACTICE AND TO PROTECT THE PUBLIC In 1995, the Family Science Section of the National Council on Family Relations approved *Ethical Principles and Guidelines* (NCFR, 1995a) for use by family scientists. These guidelines dealt primarily with ethical issues inherent in teaching and research in academic settings. In 1997, the Minnesota Council on Family Relations published *Ethical Thinking and Practice for Parent and Family Educators* (MCFR, 1997) for use by family life education practitioners. This publication provides information and guidelines useful in making ethical decisions and is discussed in more detail later in this chapter. The fact that a need was perceived for these ethical guidelines and codes provides further evidence of the recognition of family life education as a profession within itself.

This step-by-step discussion of East's (1980) criteria for defining a profession shows that family life education is indeed a profession. The heart of professionalism, however, lies in the skills and qualities of those who practice or deliver services to the public.

PERSONAL SKILLS AND QUALITIES OF THE EDUCATOR

By its nature, family life education often deals with personal and sensitive issues. Unlike an educator providing instruction in a "hard science" such as math or chemistry, the family life educator deals in matters of personal decision making, growth and behavior change, and such sensitive issues as sexuality, communication skills, parenting, and money management. The feelings, motives, attitudes, and values of the learners are central to the learning process (Darling, 1987). A major component of family life education involves helping participants to "analyze, clarify, and determine their own values and value system" (Family Service Association of America [FSA], 1976, p. 10). Participants may tend to respond with more emotion or defensiveness due to the personal nature of the topics discussed.

Awareness of Attitudes and Biases

Because of the sensitivity of these issues, family life educators need to be in touch with their own feelings or biases or both. They need to be comfortable with other people's feelings and accepting of various points of view. Many family degree programs require students to examine and study their own family of origin and family roles, rules, and values to increase their awareness of the influence of their own family experiences (Bahr, 1990). This also helps to identify conflicts that may influence their ability to effectively practice family life education.

Awareness of one's own biases toward such things as culture, race, physical ability, gender, and socioeconomic status is necessary in order to practice effectively. Family life educators need to consider the following questions: How do I view differences among people? Are differences something to value and celebrate, ignore, or fear? If working with a population different from my own, do I see my role as helper, leader, advocate, or partner? Family life educators need to take time to seriously consider their perceptions and attitudes about such things as individual and societal responsibility for poverty. Are poor people poor because of the choices they've made or because of circumstances beyond their control? The educator's perspective on these issues can influence the way in which he or she practices and interacts with an audience. Oftentimes our perceptions and attitudes are so ingrained that we don't even know we have them. It takes conscious effort and thought to really examine the way in which we see the world. This work can be uncomfortable and challenging. But if educators fail to face these issues, they run the risk of compromising their ability to practice as effectively as possible, and they cheat themselves out of a wealth of opportunities to grow and learn from those around them.

Personal Skills and Qualities

The National Council on Family Relations (1984), as part of the Certified Family Life Educator program criteria, identified certain characteristics as critical to the success of a family life educator. They include general intellectual skills, self-awareness, emotional stability, maturity, awareness of one's own personal attitudes and cultural values, empathy, effective social skills, self-confidence, flexibility, understanding and appreciation of diversity, verbal and written communication skills, and the ability to relate well with all ages and groups on a one-to-one basis.

Clearly, personal traits and characteristics play an important role in the success of a family life educator. A self-assessment (Box 2.1) gives the reader an opportunity to evaluate personal attributes and identify areas that need improvement. Working with a mentor or supervisor, peer evaluations, and observing experienced educators are some of the ways to enhance professional development.

Developing a Personal Philosophy

Although certain personal qualities can enhance a family life educator's effectiveness, it is also important to develop a philosophical basis for teaching about families. In order to be effective educators, they must have thoroughly considered where their beliefs lie. How do they define a family? What is the purpose of family life education? They must be clear about the benefits of family life education and how it can be most effectively accomplished. Dail (1984) determined that a philosophy of family life education is important for the following reasons: It provides a sense of direction and purpose; it allows the educator to be in touch with himself or herself; it enables assessment of educational problems; it clarifies the relationship of family life education to the needs and activities of the larger society; and it provides a basis for understanding the reality of the family, its value in society, the nature of family membership for the individual, and the role of family life education. Having a personal philosophy provides a deeper meaning to the educator's life.

Dail (1984) identified four beliefs that need to be addressed when constructing a philosophy of family life education. They include:

- Beliefs about the family and the quality and nature of family life
- Beliefs about the purpose of family life education
- Beliefs about the content of family life education
- Beliefs about the process of learning for families

Take a few minutes to consider your own beliefs about the following.

BELIEFS ABOUT THE FAMILY AND THE QUALITY AND NATURE OF FAMILY LIFE   Family life educators must look at their own beliefs about how to define family. A family life educator who does not consider a gay or lesbian couple to be a family, for example, needs to be aware of this bias, as it could influence his or her ability to effectively work with such a couple.

BOX 2.1

Assessing Your Personal Qualities as a Family Life Educator

Listed below are qualities seen as critical for effectiveness as a family life educator. Rate yourself on the following scale:

1   Needs much improvement
2   Needs some improvement
3   Average, but not well developed
4   Above average, moving toward competency
5   Competent in this area

☐ *General intellectual skills.* Ability to gather, read, and process information and to apply it to a topic and to group needs; to articulate concepts and ideas; to organize materials and stay on track when presenting them; to hear and incorporate ideas of others.

☐ *Self-awareness.* Ability to recognize and articulate one's own personal opinions, attitudes, and cultural values and not to assume that they are everyone's opinions, attitudes, and values; to understand personal tendencies to assume certain roles in a group, such as caretaker, controller, placater, dominant authority; to acknowledge one's own strengths and limitations.

☐ *Emotional stability.* Ability to recognize one's own level of emotional comfort or discomfort in a given situation; to express emotions in appropriate ways and at appropriate times; to maintain calmness in the face of crisis or confrontation and to refrain from personal attack on another person, either verbally or physically.

☐ *Maturity.* Ability to handle success, disappointment, frustration, or confrontation with dignity and understanding; to acknowledge one's own mistakes and weaknesses and not blame others; to move past grievances and continue to see each person as someone with value and potential.

☐ *Empathy.* Ability to put oneself in another person's place; to reflect the feeling to the other person; to understand her or his dilemma.

Family is like an inkblot test: we see in it whatever we think is important. . . . Families are this or families are that. . . . From "family values" to "dysfunctional families" the term family is so loaded with meanings that even the idea of families is quite messy and adds to the confusion of discussions. (Wigger, 1998, p. 16)

Box 2.2 includes an exercise in considering what criteria are used in defining a family. It includes a listing of various group formations. Students are asked to independently determine if they would consider each grouping to be a family. Class discussion often reveals varying opinions about what constitutes a family and what does not, often with fairly soft criteria.

In addition to how they define a family, educators need to have an understanding of how they think a family should be. What role does the family play

☐ *Effective social skills.* Ability to feel comfortable and enjoy the company of others; to share in group activities; to engage in conversation and to actively listen to others.

☐ *Self-confidence.* Ability to speak and act decisively in personal conversation or in front of a group; to accept the challenge of one's ideas without defensiveness and to state one's position with enthusiasm and documentation, not personal criticism or attack; to acknowledge personal strengths and accept words of appreciation graciously.

☐ *Flexibility.* Ability to adapt plans to suit a changed situation; to recognize when change is needed and be willing to try a new approach.

☐ *Understanding and appreciation of diversity.* Ability to acknowledge differences in others' values, attitudes, and lifestyles; to respect and appreciate cultural and ethnic differences in dress, customs, and language; to understand socioeconomic differences in income, education, and status and how they affect lifestyles and decision making; to actively resist gender, racial, and socioeconomic biases or stereotypes.

☐ *Verbal and written communication skills.* Ability to speak articulately, convincingly, and concisely; to write clearly in language that is not "over the heads" of one's audience; to use illustrations and examples that support one's points; to know when an audience has been "overloaded" with information.

☐ *Ability to relate well with all ages and groups and on a one-to-one basis.* Ability to talk with and not down to any group or person; to resist stereotypes and boredom; to appreciate humor and sharing; to practice patience in listening and interacting.

in an individual's life? Where does the family fit within society? What needs to be in place for a family to function optimally? Understanding his or her own beliefs about the role of a family and the characteristics needed for healthy functioning provides the educator with a goal to strive for and a foundation on which to base his or her programs and other services. Allen and Baber (1992) contend:

> Family life educators can strengthen family life by adopting a perspective that values diversity, equality, and full participation in society for everyone. This agenda may be accomplished . . . by a renewed commitment to professional accountability as a family life educator, the on-going reevaluation of personal beliefs about families that affect one's teaching and authenticity, and the meaningful involvement of

BOX 2.2

What Makes a Family?

1. A newly married couple moves into their first apartment together. They have both agreed that they do not want to have any children. Are they a family?
2. A man and a woman have shared an apartment for the past two years. They share equally in the maintenance and cost of the household. They have made a personal commitment to each other and plan to stay together for the rest of their lives although they have no plans to marry. Are they a family?
3. A man and a woman have shared an apartment for the past two years. They share equally in the maintenance and cost of the household. They are good friends but are dating other people. Are they a family?
4. A group of 10 people (5 men, 3 women, and 2 children) live together on a farm. They share responsibility for the maintenance of the household, including growing their own food. All household members take part in the care of the two children. The group is committed to living together harmoniously. Are they a family?
5. Two gay men live together in a house. They have made a personal commitment to each other. Are they a family?
6. Two gay women live together in a house. They have made a personal commitment to each other and were legally married in the state of Hawaii. Are they a family?
7. A divorced woman lives with her son from her marriage and her daughter from a relationship with another man whom she no longer sees. Are they a family?
8. A man and a woman share an apartment. They have a personal relationship and are committed to staying together as long as the relationship is beneficial to them both. Are they a family?
9. Two divorced heterosexual men live together in a house with their children and share the expense and maintenance of the household. Each man sometimes cares for the other's children while the other is working. Are they a family?
10. A woman lives alone but speaks daily with her sister and brother who live in another state. Are they a family?
11. A brother and sister live with their grandparents while their divorced mother attends school in another city. The mother stays with the children and her parents on the weekends. Are they a family?
12. A widower moves in with his son and his wife. Are they a family?

teachers and students in political activities that actually contribute to empowerment and social change. (p. 383)

BELIEFS ABOUT THE PURPOSE OF FAMILY LIFE EDUCATION   The family life educator must understand the purpose of family life education in order to develop appropriate goals and objectives. Is the goal of family life education to change behavior? Is it to provide insight, skills, and knowledge? Is it proactive or reactive? Is it to provide support? Is it to promote a particular ideology or belief system?

Family life educators must be clear about what it is they want to accomplish and why.

BELIEFS ABOUT THE CONTENT OF FAMILY LIFE EDUCATION   The family life educator must consider which topics are appropriate to include in family life education settings. Are there certain topics that are inappropriate? When should a referral to another type of professional be made? Is program content free of bias and stereotype? How appropriate and up-to-date are sources of information?

A professional family life educator needs to recognize when inappropriate topics are being discussed. For example, issues of sexual or physical abuse are not appropriate for most family life education settings. Persons dealing with these issues should be referred for counseling or therapy. A family life educator who attempts to deal with such issues directly or allows lengthy discussion in a group setting would not be acting professionally. Later in this chapter we discuss William Doherty's levels of family involvement model, which provides guidance for some of these issues.

Effective family life educators will want to be sure that their program content is free of bias and stereotypes. Course content should consider family members of all ages; portray nonsexist roles for family members; include information about families of different racial, ethnic, and cultural groups; recognize the uniqueness of individuals and families regardless of age, sex, race, ethnicity, and cultural and socioeconomic background; recognize that composition of families varies; and be based on current research (Griggs, 1981). Though focused on early childhood education, Louise Derman-Sparks's *Anti-Bias Curriculum: Tools for Empowering Young Children* (1989) is an excellent resource for addressing these issues in any setting.

Professional family life educators need to be familiar with appropriate sources of information. They need to be able to make referrals and to research topics when necessary. Membership and involvement in a professional association can increase awareness of relevant resources, organizations, programs, and individuals. In addition, it can provide access to current research and literature in the field.

BELIEFS ABOUT THE PROCESS OF LEARNING FOR FAMILIES   The family life educator needs to be concerned about how families learn and function as a group, as well as how the group affects the learning and thinking of individual members within it (Dail, 1984). Do groups learn differently than individuals do? How can small groups be used most effectively? Are the developmental, social, and emotional needs of the group important? How important are learning goals and evaluation? How does the education of one family member affect others in the family?

An understanding of human development and the learning process will enable the educator to use the most effective techniques for each audience and each individual. In addition, an educator who understands families as a system will know the value of including all family members in the learning process.

When that is not possible, he or she will consider the implications of introducing new information, such as parenting methods, into the family and will be prepared to help the other family members adjust to a new way of thinking or acting. Chapter 3 discusses various teaching methods and learning experiences in more detail. The important concept regarding methodology to consider in this chapter is awareness of one's own personal beliefs about how individuals and families best learn.

Constructing a personal philosophy can be a difficult process. It involves questioning, evaluating, and accepting and rejecting ideas. It is just that—a process—and it is continually evolving as the educator grows and learns. The time and effort spent in developing a personal philosophy of family life education will be well worth it. The family life educator who has a solid understanding of his or her own personal philosophy of family life education will be better equipped to assist individuals and families to lead more satisfying and productive lives.

THE LEVELS OF FAMILY INVOLVEMENT MODEL

An important trait of a professional is the recognition and acceptance of one's own abilities and limitations. This issue has been referred to as *levels of involvement* between the educator and the learner (Doherty, 1995). A fine line often exists between the roles and responsibilities involved in family life education and those involved in counseling and therapy. Professionalism can often be questioned when an educator is perceived as stepping over the line by participating in activities beyond his or her level of knowledge and expertise. But where does education end and therapy begin? William Doherty developed a model to help educators identify appropriate levels of involvement for family life education. An understanding of these levels and one's own capabilities is another important component of professionalism.

Family life educators must deal with some level of personal and sensitive issues in order to be effective, but working beyond an appropriate level can have harmful effects. Doherty's model involves a "continuum of intensity, describing interactions and defining necessary skills and understanding for working successfully at each level" (Early Childhood Family Education Demonstration Site Coordinators [ECFE], 1997, p. 2). Doherty presented this model to family life educators involved in early childhood education in Minnesota in 1993. The model allows participants to clarify their role with families, define the intensity of involvement desired, and identify personal development issues needed for optimum performance.

The five levels of the family involvement model (Box 2.3) are arranged hierarchically, from minimal involvement with families (Level 1) to family therapy (Level 5). Levels 1 and 5 are outside the range of involvement for the family life educator, as they include either too little personal interaction or too much.

Level 1: Minimal Emphasis on Family

This level of interaction is focused on the institution or organization rather than on a family or family members. Professionals develop programs with little consideration for the needs or interests of parents and family members. They are not considered important to the situation and are included only for legal or practical reasons. An example might be a school that brings in a child's parents for a conference only because they legally have to rather than as part of a team approach. The parents are not seen as playing an important or active role in the situation. The teacher does all the talking and gets little input or feedback from the parent. Another example of Level 1 involvement might be a case manager who interviews a client about financial assistance but has no interest in other matters of personal family coping. The effectiveness of Level 1 interactions is limited by the superficial involvement of the professional with the family or family member.

Level 2: Information and Advice

This level involves sharing of knowledge and information about relevant issues such as child development, parenting, and family interaction. This might include sharing literature, distributing a newsletter, or making presentations in classes and workshops. The family life educator operating at this level must have good communication skills, be able to facilitate discussion, answer questions, be aware of appropriate resources, and be able to make appropriate recommendations. The strength of this level is that it is relatively low risk, involving the sharing of information rather than value judgments and personal input. However, interaction is limited for this same reason, as little personal discussion occurs at this level.

Level 3: Feelings and Support

This level includes the information-sharing component of Level 2 but adds consideration of feelings and personal experiences as part of the educational process. Level 3 combines cognitive (thinking) and affective (feeling) domains. Family life educators involved at Level 3 are able to "listen empathetically, probe gently for feelings and personal stories, create an open and supportive group climate, engage in collaborative problem solving, and tailor recommendations to the specific situation of the parent or family member" (Doherty, 1995, p. 354). Level 3 is generally considered to be the optimal level of involvement for most family life education activities, because it involves a combination of information sharing, feelings, and support appropriate to most family life education situations. Involvement at Level 3 might occur in workshops ranging in length from 2 hours to 2 days, as well as ongoing classes and support groups.

An important distinction in Level 3 is that it generally involves the normative stresses of family life rather than more traumatic or irregular occurrences. For example, the difficulty of balancing work and family, parenting issues, and financial management issues would all be considered to be normative stresses and would be appropriately handled at this level through discussion, sharing of personal stories, and recommendations for action. More intense and irregular occurrences, such as physical or sexual abuse, are issues that would require more extensive discussion and responses and would not be appropriate for this level. Therefore, family life educators operating at Level 3 must be able to protect participants from sharing too much personal information. This is important not only for the person involved but also for other group members who might be uncomfortable with a level of disclosure that is beyond their expectations. The family life educator needs to be able to identify when a participant has needs that go beyond the scope of the group and be ready to identify an alternate setting outside the group that is better suited to the participant's need.

In order to operate effectively at this level, the family life educator must be aware of and comfortable with his or her own emotional responses. Doherty (1995) cites four mistakes often occurring at Level 3. These are:

- Moving too quickly back to the cognitive level when too much emotion or personal information is shared because of the educator's own personal discomfort
- Moving attention away from the parent to the group without adequate opportunity for discussion
- Giving advice or recommendations before the participant has provided sufficient information or adequately shared his or her feelings
- Pushing too deeply into the experiences or feelings of the participant

Level 4: Brief Focused Intervention

Level 4 includes the skills and activities found in the first three levels but goes further to include assessment of the situation and development of a plan of action that goes beyond the activities of Level 3. Level 4 actions usually involve more extensive and systemic change and are, therefore, more appropriate for individuals and families with more serious and compromising situations or for high-risk populations. For example, suppose spousal abuse is uncovered as part of a parenting support group conversation that normally operates at a Level 3 involvement. A skilled educator would want to move the client toward help outside of the parenting group, that is, to a Level 4 type of involvement that might include counseling or intervention.

Family life educators operating at Level 4 need skills in assessment and intervention. These skills require training beyond that provided in most non-therapy degree programs such as family studies or family life education. Level 4 "represents the upper boundary of parent and family education practiced by a minority of professionals who choose to work with special populations of parents and seek special training in family assessment and basic family interventions" (Doherty, 1995, p. 355). At this level it is important that there be an explicit understanding between the educator and the individual regarding the level of involvement both are engaged in.

The most common mistakes at Level 4 include:

- Unintentionally moving from Level 3 to Level 4 and then getting stuck or overwhelmed
- Engaging in deeper problem-solving discussions without the permission or agreement of the person involved
- Moving too quickly from Level 3 discussion into assessment and intervention
- Remaining at Level 4 when it is not proving to be effective

Doherty argues that although Level 3 is most typically the appropriate level of involvement for most family life educators, they also need to be familiar with Level 4 in order to decide when involvement is or is not appropriate. Family life educators often work with families with special needs and issues that may not be sufficiently addressed through Level 3 involvement. Professional family life educators need to be able to identify when a more active problem-solving approach is needed. They need to work collaboratively with professionals in related fields who may be better able to help. Level 4 "is an approach that requires careful programmatic decision making, staff preparation, acceptance by the parents and family members who participate and close working relationships with therapists and other professionals in the community" (Doherty, 1995, p. 356).

Level 5: Family Therapy

Level 5, family therapy, is clearly beyond the scope appropriate to family life education but is included in Doherty's model as part of a continuum. Family therapy involves more lengthy and intensive discussion of more personal and serious issues. Family life educators are not typically trained in issues and skills needed to operate at this level. It is when family life educators work at this level without the proper training that issues of professionalism can be called into question.

Doherty's levels of family involvement model provides a much-needed framework from which to address the sometimes overlapping issues involved in family life education and therapy. Professionals working in both fields must work collaboratively to best serve individuals and family members. An effective family life educator will recognize issues that go beyond the scope of family life education and be prepared to provide referrals to more appropriate professionals and resources.

BOX 2.3

Levels of Family Involvement for Parent and Family Educators Model

LEVEL 1: MINIMAL EMPHASIS ON FAMILY

Interactions with parents are institution centered, not family centered. Families are not regarded as an important area of focus, but parents are dealt with for practical or legal reasons.

LEVEL 2: INFORMATION AND ADVICE

KNOWLEDGE BASE: Content information about families, parenting, and child development.

PERSONAL DEVELOPMENT: Openness to engage parents in collaborative ways.

SKILLS:
1. Communicating information clearly and interestingly.
2. Eliciting questions.
3. Engaging a group of parents in the learning process.
4. Making pertinent and practical recommendations.
5. Providing information on community resources.

LEVEL 3: FEELINGS AND SUPPORT

KNOWLEDGE BASE: Individual and family reactions to stress, and the emotional aspects of group process.

PERSONAL DEVELOPMENT: Awareness of one's own feelings in relation to parents and group process.

SKILLS:
1. Eliciting expressions of feelings and concerns.
2. Empathetic listening.
3. Normalizing feelings and reactions.
4. Creating an open and supportive climate.
5. Protecting a parent from too much self-disclosure in a group.
6. Engaging parents in collaborative problem-solving discussion.
7. Tailoring recommendations to the unique needs, concerns, and feelings of the parent and family.
8. Identifying individual and family dysfunction.
9. Tailoring a referral to the unique situation of the parent and family.

LEVEL 4: BRIEF FOCUSED INTERVENTION

KNOWLEDGE BASE: Family systems theory.

PERSONAL DEVELOPMENT: Awareness of one's own participation in systems, including one's own family, the parents' systems, and larger community systems.

SKILLS:

1. Asking a series of questions to elicit a detailed picture of the family dynamics of a parent's problem.
2. Developing a hypothesis about the family systems dynamics involved in the problem.
3. Working with the parent for a short period of time to change a family interaction pattern beyond the one-to-one parent/child relationship.
4. Knowing when to end the intervention effort and either refer the parent or return to Level 3 support.
5. Orchestrating a referral by educating the family and the therapist about what to expect from each other.
6. Working with therapists and community systems to help the parent and family.

LEVEL 5: FAMILY THERAPY

This level is outside the scope and mission of parent and family education. The following description is offered to show the boundary between Level 4 parent and family education and Level 5 family therapy.

KNOWLEDGE BASE: Family systems and patterns whereby distressed families interact with professionals and other community systems.

PERSONAL DEVELOPMENT: Ability to handle intense emotions in families and self and to maintain one's balance in the face of strong pressure from family members or other professionals.

EXAMPLE SKILLS:

1. Interviewing families or family members who are quite difficult to engage.
2. Efficiently generating and testing hypotheses about the family's difficulties and interaction patterns.
3. Escalating conflict in the family in order to break a family impasse.
4. Working intensively with families during crises.
5. Constructively dealing with a family's strong resistance to change.
6. Negotiating collaborative relationships with other professionals and other systems who are working with the family, even when these groups are at odds with one another.

Note. From "Boundaries between parent and family education and family therapy. The levels of family involvement model" by W. J. Doherty, 1995, *Family Relations, 44,* pp. 353–358. Copyright 1995 by National Council on Family Relations. Reprinted with permission.

ETHICAL GUIDELINES

Let us revisit two of the family life educators introduced earlier in this chapter to look at the issue of professional ethics.

> *Carl has a baccalaureate degree in art history. He has worked for the past 9 years as a youth coordinator for the YMCA and organizes activities and classes for neighborhood kids identified as high risk. Carl learns that Chris, a child he has a close relationship with, has become involved in gang activity. The child's parents have told Carl that they want him to keep close tabs on their son. They don't know about their son's involvement with the gang. Should Carl talk to the parents?*

> *Gretchen has a degree in child development. She organizes a parent group in her neighborhood for other stay-at-home moms and dads with kids under 2 years old. The group meets regularly and discusses a predetermined topic each time. Members rotate responsibility for researching the topic and presenting information. Much of the meeting is spent in casual conversation and support. Lately, one parent, named Connie, has been monopolizing the discussion and has disclosed information about her relationship with her husband. Some of the other group members appear to be uncomfortable with the level of disclosure going on but Connie seems to be in need of the group's attention and input. What should Gretchen do?*

Professionals in fields ranging from medicine to law to auto mechanics are faced with ethical issues at one time or another. Family life education is no exception and may, in fact, be more susceptible to ethical dilemmas due to the sensitive and personal nature of some of the issues faced in practice. Because family life education often deals with values and belief systems, it is imperative that the professional family life educator have an understanding of the role of ethics in his or her professional life.

The development of a code of ethics is an important indicator of the development of a profession (East, 1980). As professionals, family life educators need access to ethical guidelines for practice, as well as the capability to consider and act upon these guidelines. "Ethical codes guide our professional interactions with each other as well as with our constituents. A code lets the public know what it can expect from those who call themselves professionals and helps us as practitioners face with confidence some of the difficult decisions that come with our work" (Freeman, 1997, p. 64).

Codes of ethics are designed to prevent harm to consumers and professionals and to the professions themselves (Brock, 1993). Ethics codes for the helping professions commonly address five principles of ethical practice that are based on the teachings of Hippocrates (Brock, 1993). These are:

- Practice with competence
- Do not exploit
- Treat people with respect

- Protect confidentiality
- Do not harm

The concept of ethics and ethical guidelines has only recently entered the professional discussion and literature of family life education. For many years, literature regarding family life education supported the notion that a code of ethics for family life education was unnecessary, because the nature of family life education did not involve an intensity level that could result in the potential for harm. Marriage and family therapy was seen as more intense and, therefore, more in need of control and regulation (Brock, 1993).

Research began to support the effectiveness of preventive and psychoeducational efforts with individuals and families with more severe clinical problems, such as family illness, mental illness, and so forth. The diversity and complexity of today's families required family life educators to increase and modify their roles. With this increased complexity, the potential for doing harm grows as well (Palm, 1998).

In 1992, the Parent/Family Education section of the Minnesota Council on Family Relations (MCFR) began work on developing a code of ethics specifically for use by practitioners in parent and family education. They recognized that family life education was an emerging field and that many practitioners faced ethical dilemmas in relative isolation and with limited guidance (MCFR, 1997). They based their efforts on a model used by the National Association for the Education of Young Children (NAEYC) to develop a code of ethics for early childhood practitioners.

The Ethics Committee of MCFR developed and carried out a series of workshops with parent and family educators from 1995 to 1997. These workshops involved the use of case studies to identify agreed-upon principles for practice within family life education, as well as steps to follow in dealing with ethical dilemmas.

The committee's discussion with William Doherty of the University of Minnesota resulted in a multiperspective approach to ethics. Such an approach blends the concepts of relational ethics, ethical principles, and core human virtues. Relational ethics emphasizes the context of the relationship between the people involved. It asks, "Who are the stakeholders?" and considers the role of each person in relation to the other. The principles concept considers agreed-upon principles for practice and such standards as "We will do no harm to children and insist on the same from others" and "We will define our role as family educators and practice within our level of competence."

Doherty's inclusion of a virtue approach is an exciting step in the process of developing ethical guidelines, for it recognizes the importance and prevalence of the human element in family life education. The previous way of defining professional behavior focused on technical competence. The introduction of virtues into the equation recognizes moral competence. "Good practice in family life education should be tied to internal standards of excellence" (MCFR, 1997, p. 2).

BOX 2.4

Process for Considering an Ethical Dilemma

Step 1	Identification of important relationships
Step 2	Application of principles
Step 3	Identification of contradictions
Step 4	Application of virtues
Step 5	Consideration of possible actions
Step 6	Selection of action

From *Tools for Ethical Thinking and Practice in Family Life Education* by the National Council on Family Relations, 1999, Minneapolis, MN: Author.

Doherty identified core virtues that should exist in most professions. These include justice, truthfulness, and courage. But there are also virtues that are inherent in family life education. Professionals attending the ethics workshops provided a long list of virtues, from which three essential virtues emerged. They are *caring, prudence/practical wisdom,* and *hope/optimism.* It is believed by some that these virtues need to be present within the practitioner in order for him or her to implement effective family life education.

Tools for Ethical Thinking and Practice in Family Life Education is available through the National Council on Family Relations (NCFR, 1999). It provides a more detailed description of the concepts, as well as a step-by-step process for use in dealing with ethical dilemmas. Box 2.4 provides a summary of the six steps.

It should be noted that in 1995 the Family Science Section of the National Council on Family Relations approved ethical guidelines for family scientists. Although many concepts are similar or identical to those in family life education, the focus is more on academic teaching and research issues.

Personal morals are not sufficient when dealing with ethical dilemmas in a work setting. Practitioners need to understand and internalize their profession's core values. Because of the nature of their work, family life educators are expected to balance the needs of a variety of clients. They have an ethical responsibility to children, parents, colleagues, employers, and society. Oftentimes ethical dilemmas arise out of the conflicting needs or interests of those involved (Freeman, 1997). Consideration of ethical principles and the implementation of an ethical-guideline process can provide family life educators with guidance to help make a decision that is right for them and for the situation.

IMPORTANCE OF ONGOING PROFESSIONAL DEVELOPMENT

As you walk up to the stage to accept your degree and prepare to throw your mortarboard in the air, it is tempting to think that your time as a student is over. You have completed the course work needed for your degree, taken your last test, and submitted your last paper. Now it is time to roll up your sleeves, get to work, and put all the knowledge to good use!

Newly graduated professionals often give little thought to the need to continue their education beyond graduation (Darling & Cassidy, 1998), but it is an integral part of professionalism. Qualified professionals must stay current on research and developments within their field.

Continuing education and professional development can be accomplished through a number of avenues. Some examples include attendance at workshops, seminars, and professional conferences; review of current research through professional publications such as newsletters and journals; presentation of research at professional meetings; and networking with others in the field through membership in professional organizations and associations.

Most certification and licensing programs require professionals to earn a minimum amount of continuing education credits (CEUs), sometimes called PDUs (professional development units), in order to maintain the designation or license (National Certification Commission, 1998). Professionals need to actively seek continuing education opportunities and to maintain records that document attendance at meetings and professional activities. Membership in one or more professional organizations can provide numerous opportunities for continued growth.

SUMMARY

We have looked closely at the field of family life education and issues of professionalism. We have determined that the field of family life education does indeed meet many of the criteria set forth by experts in defining a profession. We have looked at the importance of developing a personal philosophy, including personal insights, values, and beliefs about families and family life education. Personal qualities and traits needed for effective practices were considered. Doherty's levels of family involvement model provided helpful parameters for identifying boundaries for effective practice. Finally, we discussed the importance of ethical guidelines in assuring best practices. These considerations provide the foundation for further discussion about the practice of family life education.

QUESTIONS/PROBLEMS FOR DISCUSSION AND REVIEW

Class Discussion

1. Which of the people described on the first page of this chapter would you consider to be a "professional" family life educator? Why?

2. How do you define "family"?

3. What is the goal of family life education?

4. Can a person have a different set of values in his or her personal life than in his or her professional life? Why or why not?

Research Problems

1. Trace the development of another social science profession (e.g., social work, marriage and family therapy) applying East's criteria.

2. Interview a representative sample of family studies majors in your department and a sample of family life educators in your area. Compare their responses to the ethical dilemmas presented in the case studies in this chapter. On what bases do they make their judgments?

3. Using Doherty's levels of family involvement model, determine the proper course of action for a family life educator when a parent in a parent education group reveals having been physically abused by his or her spouse.

Case Study Design

Read through the two ethical dilemmas described on page 42. What should Carl do? What should Gretchen do?

PART II

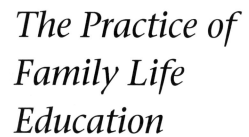

The Practice of Family Life Education

CHAPTER 3

Relating Theory to Practice

The trend is definitely disturbing: Teen pregnancies at younger and younger ages have been on a continual rise since the 1950s. Although the latest figures from the National Center for Health Statistics (1998) show an encouraging downturn in the number of teen pregnancies, the figures still cast a long shadow. Young single parents tend to drop out of high school and have few marketable skills that would lift them out of poverty. Many of their children suffer from lack of resources and possible neglect. There is great national concern for the mothers, the children, the communities in which they live, and society as a whole.

What can be done to support these families and move them toward self-sufficiency and competent parenting? How can young men and women be influenced to postpone parenthood until they are adequately educated and able to make more mature decisions? Many things are being tried by various societal institutions: government, through changes in laws and policies; the education system, through more—and earlier—sex education in the schools; the social system, through programs to get family members more involved with each other in positive ways.

Unfortunately, very few of the efforts to date have been based on established theories of social and behavioral change and proven effectiveness. "Too often, prevention efforts are based on common sense, good intentions, myths about adolescent development, and the heroic efforts of committed staff" (Bogenschneider, 1996, p. 127). For example, before the 1992 presidential election, an alliance of politicians pressed for adoption of governmental policies that they felt would reverse the breakup and decline of two-parent families. These included lowering the tax burden to reduce financial stress that contributes to divorce; investing in education, job training, child care, and health care (social supports that would assist families toward self-sufficiency); and cutting welfare benefits to discourage welfare dependency and low-functioning families. Although some attention was given to reeducation and prevention services, they

49

were not a major focus of the proposals (Zimmerman, 1995). This comes some 20 years after a rigorous assessment of a family support model conducted by the Yale Child Welfare Research Program determined that services to families can bring social benefits to children—and their mothers—but only if services are sustained and comprehensive (Ziglar & Gilman, 1990). The Yale project employed a multidisciplinary approach, including health care, monthly home visits for problem solving and parent education, and child care as required. The long-term effects on children and parents were very positive and measurable. After 10 years, children who had received intervention were better adjusted to school and had greater school attendance; mothers who had received intervention had a higher rate of self-support and employment. They also had pursued more education and chosen to bear fewer children than the control-group mothers. "If we have learned anything over the decades of child study, it is the need to be broad-based and family-centered. There are no instant, one-shot solutions" (Ziglar & Gilman, 1990, p. 244).

As valid studies of healthy family functioning and family wellness accumulate, the family focus on education and preventive services is confirmed. Kilpatrick and Holland (1995), in developing a model for community human services, determined that education that reinforces family efforts is the most effective prevention tool. They outline three types of human-service agenda: (1) for survival, (2) for self-empowerment, and (3) for self-realization and prevention of relationship problems. Agenda types (2) and (3) are especially related to the skills of family life educators who understand family dynamics and family systems theory. Coupled with knowledge of learning theory and effective teaching methods, education for positive behavior change should certainly be enhanced. Bogenschneider (1996), in presenting an ecological risk/protective theory for building prevention programs, stresses that our most effective prevention efforts are based on strong theoretical and empirical foundations that shape program conceptualization, design, implementation, evaluation, and institutionalization. Yet she laments that "promoting health or wellness is less effective in mobilizing parents, community leaders, and policymakers than is attacking problems or crises" (p. 129). Aulette (1994) points out that theory can serve not only as a guide to social change but also as a force for change, whether the societal concern is teen pregnancy, parent competency, or any other relationship issue.

THE ASSUMPTIONS OF FAMILY LIFE EDUCATION

The general intent of the family life education movement has been (1) to encourage the growth potential of individuals and families and (2) to reduce family-related societal problems through family-focused educational opportunities (Arcus & Thomas, 1993). Through the years, a myriad of family life education programs have been developed to address some part of this two-pronged focus. A variety of goals and objectives have been used. The most common are (1) gaining insight into self and others, (2) learning about human development and behavior in the family setting over the life cycle, (3) learning about marriage and family patterns and processes, (4) acquiring skills essential for family living, (5) developing the individuals' potentials in their current and future roles, and (6) building strengths in families. "One of the assumptions in family life education appears to be that, if these and other similar objectives are met through family life education programs, then families will be better able to deal with problems, to prevent problems, and/or to develop their potentials" (Arcus & Thomas, 1993, p. 5).

How this assumption influences program design depends upon the educator's perspective on the purpose of family life education (Miller and Seller, 1990). The *transmission* perspective equates accumulation of facts with mastery of subject matter and skills. The learners are expected to be attentive to the teacher and basically passive consumers. (They may ask or respond to a question, but no further involvement is expected.) The purpose of family life education from this perspective appears to be the transmission of facts, skills development information, and values information that prepare one to fit into society. The *transaction* perspective implies more involvement between the teacher and the learner. The learners are viewed as autonomous beings who are capable of rational thought and active involvement in their own learning experience. Therefore, the purpose of family life education from the transaction perspective would focus on developing cognitive skills and critical thinking abilities in order to use them in individual problem-solving situations. The *transformation* perspective recognizes the personal element of knowledge and the strong influence of social interaction and cultural context in determining personal behavior and values. Although learners are seen as diverse and unique, they also share many basic human needs and concerns. The purpose of family life education from this perspective would be to facilitate social interaction that results in personal and social change.

A review of the stated aims and objectives of family life education by Thomas (1988) determined that most descriptions of family life programs reflect the transmission perspective, even though program designers often desire personal and social transformation as an outcome. In a critical analysis of the assumptions of family life education, Morgaine concludes that the practices of the field must be "reconceptualized" if programs are to reach the ultimate goal of family life education, namely, to "strengthen and enrich family well-being" (Morgaine, as cited in Arcus & Thomas, 1993, p. 5).

USING THEORY TO DESIGN PROGRAMS

In order to understand how growth and change in an individual or a family occurs, it is important to be familiar with several major theoretical models related to families. The process of change does not easily fit into any single model

(Winton, 1995). Human beings and families are truly unique in their experiences and makeup. Most family counselors conclude that no two children have the same parents, because each child is born into a different time and context of relationships. Every person is unique and reacts somewhat differently to the same set of circumstances because of other variables in her or his environment. So it is that family scientists must always expect a certain degree of error in their conclusions and discuss "probabilities" of cause and effect. With that qualification, we now discuss the basic tenets of family systems theory, human ecology theory, exchange theory, and family developmental theory.

Family Systems Theory

Earlier in this chapter, the Yale Child Welfare Research Program design (Ziglar & Gilman, 1990) and the model for community human services (Kilpatrick & Holland, 1995) were mentioned as programs that stress the important role that the family plays in program success. Family systems theory helps us to understand why this is so. Basically, family systems theory views the family as a living organism operating within certain boundaries, rules, expectations, and interaction patterns between its members. These patterns have been passed down and adapted through many generations. They may be helpful or destructive to family members, but regardless, they are very powerful in determining the behavior of each individual. The family system exerts such a strong influence on the individual because the system depends on certain patterns of interaction to maintain its familiar and comfortable "shape." Like the carefully balanced mobile that Virginia Satir (1972) used to describe the family, the system works to keep everything in balance. When change occurs in any part of the system, the whole system is affected and becomes unbalanced. The system then must either support and accommodate the change or resist it. Often it is easier to maintain the status quo (homeostasis) by resisting the change than to exert the energy it will take from every part of the system to accommodate a change. Furthermore, the family system is part of several larger systems, including the community, the culture, and peer networks. These also exert a strong influence on the shape of the family and may have to be confronted or altered if the family system changes.

Let us apply the family system concept to the topic of teen pregnancy prevention. Usually, programs of sex education and pregnancy prevention are designed by educators to involve the child or teen only. Little input from parents or program participants is sought in planning the program, and seldom is follow-up or long-term reinforcement included in the program design. The end result is scant family reinforcement of the ideas or skills presented in the program. The system remains uninvolved and unaffected. Furthermore, the teen functions within a peer system that emphasizes conformity and short-term gratification. Attempts to "buck the system" are quickly squelched through ridicule, intimidation, or isolation from the group. Is it any wonder that many of our programs show few positive changes, either short or long term?

On the other hand, if a family system functions in a healthy manner, it can reinforce and influence positive growth for the individual as well as the system. A classic and extensive study of psychological health in family systems by Lewis, Beavers, Gossett, and Phillips (1976) determined that families need to have access to preventive programs that are based on sound research about the types of interactions that build "healthy," well-functioning families. But "What is meant by 'health'? What is meant by 'normal'?" the authors query (p. 12). They proceed to discuss four perspectives of health that are used by behavioral and medical research: (1) health as absence of overt pathology, (2) health as "optimal functioning," (3) health as average or normal functioning, and (4) health as process, recognizing the ability of a system to change over time. Whether or not one chooses to define "health" from any of these four perspectives, the particular system's characteristics can serve as a basic reference point.

Lewis et al. (1976) also strongly stress that health cannot be studied independently of time, place, and cultural or ethnic context and values. Epstein, Bishop, and Baldwin (1984) give an example of this as it relates to understanding and evaluating certain family responses:

> [When] we describe how a healthy, or, in our view, a normal family should look on each of the dimensions, often such a description involves a value judgment. For instance, we would say that family members ought to be able to show sadness at the appropriate times and to the degree called for by the situation. The judgement of appropriateness with respect to sadness is not clear-cut and varies among cultures. We take the position that knowledge of the culture to which a family belongs is necessary for understanding a family and that judgements of health or normality are relative to the culture of the family. (p. 117)

Unfortunately for persons outside of the mainstream cultural group in America (i.e., the White middle class), many family life education programs or texts in the 1970s did not address differences in class, cultural values, or lifestyles (Rodman, 1970). The research of Scott-Jones and Peebles-Wilson (1986) uncovered a gender bias as well. They determined that many parent education programs were aimed at the middle-class, White female parent and that the scheduled times (plus fees charged and level of English-language competency needed to complete learning materials) automatically excluded those of a certain socioeconomic status and most males, as well. Hopefully, the increasing awareness of cultural and gender diversity—and its impact on program design and effectiveness—has addressed these earlier deficits.

To summarize, the influence of the family system on an individual's behavior and choices is very powerful and should be considered and utilized in the design of family life education programs.

The timing of educational intervention is another critical factor. Lewis et al. (1976) call this an "urgent need" for program design and stress the importance of focusing on the young family:

> In a useful analogy, young families may be likened to an infant. The family as an organism undergoes a series of developmental sequences. Over time a family's characteristic style of reacting may become increasingly "fixed." Young families, therefore, are reasonably unencumbered by family developmental events and may represent organisms unusually responsive to education. (pp. 4–5)

Because the new pair is forming a new family system, the probability of incorporating healthier patterns is much more likely than in a long-established system, provided new skills and options are presented effectively and reinforced through practice by the pair.

Human Ecology Theory

The external systems already mentioned (cultural context, time, place, gender, lifestyles) emphasize the interdependence of human communities and their various environments. This emphasis forms the basis of human ecology theory.

Families do not exist as isolated systems. They are constantly interacting with their environment and the resources (or lack there of) it provides. These resources include useful goods and services that families must have for their own needs and also what they can give back, such as productive work and family and community support. Andrews, Bubolz, and Paolucci (1980) explain:

> The flow of energy to and through the family system activates the decision-making and decision-implementation processes. Internally, the energy is transformed to support the production, consumption, and socialization functions of the family. The outputs to the environment are used by other systems, activating reciprocal exchanges and bonds of interdependence. (p. 35)

For example, in planning a grief support group for widows, the family life educator must consider not only the group's emotional and social needs but also such factors as time, transportation, and health constraints. Cost of materials and supplies, reading levels, and child care are other typical ecological factors that must be considered when planning programs. On the "output" side of the ledger, it is important to remember that self-esteem is bolstered when persons feel that they have something to give back to the community and have power to make changes in their living environment. One small personal example supports this theory as an effective educational tool. I (Powell) was facilitating a welfare-to-work series of sessions on effective communication in the workplace. The meetings were taking place in a vacant apartment in the housing project in which most of the women lived. Tables and chairs had been moved into the apartment, but unfortunately the apartment heater was not working.

There were numerous voiced complaints, and the group's shivering and discomfort greatly affected their ability to engage in the sessions. Coincidentally, the lesson for the day was how to communicate and effect change in your home and work environments. The program leader had called the management office repeatedly with no results, and I suggested to the group that a letter might get more attention. Together, the group composed a letter; everyone signed it, and someone was dispatched to deliver it to the apartment manager. By that afternoon, we had a written promise from management that the heater would be fixed immediately. The group was elated. They received a "power boost" and a great lesson regarding how they could affect the environment in a positive way. Human ecology theory goes much deeper than that, considering natural, human-behavioral, and human-constructed environments and how each becomes an energy transformation system (Bubolz & Sontag, 1993). But the bottom line is that physical resources of families (air, water, land, food, temperature, space, and energy) are critically important factors that influence the ability to perceive problems and envision solutions (Rettig, 1988). Whereas human ecology theory focuses on external factors of influence, exchange theory looks at internal influences on decision making and behavior, such as one's perception of self and internal motivations.

Exchange Theory

Social exchange theory was articulated by behaviorist George Homans (1958, 1961) and sociologists Thibaut and Kelley (1959). They reasoned that all individuals are motivated to act on a cost-reward basis, seeking to minimize costs and maximize rewards. If a certain behavior is seen as rewarding, it will tend to be repeated; if it is seen as too costly (whether in terms of money, time, or emotional effort), it will be discouraged. Homans (1958) also surmised that people will be drawn to those who possess desirable qualities or characteristics, such as people who have high income, status, or prestige or who are physically attractive. The qualities considered to be desirable may vary greatly from culture to culture, however. Reverence for the elderly and their opinions is a good example of this cultural variation. In some cultures, the elderly are considered wise and their input valuable; in other cultures, the elderly are generally tolerated or ignored. When applied to program design, the use of role models who have appeal for the particular group, either as group facilitators or guest speakers, can reinforce motivation for desirable change.

It is not always easy to ascertain who will inspire admiration and respect as a leader. In one situation I (Powell) personally experienced, the group of learners was of a different race and socioeconomic level than I, yet we seemed to get along quite well. I asked the program director if they had tried to recruit "successful" persons of the same race as the participants to serve as role models and teachers. "Yes, and we actually have had some come to lead the group, but the women didn't like them." Rather surprised, I asked why. "Because they felt that the leaders were talking down to them," she responded. I am not sure what happened that resulted in the lack of connection, but it's important to remember that respect for what a teacher says is a quality that transcends cultural similarities or external trappings of success. Respect must be earned, not assumed.

Jane Vella (1994), a community development educator from North Carolina, has designed and led community education programs for adult learners in more than 40 countries around the world. The seminars often involve several hundred people and a language group or culture different from her own. Vella recalls an invitation to come to El Salvador to teach what she knew about community development organization.

"I knew I could not do that with accountability if I did not first find out what they knew, what their life was like, how they thought about it, what they still needed to learn," she observed (p. 126). So Vella spent several days visiting clinics, schools, and farms in the area before she began her classes:

> We chatted with village leaders and priests and teachers and wives. We played with endless numbers of beautiful, brown-eyed babies, their mothers' eyes shining with pride as I praised each one. Again I saw how basic human courtesy, expressed in respect for each individual and for the cultural practices, is such a profound instrument for learning. I was learning because they respected me. They were learning through my respect. Perhaps, under the umbrella of respect, learning is always mutual. (Vella, 1994, p. 128)

Exchange theory is applicable in this example because it demonstrates how the role of respected leader and role model can be achieved through the exchange of information, sharing of opinions, and obvious respect for the culture and customs of the learners. As the two different cultures in Vella's experience came to admire each other, a sense of equality between teacher and learners developed, and everyone was then ready to learn.

The use of tangible or intangible rewards, also an emphasis in exchange theory, can enhance the effectiveness of educational programs as well. The age and identified needs of group members will determine what type of reward system will be most effective. For example, adolescent drug treatment programs often use television privileges and weekend passes to encourage cooperation and group participation. Although the rewards may work to produce desired behaviors, they may also be viewed by the program participants as coercion rather than reward, and the desired behaviors will likely fall away after the participants leave the program. On the other hand, genuine acknowledgment by a respected leader of good work done or the discovery of personal gifts or talents that bring respect from others are often more lasting rewards. This may lead to sustainable behavior changes if coupled with a family and peer group system that support and encourage the new behaviors (another type of reward).

For adult groups, rewards will vary, but most will be intangible. The thrill of gaining new knowledge and personal awareness may be enough for some (and may be all the program was designed to do). For others, it may be the hope of a better self-image, a more peaceful household, better communication, more control over life decisions, or a successful job search. If a new behavior is tried and gets positive results, it is likely to be repeated and reinforced. If it is tried and rebuffed, the new behavior is likely to be discarded. As a leader, I often remind program participants that new behaviors take work and practice in order to be successful. I did not learn to ride a bike on my first try (or my 10th!), but I wanted to learn badly enough that I was willing to suffer the wobbles and falls in order to keep on trying. The same is true of any new behavior.

Exchange theory is often used to explain why couple relationships last or end. If partners perceive that they are receiving benefits from the relationship that are equal to or exceed the costs of sustaining a long-term commitment, then they are likely to maintain the partnership. New behaviors can be taught and perceptions can change, but it usually takes commitment from both members of the couple to work at changing old interaction patterns. Some behavioral marital therapy programs design short-term rewards and contracts to encourage couples to keep trying to establish new relationship patterns. This use of exchange theory is one way to heighten the possibility of success for couple growth.

Family Developmental Theory

Family developmental theory proposes that the family unit grows and changes in stages and over time, just as individuals do. Winton (1995) points out that because families do not necessarily develop in a unilinear fashion (always proceeding in the same way and through the same stages), the division of family development into stages is "an arbitrary and artificial enterprise" (p. 13). For example, Duvall (1977) described an eight-stage developmental cycle that begins with the childless newlywed couple and ends with aging family members. For each stage, certain roles and developmental tasks are delineated (see Table 3.1). One problem immediately seen is that all couples do not begin new family development as a childless newlywed couple. There may be children present from previous marriages. One partner may have been married before and the other not. Many variables exist even for the first stage. Furthermore, all couples do not choose to have children in a "cluster," particularly if they are in a second or third marriage. And they may choose not to have children at all. There may be two separate sets of children, so that the family will be in two (or even three) developmental stages at the same time!

Hill and Rodgers (1964) determined a more general, five-stage model based on the change in family size over time. Beginning with a stability stage for the childless married couple, the family expands with the birth of children, then stabilizes during a period of child rearing, contracts when the children start to leave home, then is stable again during the postparental stage. This stage theory also has major exceptions, such as the tendency of many couples to divorce

TABLE 3.1 Stage-Critical Family Developmental Tasks Throughout the Family Life Cycle

Stage of the Family Life Cycle	Positions in the Family	Stage-Critical Family Developmental Tasks
1. Married couple	Wife Husband	Establishing a mutually satisfying marriage Adjusting to pregnancy and the promise of parenthood Fitting into the kin network
2. Childbearing	Wife-mother Husband-father Daughter-sister Son-brother	Having, adjusting to, and encouraging the development of infants Establishing a satisfying home for both parents and infant(s)
3. Preschool age	Wife-mother Husband-father Daughter-sister Son-brother	Adapting to the critical needs and interests of preschool children in stimulating, growth-promoting ways Coping with energy depletion and lack of privacy as parents
4. School age	Wife-mother Husband-father Daughter-sister Son-brother	Fitting into the community of school-age families in constructive ways Encouraging children's educational achievement
5. Teenage	Wife-mother Husband-father Daughter-sister Son-brother	Balancing freedom with responsibility as teenagers mature and emancipate themselves Establishing postparental interests and careers as growing parents
6. Launching center	Wife-mother-grandmother Husband-father-grandfather Daughter-sister-aunt Son-brother-uncle	Releasing young adults into work, military service, college, marriage, etc., with appropriate rituals and assistance Maintaining a supportive home base
7. Middle-aged parents	Wife-mother-grandmother Husband-father-grandfather	Rebuilding the marriage relationship Maintaining kin ties with older and younger generations
8. Aging family members	Widow/widower Wife-mother-grandmother Husband-father-grandfather	Coping with bereavement and living alone Closing the family home or adapting it to aging Adjusting to retirement

Note. From *Marriage and Family Development* (6th ed.) by E. M. Duvall and B. C. Miller, 1985, New York: Harper and Row. Copyright © 1985 by Allyn and Bacon. All rights reserved. Reprinted with permission of Allyn and Bacon.

during the years of child rearing and the rising number of adult children who return home, many with children from a former marriage.

Later work by Mattessich and Hill (1987) stressed the importance of the theory for describing and explaining the processes of change in families. They noted that the sequence of stages is triggered by the internal demands on the family, biological, psychological, and social, combined with the external expectations and ecological restraints of the larger society. Rodgers and White (1993) suggested a revised theory that acknowledges that not all family change is developmental. At every level of analysis, the individual, the relationship, the family group, and the institution itself have an impact on the future direction of the family.

So what is the value of a family developmental model? Even with such numerous and widespread exceptions, developmental models can offer insight into the typical direction of development a family will take. Analyzing the new roles, adjustments, and developmental tasks that are needed in each stage can help families prepare to a degree for what is coming next. Noting typical development and the numerous exceptions can emphasize the complexity of developing and maintaining strong family systems. Discussing family development can also defuse unspoken simplistic myths about how a family ought to look or be.

Using developmental theory, family life educators can address programs to couples in a particular family developmental stage: newlyweds, new parents, parents with teens, empty nesters, or stepfamilies, to name a few. Such stage-specific programs have a greater probability of long-term effectiveness, because they address current issues that the person or family is facing and provide support and insight from other group members who are having similar experiences. Today, additional developmental stages have emerged for some families. There are grandparents raising a second family of grandchildren or the divorced older adult who struggles to redefine a family system. With few guidelines from the past, persons who are thrown into unexpected or unfamiliar roles may be eager for new insight and support from those in similar circumstances. A final word of caution: It is important that educators not assume that everyone in the group (even a group of newlyweds) has the same family developmental pattern. Educators should assure participants that differences in developmental paths do not mean deviance. Although some of the new developmental stages may be challenging, they can also be rewarding and growth-producing, provided individuals and families have good coping skills and a network of support.

MODELS AND PRINCIPLES FOR LEARNING

Educators who operate within a theoretical framework must still develop models and principles for program design. Vella (1994), after many years of experience in program design, implementation, and analysis, concludes that a program, even short term or in less-than-ideal situations, can be effective if the following principles are incorporated:

- *Needs assessment:* uncovering the specific needs of the learners in the program through their participation in naming these needs

- *Safety in the environment and the process:* defusing fears of the group and establishing ground rules and ways of sharing that the group is comfortable with
- *A sound relationship between teacher and learner for learning and development:* persuading learners to trust and identify with the teacher in order to learn from her or him
- *Careful attention to sequence of content and reinforcement:* preparing and understanding how much (or how little) learners can absorb at any one time; with a variety of reinforcing activities
- *Focus on praxis:* acting and reflecting on the part of the learners
- *Respect for learners as subjects of their own learning:* "drawing in" and valuing the contributions of learners' life experience and insight
- *Cognitive, affective, and psychomotor aspects of learning:* incorporating ideas, feelings, and actions into the learning experience, if possible
- *Immediacy of the learning:* making immediate application of the principles and information learned
- *Clear roles and role development:* accepting and honoring the "teacher" role but moving toward a "learners together" role, which encourages dialogue and freedom of application
- *Teamwork:* using small groups to complete tasks or projects
- *Engagement of the learners in what they are learning:* encouraging active, rather than passive, involvement, which results in new pathways of learning that the teacher can validate rather than ignore
- *Accountability: How do they know they know?* validating their accomplishments through assessments, role plays, praxis

To summarize, Vella (1994) emphasizes the basic educational concepts of Paulo Freire, who contrasts the "banking system" of teaching (in which the professor comes and tells you what she knows so that you know it too, with no reference to what you already know or what you need to know) with the "problem-posing approach" (in which the group works in and through dialogue; Freire, as cited in Vella, 1994, p. 126). She concludes that problem-posing dialogue structures a partnership for learning and is a much more effective model of education because it respects the learners and their needs.

Mace (1981) also points to several key concepts that have been seen through theory and experience to create and enhance the climate for growth and change in educational settings:

- *Enough time together to build a sense of community and mutual trust:* a minimum of 15–18 hours of sustained time together, a time frame that can be met by a weekend seminar or a 3-hour class 5 days a week
- *Trained leaders who can establish rapport with the group and who model the skills being taught:* ability to establish "connections" with the group and

do more than present facts: to model, give examples from their own life history, ask for examples from others

- *Dynamic presentation of a body of information based on a well-developed theoretical frame of reference:* information that is up-to-date, appropriate, and theoretically sound

- *Direct application of information to one's personal life and relationships:* each learner making the connection between the subject matter and the application, whether through writing assignments, role plays, or sharing personal experiences

- *Follow-up and reinforcement of classwork with outside assignments or materials:* handouts, additional exercises, specific assignments to help the new information "stick" in the mind and encourage application of new principles

- *Opportunity for personal reflection and decision making:* a personal goal, a decision to start a new habit, and articulating steps on how to do this, to encourage personal reflection and application

The process of education with adults is sometimes referred to as *andragogy* and is derived by combining the Greek noun *agoge* (the activity of leading) with the stem *andr* (adult). Gross (1993) delineates several methodologies that are highly effective with adult learners: buzz (task-oriented) groups, role playing, and, most important, the discussion group. A discussion group can range in size from 3 to 15 participants. This small-group discussion allows optimum "two-way learning" to take place as both the teacher and the students share knowledge and participate in the learning experience. Vella (1994) adds that the small group provides an element of safety for the person who is reluctant to speak up in a large-group setting. The small group quickly becomes a learning team, building cooperation and support so that the team becomes a constructive competitor with other groups. Chapter 5 elaborates on the dynamics of group formation and interaction.

Moss and King (1970) point out that different approaches to family life education employ various methodologies. The *group-oriented approach* focuses on group processes in problem solving and decision making, the *sensitivity approach* on the development of individual awareness, and the *thinking-oriented approach* on intellectual development. The methodology and focus of andragogy obviously differ somewhat from effective methodologies used with children and young adolescents. The needs and limitations of other ages are reviewed in Chapter 4.

DEVELOPING EFFECTIVE EDUCATION STRATEGIES

Does real education involve more than simple accumulation of facts? If you answered yes, then you agree with education specialists who emphasize that education involves the ability to actually use knowledge to make choices and to act on the basis of reason (Arcus & Thomas, 1993; Mace, 1981; Peters, 1967; Vella, 1994). "Making choices" and "acting" on the basis of reason imply a much deeper level of involvement by the student and certainly are required if many of the stated goals and assumptions of family life education are to be accomplished. Yet few teachers in our education system in general or family life education in particular consistently go beyond factual presentation and immediate audience response.

Mace (1981) stressed the original meaning of the word *education,* which is derived from the Latin verb *duco (to lead, conduct, draw,* or *bring)* combined with the prefix *ex (out of, from).* Thus education originally referred to drawing out of the student what was already there but unknown or unarticulated. Mace observed:

> This is not, however, the sense in which we customarily use the word "education" in academic circles. We place the emphasis less on drawing out what is already there, and more on pumping in what is definitely *not* already there. What we pump in is *information,* so that the student may process it as *knowledge,* which is simply information systematically filed in the brain's computer system in such a way that it is later available for instant recall. (p. 599)

Although such ability to recall facts is certainly necessary for cognitive (intellectual) growth, Mace stressed the importance, particularly for family life educators, of distinguishing between "learning for knowing and learning for living."

"As family life educators, therefore, we have to ask ourselves how our students make the transition from the classroom, where they learn to *know,* to the more private environment in which they learn to *live*" (Mace, 1981, p. 600). Mace offered a model for the journey from factual input to behavioral change; although it is a difficult road for any individual:

> I asked myself whether I really believed that the people who heard me speak, or who read my books, were somehow released from their paralysis, and set free to change their relationships for the better . . . but I could not persuade myself that I . . . made any significant difference in the way they behaved at home—the tight bonds of long-established habits are just too powerful. (p. 600)

So what are the established levels and necessary environments for learning that motivate personal behavior change? Mace proposed that one must go through several steps: from the *acquisition of knowledge* (the gathering of facts that "stick" in the brain and are available for recall) to *insight* (the understanding of how a certain piece of knowledge could apply to one's personal life and situation) to *experimental action* (the actual application of a new piece of knowledge to personal behavior to see what will happen) to *commitment to change* (the determination to make a behavior change and the ordering of one's life to accommodate this change) to *relational reorganization and acceptance* (the acceptance and support of the change by significant others in one's life).

Let us apply these steps to the straightforward behavioral change needed for "Ann" to lose weight. Ann has read books and seen programs on the health haz-

- promotes the functions of healthy family systems
- supports and encompasses the family in its unique social and cultural context
- reinforces family efforts
- is sustained and comprehensive (over time, over life experiences)
- focuses on prevention rather than remediation
- builds in levels of learning that encourage personal transformation and behavioral/attitudinal change
- includes at least 15–18 hours of learning experience, followed by options for long-term reinforcement
- incorporates learning activities for all learning styles
- engages the learner in praxis (action with reflection)
- applies information to personal life experience and demonstrates immediate usefulness
- respects learners' experiences, culture, and values orientation
- models learning skills and invites discussion/commentary
- uses small-group discussion format
- is well prepared and up-to-date
- involves short "lectures" followed by prepared learning activities and discussion
- is based on assessed needs of group

BOX 3.1

Family Life Education Is Most Effective When It . . .

ards caused by obesity (acquisition of knowledge). She is also aware of feeling unhappy with her body image and believes that she would feel better and get better responses from friends and coworkers if she were slimmer (insight). She decides to try a new diet that she read about in a magazine (experimental action). The first couple of days go well, but then she begins to long for her favorite comfort foods and finds it to be a lot of trouble to always be counting calories and fat grams. Her resolve weakens, and she starts to give in and give up. But she goes back and reads the article again. It suggests she make a list of the good things that will come from losing weight. It also suggests new menus that sound interesting and not too difficult. Some of Ann's friends are not very helpful. They applaud her efforts but say she shouldn't let the diet control her life; it won't hurt to cheat now and then. They urge her to eat a little more when they go to lunch together. Some say her personality will change if she gets too thin. For now, Ann decides not to listen to them. She is determined to follow through (commitment to change and growth). She calls a friend who has decided to go on the diet with her. They talk about the temptations, and they encourage each other. They decide to share cooking duties during the week and to make larger quantities that they can freeze to eat later. They set a date to go shopping for new clothes after a month has passed. As Ann's weight drops, she begins to get compliments from some of her coworkers and friends. Others seem to be jealous and make comments about how long it is taking and so forth. But Ann is getting enough reinforcement to keep going (relational reorganization and acceptance).

For illustration's sake, this story has a happy ending; but Ann's successful journey has not been an easy or a guaranteed one, as any of us who have tried to lose weight can testify. When the learning model is applied to topics such as parenting or enhancing interpersonal skills, the challenge is even greater. It takes sustained attention and consistent reinforcement to incorporate new behaviors. Yet many times the family life educator is asked to present programs of one hour or less on family life education topics ranging from developing intimacy to parenting the difficult child. Is anything accomplished by such short-term contact? What about the weekend seminar or retreat? Or the 50-minute sex education class once a week for 6 weeks? Do people retain any of the facts presented long enough to apply them and incorporate them into their lives? Malcolm Knowles's research (1989) concluded that average people retain 20% of what they hear, 40% of what they hear and see, and 80% of what they do or discover for themselves. He also determined that learning is most effective when the learner feels respected by the teacher, can relate the information to his or her own life experience, and can see immediate use for the information.

Learning Styles

Just as people even in the same family have different personalities and preferences, so persons, old or young, have different learning styles. The emphasis on learning styles has been a recent focus of education research, and several explanatory models have emerged (Gregorc, 1982; Kolb, 1984; Sternberg, 1988). The Gregorc model encompasses learners of all ages and is based on a two-pronged assumption:

1. We take in information (perception) in two ways: concretely and abstractly.
2. We use information (ordering) in two ways: sequentially and randomly.

This results in four primary learning style combinations: concrete sequential (CS); abstract sequential (AS); abstract random (AR); and concrete random (CR).

CONCRETE SEQUENTIAL (CS)   CS learners are generally perceived as orderly, disciplined, and organized persons. They prefer a plan that leads from point A to point B, and they become uncomfortable veering from that plan. CS learners are usually dependable, hardworking, and stable. They are often tempted to "pick up the slack" or "do it for" the less organized or slower paced learners:

> *Mary is always on time to the seminar and has her homework assignment ready to hand in. She keeps all of her notes and assignments in a special notebook that she brings with her every time. She usually brings extra paper and pens for her group members who may have forgotten, although they pay the price of enduring Mary's smug expressions. Mary prefers lecture, handouts, and personal work assignments to the small-group discussions, which she describes as "a waste of time."*

ABSTRACT SEQUENTIAL (AS)   AS learners tend to be analytic thinkers who prefer to acquire knowledge through a vast number of sources. They are usually thorough, logical, and deliberate in their consideration of a topic. They do not like to be rushed and generally take more time to make decisions than the other learners:

> *Joseph wants extra reading assignments on the seminar's topic for the week. He sometimes brings in news articles related to the topic and he enjoys discussing the pros and cons of any idea. He is hard to pin down, however, especially when the group has to reach consensus on a question within a short time period.*

ABSTRACT RANDOM (AR)   AR learners are defined as sensitive, compassionate, and perceptive. They are quick to pick up on the needs of others, and they are natural nurturers. If people are upset, AR learners readily assume guilt and work to avoid open conflict. They are spontaneous, flexible, and idealistic:

> *Earl is quickly bored with lectures and paper and pencil tasks. He prefers small-group discussion and brainstorming about problem solutions. It fascinates him to hear other group members' personal stories, and he enjoys sharing his own personal experiences. He has little patience with someone who hogs all the time (either as presenter or discussant), but he doesn't know how to voice his frustration without making someone angry. When decisions have to be made Earl may voice his opinion, but he will "go with the flow" and quickly adapt to what the majority wants to do rather than risk an argument or disapproval from someone in the group.*

CONCRETE RANDOM (CR)   CR learners are the most challenging for a teacher or presenter. They are strong-willed, curious, and realistic. Their quick and creative minds are easily bored. CR learners crave adventure and innovation. The CR learner, whose independent and innovative thought processes challenge traditional teaching situations and methodologies, may often wind up in trouble with the teacher.

> *Susan is often late to the seminar and usually arrives in a state of agitation. Her life seems to go from crisis to crisis, and she much prefers to recount this real-life experience to the group than to focus on the topic being discussed. When she settles down and is given a specific task that allows for creative expression and personal application, she works intensely and quickly. She is often ready to move on to another task before most of the members have finished. Susan is also quick to laugh and to make jokes or puns, often interrupting the flow of the session with her spontaneous creativity.*

Although no one style is the "right" one, the concrete sequential learner tends to be seen as the "model student." Learners who do not fall naturally into the CS category are often judged to be undisciplined, disorganized, or unmotivated. Their learning strengths go unrecognized and unrewarded. Furthermore,

Concrete Sequential (CS)	**Abstract Sequential (AS)**
hardworking	analytic
conventional	objective
accurate	knowledgeable
stable	thorough
dependable	structured
consistent	logical
factual	deliberate
organized	systematic

Abstract Random (AR)	**Concrete Random (CR)**
sensitive	quick
compassionate	intuitive
perceptive	curious
imaginative	realistic
idealistic	creative
sentimental	innovative
spontaneous	instinctive
flexible	adventurous

teachers tend to approach a topic using their own learning style and ignore all others, with frustrating results for both teacher and many learners. As greater understanding of personality types and preferences has developed in the last 20 years, the awareness that people also learn in different ways has grown. Other styles of learning have been identified and are better understood. The learning styles are further defined in Figure 3.1. Before reading on, consider which combination best describes your own learning style. Each style has strengths and challenges. What would you say are the challenges of your style?

Sensory Modalities

Learners also perceive and take in information using a variety of senses. These modalities have been categorized as *auditory, visual,* and *kinetic* (Barbe, 1985). Although each person may have a dominant modality, she or he can use all three in the process of learning. Retention and application of information is enhanced when all sensory modalities are incorporated in the learning experience. How various learning techniques can be applied to the modalities is illustrated in Figure 3.2. Some of the learning exercises obviously involve more than one modality, serving to enhance effectiveness. Ideally, family life education presentations and programs will incorporate all three learning modalities in creative combinations.

Auditory Learning	Visual Learning	Kinesthetic
Presentation/lecture	Computer graphics	Puzzles, games
Songs, poems, stories	Demonstration/modeling	Note taking
Discussion	Personal inventories/assessments	Question cards
Humor		Role plays
Audiotapes	Brainstorming on charts, blackboard	Pencil and paper tests
Debate		Journaling
	Cartoons	Drawing
	Books, reading assignments	Manipulative materials (clay, pipecleaners, dominoes, etc.)
	Slides, transparencies, posters	Movement into groups (dyads, triads, etc.) or lines (opinion continuums)
	Films, videotapes	Reporting assignments (give a task to do in class or out of class)

FIGURE 3.2
Learning Modalities and Classroom Experiences.

Source: From *Growing Up Learning* by W. B. Barbe, 1985, Washington, DC: Acropolis Books.

What about the Short-Term Program?

We return now to the question of the value of the 1-hour program for effective education. Although the brief, one-time program is severely limited in its effectiveness, it can be the beginning point for developing individual awareness and intellectual development. It may be a safer way for people who are skittish about attending long-term parenting or marriage enrichment programs to "test the waters," have negative stereotypes challenged, and lay a positive foundation for future involvement. Unfortunately, many institutions assume that they have done all they need to do to educate when they have a speaker come to talk about parent education or sex education. Our own educational challenge as family life educators is to raise awareness among community leaders regarding the limitations of short-term programs and encourage alternatives that we know—from theory, educational models, and experience—will be more lasting and life changing.

SUMMARY

The value of theory-based program design and development was discussed in this chapter from the viewpoint of the educator and the learner. This discussion included a review of family systems theory, human ecology theory, exchange theory, and family developmental theory. Basic teaching assumptions and how assumptions relate to teaching effectiveness were addressed. The experience and conclusions of Vella (1994) and Mace (1981) stressed the importance of models and principles of learning that focus on interactive learning and build retention. A review of the learning styles typology developed by Gregorc (1992) and a discussion of sensory modalities for learning concluded the discussion.

QUESTIONS/PROBLEMS FOR DISCUSSION AND REVIEW

Class Discussion

1. Recall and describe the best teacher you ever had. How did her or his methods correspond with the list of effective teaching strategies listed in Box 3.1?

2. Determine which of Gregorc's learning styles (Figure 3.1) best describes your personality. Then discuss as a group the different learning styles among the group members. How can a group with so many different styles learn to work effectively together? How would you as an educator or group leader design a program that would affirm all of the learning styles?

3. Using your own family constellation, how do you see it fitting with the developmental stage theory articulated by Evelyn Duvall and Brent Miller (Table 3.1)? If there are exceptions in many families, does that make the theory invalid or useless? Why or why not?

Research Problems

1. The area of emphasis on family wellness and family strengths has been prominent in family research during the last few years. Review several of these studies. Are there commonalities between them? What overarching principles seem to be incorporated in all? Compare with the characteristics of healthy family systems.

2. A book by Judith Rich Harris, *The Nurture Assumption* (1998), has stirred much discussion over the value of parental influence on children in the course of their development. Read the book and consider the research on which Harris bases her conclusions, looking particularly at its thoroughness and possible bias. Are there influences or issues she may have ignored? What counterarguments have been presented in journal articles and Internet discussions? Are these arguments or defenses supported with valid research? What conclusion do you personally reach about the issue?

Case Study Design

If you are developing a program based on the case studies in Chapters 1 or 11, review the program now by applying the criteria for effective programs listed in Box 3.1. What might you want to add or change about the shape of your program design?

CHAPTER 4

Addressing the Needs of Your Audience

AN IMPORTANT FIRST STEP in establishing programs for children, youth, adults, and families is to determine the needs of the specific group you are working with (National Commission on Family Life Education, 1968). This allows the educator to develop program priorities and to know more about the major concerns of the learners and to therefore be more effective.

The first two "operational principles" of family life education, as defined by Arcus, Schvaneveldt, and Moss (1993), support the value of the needs assessment process (p. 14). Principle 1 states: *Family life education is relevant to individuals and families throughout the life span.* At all ages and stages, people experience normative changes (births, deaths, moves) and nonnormative changes (divorce, parenting a special needs child, serious accident or injury). Each of these situations brings the need for certain resources and education in order to most effectively cope and adjust. Principle 2 follows logically after: *Family life education should be based on the needs of individuals and families.* But needs are not as easy to pin down as it first may appear.

Let us look again at the design of a sexuality education program for adolescents. One teen, when asked what she needs to know about sexuality, might say: "I need more information about birth control and what to do if I get pregnant." Another teen could answer, "I need to know how to say 'no' without hurting someone's feelings." Yet another teen responds, "What I really want to know is how to satisfy my girlfriend: Where are the 'spots' that turn her on?"

A parent, if asked about the program design, could say: "My children need to know more about what causes pregnancy, how to protect yourself, and why you shouldn't have sex before you're married." Another may say, "He needs to learn respect for other people and their choices." A third parent speaks up: "They don't need a lot of information. They just need to know that sex before marriage is wrong." The educator will probably have her or his own agenda of needs, based on developmental stages and tasks and the knowledge of adolescent stressors. He or she believes that adolescents need information on pubertal changes in their bodies and emotions; they need practice in good decision-making skills; they need to know the difference between love and infatuation; and they need to know what it really means to be a parent to an infant. A special-interest group or a government grant may put limitations on the program content. Guidelines could specify that the adolescents be taught only certain information, such as how to prevent sexually transmitted disease. They may also prohibit discussion of other related topics, particularly those that are seen (by at least some of the community) to go against the community's prevailing value standards. So how does the educator sort out all of the various voices and expectations? How does the educator decide what the needs are and which ones to address in the program? You can see why it is easier not to ask in the first place! Yet educators must not overlook this important first step in developing a program that really fulfills its primary objective: to promote "learning for living."

RECOGNIZING TYPES OF NEEDS

Three basic types of needs are addressed in family life education programs: felt needs, ascribed needs, and future needs (Arcus et al., 1993). All are important in determining program design, and all are assessed in different ways. Additionally, the educator must identify what are the developmental needs and abilities of the audience to take in and process information. Otherwise, a program with good, relevant content will still miss the mark of providing relevant, useful information and experiences.

Felt Needs

These are the needs that potential learners specifically tell you about. Felt needs are very personal and based on the learners' experience with the topic. They may be not only individualistic but also culture centered. Felt needs tend to address immediate problems with a hope for quick answers—which may or may not be possible. Regardless, the needs and concerns of the learners should be acknowledged by the educator and addressed in some fashion during the program. Otherwise, the learners will feel frustrated and doubtful about the value of the program to their personal situation, and they will "vote with their feet," says program developer Jane Vella (1994). Expression of felt needs helps the leader to get to know the learners better and to establish rapport and empathy with them. It also provides points of reference for moving from the specific issue or concern to a more general topic of discussion or a deeper level of need. "Modeling a true attitude of inquiry and learning is perhaps the most useful thing a teacher of adults can do" (Vella, 1994, p. 50).

Ascribed Needs

"To ascribe" is defined in the WordNet Vocabulary Helper (1997) as "to assign" or "to attribute." Ascribed needs are those identified by someone other than the learner and assigned to the person or group as a need. For example, a pediatrician may determine that an infant is undernourished and conclude that the young mother needs information on nutrition, even though the parent has no awareness of that need. A parent educator who has studied the latest research on brain development may determine that the new parents' group he is leading needs to learn more about the importance of infant stimulation and giving affection—even though the group may not have mentioned this as a felt need. A teacher in the university knows that her students need information on family systems theory because their future career plans will draw upon such knowledge, whether they know they need it or not!

The area of ascribed need has its risks also, particularly when cross-cultural programs are being planned. Past history can be a valuable teacher about what *not* to do. Up until the 1970s a cultural deficit model was most often used to design programs. The main objective: to remedy a problem, or what was seen by the researchers and educators as a problem, that is, low achievement on mainstream cultural norms. "Such an approach not only undermined the strength that characterizes various cultural groups but also robbed them of their dignity as a people" (Hildreth & Sugawara, 1993, p. 177).

One of the harshest examples of this approach involved the American Indian children who were placed in boarding schools run by the Bureau of Indian Affairs (established in 1834). For more than a century, the philosophy of the schools was to "kill the Indian and save the man" (Youcha, 1995, p. 222). Children were often taken forcibly from their families and totally cut off from their cultural traditions. In some schools they were forbidden to speak their native language and were given new Anglo names. This was what the school directors decided the children "needed" in order to become assimilated into the dominant culture: to become "real," that is, "White," Americans.

More recently, the recognition and appreciation of cultural differences and family strengths has been emphasized:

> This approach makes no value judgement about the relative "goodness" of each cultural group, and there is no intervention into the life of such a cultural group for the purpose of remediation and modeling. Instead, all cultural groups are valued for their uniqueness, so that programs change to meet the needs of individuals and families rather than vice versa. As a result, the dignity, integrity, and diversity of all cultural groups are preserved. Family life education programs that are sensitive to the diverse needs, expectations, and strengths of various cultural groups and are flexible enough to adjust their programs to meet this diversity are more likely to achieve success in aiding individuals to live meaningfully and effectively in a diverse society. (Hildreth & Sugawara, 1993, p. 178)

Adjusting to a multicultural society may yield a different set of needs and program goals than just focusing on the cultural group alone. Often, groups need to work together on common goals for school, community, and society at large. Family life educators can play a critical role in designing and implementing successful programs for culturally diverse societies if they are sensitive and knowledgeable about cultural diversity (Hildreth & Sugawara, 1993).

Because some 30% of young adults in the United States are members of an ethnic or cultural minority group (Phinney, 1990), it is important to spend time observing and listening to their opinions and their needs. To simply ascribe a set of needs to them based on one's limited experience with the cultural group would be counterproductive and disrespectful. Because differences within a main culture group can be vast, no one or two persons can validly "represent" the group's opinions and needs. Surveying a large representative sample from the target population will produce a more valid needs assessment and is vital for working effectively.

Future Needs

Addressing future needs is one way of preparing children and adults for the tasks and normative developmental changes that are to come. Even highly stressful events can be better handled if one understands fully what to expect in the future and what resources are available.

"Ms. Jones," a former preschool teacher at a college laboratory school, had joined a parent support group in her community. Now, as the mother of two toddlers who were born within ten months of each other, she had her hands and lap full of squirming, crying, pushing, poking babies. The group was sharing personal experiences on the topic of "What I wish someone had told me before I had children." When it was Ms. Jones's turn, the harried mother observed, "I have a master's degree in child development and taught 20 3-year-olds every day for 4 years, but nobody ever told me it was going to be this bad!" She explained that she wouldn't change her decision about motherhood, but she would have been better equipped to handle the stresses of a difficult role if someone had told her what to expect.

Older adults need to consider the possibility of ill health and reduced income; children who are about to become the "big sister or brother" need to think about the changes that will take place in their family when the baby arrives; parents whose last child is leaving home need to consider empty-nest challenges. The Framework for Life Span Family Life Education (Appendix A, this volume) outlines in detail the developmental tasks of four distinct times of life: childhood, adolescence, adulthood, and older adulthood. Education programs developed around the various themes and developmental tasks can be very effective. But timing is everything! Too soon or too late can sabotage effectiveness (Arcus et al., 1993). For example, teaching middle-school adolescents about parenting skills is largely ineffective unless they are pregnant. Even then, their ability to realistically conceptualize what parenting will be like is limited by their level of cognitive development. A better approach is the one-on-one home visitor who starts her visits in the hospital after the young mother has given birth and is available when crises and questions arise. A support group for new mothers would also catch the teachable moment.

Developmental Needs and Abilities

A different kind of need category involves the educator's awareness of the developmental abilities of the participants. If a group of adults who are basic readers are asked to read complicated material or assessments, their needs and abilities are not being considered. If children or teens are expected to sit still and listen to a long lesson that involves little kinetic activity or interaction with the speaker, the teacher does not understand the cognitive and developmental abilities of this age group. An understanding of cognitive development, abilities, limitations, and interests (as long as this understanding is not based on stereotypes) will help the educator to assess the needs of the group and address them more effectively.

AGES AND STAGES OF NEED   Gross (1993) observes that we have different educational needs at different ages and stages of family development but that the stages also overlap as families are more often now dealing with four-generation issues. Schaie (1977/1978) succinctly summed up the basic questions and issues of four main stages of life (childhood/adolescence, younger adulthood, middle adulthood, and older adulthood) into two broad categories (see Table 4.1). For children and adolescents, the broad category is "What should I know?" For adults, it is "How should I use what I know?" This is not to imply that adults are closed to new knowledge but that their basic concern is with the application of knowledge to their lives. Irwin and Simons (1994) point out that Schaie's basic schema is compatible with the cognitive stages of Piaget and the psychosocial stages of Erikson. In this chapter, we focus on how to apply learning concepts to life experiences, the basic focus of family life education. But it is important to understand how people of various ages and abilities learn best. Cognition, according to Santrock (1992), is the process of receiving and interpreting information from our environment, through either our senses or our perception. How it is stored in memory and acted on is also a part of cognition. Piaget stressed the "acting on" part and theorized that humans act on information through assimilation, the incorporation of new information into one's existing knowledge, and accommodation, adjustment in one's attitudes and behavior because of the new knowledge. The more recently developed information-processing approach breaks cognition into smaller segments.

THE INFORMATION-PROCESSING APPROACH   This approach has been influenced and refined through considering how computers store and process information

TABLE 4.1 Schaie's Stages of Adult Cognitive Development

I. *"WHAT SHOULD I KNOW?"*		II. *"HOW SHOULD I USE WHAT I KNOW?"*		
Childhood and Adolescence	*Young Adulthood*	*Middle Adulthood*		*Later Adulthood*
Acquisition (Get Knowledge)	Achieving (Use Knowledge)	Responsible (Concern for Others)		Reintegrative (Wisdom)
		Executive (Concern for Social Systems)		

Note. From "Toward a Stage Theory of Adult Development" by K. Warner Schaie, 1977/78, *International Journal of Aging and Human Development 8:* 2, pp. 129–138, 1977–78, Amityville, NY: Baywood Publishing Company. Reprinted by permission.

and then comparing it with the human brain (Santrock, 1992). The physical brain is seen as similar to the computer's hardware and cognition to its software. A person takes information from the environment through sensory and perceptual processes (touch, taste, smell, sight, sound, emotional environment, relational interactions). This information is stored in the memory (short and long term) and used to expand thought (knowledge) and determine future behavior, which includes, first and foremost, language. This interaction and interpretation of the environment through language in turn creates more sensory and perceptual stimulation, more memory, more thought, and, hopefully, application to one's attitudes and behavior. It is at this last point—the application to one's attitudes and behaviors—that humans exceed computers, and it is at this point that family life educators hope to have a role and an influence.

Information processing in children   Children are constantly bombarded with sensory stimulation that they interact with and interpret in ways that are often quite different from the ways adults interpret the event (having had many more years of accumulated input, memory, thought, and interaction). It is important, however, for the adult to learn to understand what the child is saying and respond in a way that the child can incorporate into memory (Santrock, 1992). Three important learning processes enhance a child's long-term memory: rehearsal, organization, and imagery (McGilly & Siegler, 1989; Pressley & Harris, 1990). Rehearsal, the repetition of information after it has been presented, improves memory. Because children enjoy repeated stories and activities, it is no problem to incorporate rehearsal if the educator is attuned to the children's natural rhythm. Organization fits knowledge into categories: from naming five kinds of dogs to identifying the capitals of all the states to recognizing nonverbal signs of anger, distress, or approval. As with the rehearsal process, children in middle and late childhood are usually more capable of spontaneous organization, which improves memory retention. Imagery—the ability to picture in one's mind a scene, a story, an anticipated activity—enhances both memory and thought processes. Imagery encourages children to engage in the rehearsal of societal roles and behaviors and to play out their fears and dreams, both in the present and in the future time.

The extent to which these processes function efficiently (no "illegal function," to use a computer term, shuts them down) is determined by many influences. Age is the obvious one. But attitude, motivation, accessibility, past experiences, external and internal feelings of oppression, and health are others. Santrock (1992) summarizes: "The best way to nurture this motivation for knowledge is to allow the child to spontaneously interact with the environment. Education needs to ensure that it does not dull the child's eagerness to know by providing an overly rigid curriculum that disrupts the child's own rhythm and pace of learning" (p. 310).

Information processing in adolescents   As cognitive development continues, adolescents can use new skills for processing and using information. They can think more abstractly, logically, and idealistically. They are keenly aware of their own thoughts and what others are thinking about them, and they are very absorbed in their own social context. This may explain why research studies show that the knowledge that adolescents and young adults have about a subject does not necessarily coincide with their behavior. They may know all the facts about how pregnancy occurs, for example, and they may know that unprotected sex is very risky, but some will still engage in this risky behavior. Why is this so? For one thing, not all adolescents have reached the level of formal operational thought that fosters abstract thinking about logical consequences. Further research and testing of Piaget's original theory of the development of formal operational thinking in adolescence shows that there is much more variation in the level of formal operational thought than was first believed (Lapsley, 1989; Overton & Byrnes, 1991). Only one in three adolescents was determined to be a formal operational thinker. Many American adults never develop this level of thinking, nor do many adults in other cultures (Santrock, 1992). It is therefore wrong to assume that all adolescents and adults will process information in a way that will automatically lead to a change in behavior. Even highly educated adults are "guilty" of knowing the facts about exercise and good nutrition and yet never practicing those important habits. Why then would we assume that teens will change their behavior because they learn new facts?

A second reason why they may fail to act on the new information is that they have had little experience with the newly developed ability to do critical thinking. Although definitions of critical thinking vary, they all address the ability to think more deeply about problems and issues. This includes looking at varying points of view and discussing the merits and disadvantages of each. Critical thinking stresses the connection between cause and effect and the importance of making one's own decision about an issue, thought, or belief. Unless this critical thinking process has been encouraged and nurtured, it will not develop. Adolescents must have the freedom to speak their opinions without ridicule or judgment, but they should be challenged to state why they hold these opinions and to follow the course of an argument to its logical end. Adolescents must be regarded as persons moving toward total independence and therefore be allowed to make more of their own decisions and experience the consequences of those decisions. Programs that use people who share their stories of struggle, decision making, and the ultimate consequences will make much more of a lasting impression on teens than any carefully structured lecture. Role play, a chance to practice a social script and to discuss it afterward, will also bring more lasting impressions to adolescents and adults who are striving to develop critical thinking skills.

Information processing in young adults   The young adult of today is more likely to be single and mobile than in any previous period. In the past 30 years, the number of single adults living independently has doubled and includes three fourths of all men and women between the ages of 20 and 25. More than 20 million adults in the United States are never-married singles (Irwin & Simons, 1994). The number of cohabiting couples has increased by over 500% since the 1960s. Do these changing lifestyles affect the way one processes information? Schaie (1977/1978) proposed that young adults are in the *achieving* stage of cognitive development. They are using the knowledge they have acquired earlier to further their education, careers, leisure activities, and relationships. So family life education programs aimed at young adults should certainly utilize the small-group interaction format. Minilectures, which provide new schematics of information, followed by group discussion appeal to the young adult's desire to acquire and use knowledge.

Information processing in middle adulthood   Is there a difference between young adult and middle-aged adult thinking? Labouvie-Vief (1986) contends that the middle-aged adult is more pragmatic and at ease in a variety of situations than is the young adult. Three distinct characteristics of mature thinkers are (1) complex thinking that knows and can allow inconsistencies in thought and action to exist; (2) practical thinking that deemphasizes the idealistic "ifs" and "whens" of fantasizing; and (3) subjective thinking that feels free to disregard formal, logical rules in favor of intuition (Labouvie-Vief, 1986). In general, when compared with young adults, middle-aged adults are superior in answering questions based on real-life situations that require subjectivity and self-reliance. Whereas young adults are generally better at decision making through logical thought, some theorists and researchers term the middle-adulthood stage of life as the most creative (Cole, 1979; Simonton, 1977). Schaie (1977/1978) characterized middle-adulthood thinking as responsible and executive (see Table 4.1). The responsible aspect addresses the middle-aged adult's concern for others in the family and in society. This is the age of heavy involvement with children, aging parents, and church and/or civic organizations. Career advancement is also a primary concern. The executive aspect, which is defined by Schaie as concern for social systems, includes the leadership roles that middle-aged adults assume in business and community. Both aspects challenge the capabilities of middle-aged adults, who are very busy people. The effect on family life education programs is obvious: They need to be concise, well-planned, and accessible. Programs must demonstrate their usefulness and be time-efficient.

The ability to use creative problem solving to solve practical problems or improve a situation has been termed *postformal thinking* (Arlin, 1984). Postformal thinking recognizes the overlapping nature of the demands of everyday adult living in the contexts of work, home, friends, and society. It draws upon past experiences to define problems in better ways and to offer creative solutions. Yet it is believed that less than half of middle-aged adults engage in postformal thinking. Much of midlife thinking is more practical in nature: paying bills, raising teens, planning weddings, attending to needs of grandchildren and aging parents. It is easy to get into ruts of habituation. Kastenbaum (1984) described habituation as the growing tendency of middle-aged adults to depend on daily routines and limited expectations. They have become comfortable and complacent. This makes them less open to adaptation to new situations or challenges. Although dependence on routine can free one to focus on other tasks that require more energy, it can also become extreme—a condition termed *hyperhabituation*. At this point, any change in routine or habitual experiences is strongly resisted and feared. Fortunately, this condition is also extremely rare (Datan, Rodeheaver, & Hughes, 1987).

Information processing in older adults   Current activities of many older adults are blasting the stereotype of the "failing granny." More than 340,000 Americans aged 65 and older are enrolled in college (Peterson, 1985). Schaie (1978) describes this cognitive stage as *reintegrative,* or the age of wisdom. Many learning experiments with older adults show that comprehension is still keen, although reflexes are slower than in younger adults (Clark, Lanphear, & Riddick, 1987). Older adults tend to emphasize personal experience over straight logic. They are cautious about trying new things if the "old ways" are satisfactory to them. They tend to prefer practical solutions over "ideal" ones (Botwinick, 1967). In general, older adults are slower at problem solving and tend to ask more inefficient questions when trying to solve a problem. This is not true of more educated adults, particularly those who have continued to read, study, and remain actively involved with others (Irwin & Simons, 1994). Short-term memory is somewhat impaired. In one study, older adults had more problems reporting details of a story just heard or a passage read. However, they did well in summarizing the essential meaning of the material. They may become distracted if material that is being read or recited contains a number of pronouns or auxiliary phrases. Short sentences using basic sentence structure communicate best. Long-term memory remains strong, although recall may take longer than in the past. "Priming," or "prompting," greatly improves recall. Bahrick (1984) reported on a research study that compared recall of Spanish by younger adults who had completed a Spanish class in the past 3 years with that by older adults who had studied Spanish 50 years ago. Not surprisingly, the younger adults did better; but what was surprising was that the older adults recalled 80% of what the young adults remembered, even though more than 47 years had elapsed! The slope of decline in intelligence that psychologists of the 1960s assumed to start right after college has been greatly overrated. The most consistent finding is that a person's response rate to questions or problems slows as one ages, but, given no time limits, performance on many mental tests is equal to that of young adults.

Self-actualizing creativity is a term coined by Abraham Maslow (1959) to describe the personal intelligence that comes from experiencing a long life. Such creative wisdom can be passed from older to younger individuals, forming a valuable network of interconnectedness.

The conclusion about information-processing ability is that it varies widely among all ages. Many factors, including educational level, test-taking style, health, personality characteristics, and exposure to information through many sources, have an influence on a person's level of cognitive reasoning. But overall, problem-solving abilities are very much tied to life experience—gained through repetition, rehearsal, memory, envisioning, and creativity.

CONDUCTING AN ASSESSMENT

The Process

Vella (1994) considers the process of needs assessment to have three distinct components: (1) ask, (2) study, and (3) observe. There are two basic kinds of asking to be done. First, to start the "investigation" process, one must first seek permission from appropriate authorities—and the participants themselves—to conduct an assessment. The appropriate authority might be the school board or a principal, the church youth minister, and/or the parents (if the participants are under 18). Determining which type of permission is necessary—formal or informal—is governed by the sensitivity of the topic and the age of the participants. The prevailing cultural and political climate will also have a bearing on the type of permission one should seek to conduct a needs assessment.

In a formal permission process, a written permission form will explain who you are and what the purpose of your assessment is. The form should assure the consenting party and the participant that all participation is voluntary—no one will be forced to participate—and that all information gathered will be used anonymously. There should be a place for the consenting party to sign (see Appendix C, this volume, for an example).

Many types of consent to conduct a needs assessment are more informal and do not require a written form. For example, you may verbally request that a group of adults at a PTA meeting fill out a brief questionnaire about the upcoming program topic or explain to a school class that the teacher has given you a few minutes to ask some questions about smoking or teen dating. It may be as informal as asking an already assembled group how many are grandparents or who has teenagers, school-aged children, and so forth.

The second type of "asking" is used to uncover the felt needs of the target group for whom you are designing a program. The purpose of such asking goes far beyond getting answers to the basic question, "What do you want to know about . . . ?" Asking opens up room for relationship and the building of trust between teacher and learner. It sends the message that you really care about what they think and feel. Asking allows you to discern attitudes and cultural values of the group and to see what topics might be of interest to them that you, or they, may not have thought about before. Freire (1970) termed this "thematic analysis." It is a way of listening and understanding the themes of importance in a person's life. "When . . . learners are bored or indifferent, it means their themes have been neglected in planning the course. Motivation is magically enhanced, however, when we teach them about their own themes. People are naturally excited to learn anything that helps them understand their own themes, their own lives" (Vella, 1994, p. 5). Vella recounts an example of a phone interview needs assessment that a colleague conducted:

> A colleague of mine, Dr. Paula Berardinelli, doing training in time management skills with a group of secretaries at a major industry, sent a number of them the draft program for the training a month before the event. She indicated that she would be calling them for a ten-minute conversation on a specified day. When she spoke with them, one by one, she heard a similar set of themes about their work. She also heard, over and over, how delighted they were by her call. They cited many incidents she could use in the training—as stories for analysis, praxis material for reflection—and helped her understand some of the unspoken variables they were working with. The result was a course that was accountable to the industry and to the adult learners, who knew themselves to be subjects in a healthy relationship with the teacher. Although she spoke with only one-tenth of the group, the entire unit had heard of her needs assessment and were prepared at the outset of the day to offer their ideas spontaneously and creatively. Virtually all of the secretaries said this had never happened to them before. (pp. 5–6)

The needs assessment can be conducted in a variety of settings: as a small focus group, a phone interview, or a written questionnaire, to name a few. Types of assessments are discussed further in the next section of this chapter.

A second step in the needs assessment process is to study. The educator should take time to research and read about the age group and the culture. Read some of their popular literature. Get to know their heroes and their interests. Put assumptions and prejudices aside and study for insight and understanding. This takes time and patience, but it is invaluable for designing truly effective programs.

The third step in the process is to observe. While observing implies a passive spectator stance, it actually demands involvement and immersion by the potential teacher in the culture and values of the reference group. It also requires a willingness to become the one being taught: to "get inside their skins" in order to understand the pressures, dilemmas, and challenges that they face in their life themes.

Suppose you are asked to design a parenting program for teen parents in the local high school. Spending a day or two as an unobtrusive observer in the school's classrooms and halls can give you some idea of the teens' situations and cultural values. Going with the teacher on home visits can further clarify what the teen has to cope with as both a student and a new mother. It is important to be introduced to the situation by someone who is trusted and accepted by the prospective learners. Also, you must be able to convey interest and warmth when persons approach you with questions or comments. Genuine smiles and a relaxed attitude are a must!

One question remains: In cases in which program material is sensitive and the issues politically charged, how do you determine what needs will be addressed? If you are designing a program that is being funded through a grant or research project, you must function within the parameters of the specified content that can or cannot be discussed. To do otherwise would be unethical and would destroy your credibility. It is possible to preface your program with some words about the scope of the program to be presented. Acknowledge that all topics gleaned from the needs assessment will not be covered but that you will address the following. All of the information you collected from the assessment, shared anonymously, of course, could be useful to parents and policy makers as they consider what type of programs to plan in the future.

Assessment Techniques

There are many ways and many times to do needs assessment. Adapting the type of assessment to the group is the first step in a creative process of engaging each individual in a mutual learning experience. The amount of time you have, the context, and the available resources are some of the factors that will determine your choice of a needs assessment technique for a particular group. Vella (1994) also stresses that needs assessment is an ongoing process that continues as the leader comes to know the learners and their current levels of knowledge of and experience with the topic being discussed. Some of the ways of gathering information about the learners' concerns have been mentioned already. This section discusses the main techniques for beginning the needs assessment process.

THE FOCUS GROUP   A focus group is composed of a small group of representative persons (six to eight) drawn from the pool of potential participants in the program. The purpose of a needs assessment focus group is to gather information from participants about their concerns and attitudes on issues related to the program topic. The value of the group format versus an interview is that it provides opportunity for feedback from members about the opinions of other members. It allows for clarification and a better understanding about whether one person's opinion is representative of the group. Group interchange also generates questions or issues that might not have been thought about by one person or by the facilitator alone.

The group facilitator is usually the educator who is planning the program and leading the group. However, when a focus group is used at the end of a program for program evaluation, it is important for participants to feel that they can speak freely about program effectiveness. In that case, a neutral third party who is skilled in leading group discussion should be chosen as focus group facilitator, and the program facilitator should not be present.

How to create a climate for participation   Ask someone who works with the target group and knows them well to choose a cross section of participants to visit with you for a specified time (30 minutes to 1 hour). Include at least 10 minutes extra in the schedule for gathering time. Arrange also to have someone present to take notes during the discussion, preferably a colleague who would accompany you rather than the person who selected the group or a participant. In order to encourage a relaxed atmosphere, the setting for the focus group should be carefully planned. Spend some time arranging the room beforehand. Put the chairs in a circle, prepare light refreshments, and provide name tags. Greet the participants as they arrive, introduce yourself, and thank them for coming. At the appointed time (don't wait around for latecomers), start the meeting. Explain who you are and who the recorder is. Thank them for coming, and let them know that you need their help: You want to get to know them better in order to plan a program that really meets their needs. Start with the "easy" questions that are basically demographic: Ask for each person's name and ask a simple question or two, such as, "How many people are in your family?" "Are you the youngest, oldest, middle?" "What grade are you in in school?" "What's your favorite thing to do with your brother/sister/mother/father?" This gentle process can ease anxiety and will help to develop rapport between you and the future participants of your group.

Use open-ended questions   The second-stage questions are more directly related to your planned program topic and are generally open-ended questions (not answered by a "yes" or "no"). For example, "What do you think will be the hardest thing about being the parent of a newborn?" or "If someone made a video about child management, what do you think they should include?" or "How do you handle a disagreement between you and your spouse—or you and the grandparents—over how to discipline your child?" "What areas seem to cause the most disagreement?" Questions such as these should not be posed to any particular person but should be voluntarily answered. Encourage all to participate, but be sure to keep the participation voluntary and to acknowledge appreciatively any contribution from a group member. For example, "Let's hear from some of the rest of you. What do you think is the biggest stress in parenting?" Never ignore or slide over someone's comment. All contributions are important and worthy being acknowledged, even if they're a little "off-base." Generally, this should include a verbal restatement of what was said. This lets the person know he or she has been heard and gives time for the recorder to write the comment and time for other group members to consider their own responses. Avoid expressions (either verbal or nonverbal) of judgment or belittling. Listen to what is not being said as well as to what is being verbalized.

For groups of children or teens, the best type of question poses a hypothetical situation: "Suppose you are about to bring your new baby home from the hospital. What are the main things you will need to know how to do? What would you like to ask someone about being a parent?" or "What would you like your younger brother or sister to know about sexuality?" or (for a class on ethical decisions) "If you found a $50 bill on the sidewalk, how would you decide whether to keep it or not?" A question like this will help you understand the level of clarity or confusion about decision making. Children and teens are also good at listing things that "bug" them (about living with brothers and sisters, about dating, about being part of a stepfamily). To keep things on a positive note, you might follow a "bug" question with, "What do you like about (dating, etc.)?" With adult groups, a straightforward question will usually be effective, such as "What would you like to know more about in the area of (handling stress, managing your time, parenting adolescents, etc.)?"

THE INTERVIEW TECHNIQUE   Interviews to determine participant needs and interests can be conducted either in person or over the phone. A sample of persons from the target participant population is randomly selected to be interviewed regarding the design of a planned program. About 10% of the participant group will provide a good sample. Advantages of this technique include the sense of safety in speaking to one person instead of the whole group and a stronger sense of dialogue between two persons. Effectiveness is also enhanced by sending a letter ahead of the interview outlining the scope of the planned seminar, as was done in the example of the phone-interview technique in the previous section on the needs assessment process. By giving persons time to think ahead about the topic, the interviewer is likely to get more thoughtful and thorough feedback. The major disadvantage is the amount of time it takes.

Another way to use the interview technique, but only as a supplement to other needs assessment, is to interview persons who work with the target group, such as social workers, schoolteachers, or ministers. Their experience can often detect patterns of questions or behaviors that also need to be addressed in a program.

THE QUESTIONNAIRE   A written needs assessment can "poll" the group on their most pressing needs and allows every potential participant to respond. It can also bring to the surface issues that a person or group may not think about during an interview or group session. The questionnaire should be easy to understand and relatively short. Preferably, it should be filled out on the spot—at the beginning of a class or in the office cafeteria, with the interviewer waiting nearby. Any time the person has to do it at home, survey participation drops. It can be as simple as: *Below is a list of issues that parents of newborns usually have to deal with. Please check the ones that you would like to have discussed in the upcoming seminar on "Baby Bliss and Baby Blues." You may check as many as you wish.* At the end of the questionnaire, always invite other suggestions or comments by leaving several blank spaces for write-ins. These comments will address some of the most pressing needs of your group. You may already be thinking that a questionnaire like this could generate too many topics to cover in one seminar (unless it's very long). What can you do about that?

In order to be responsive to all the needs that have been expressed, you can do several things. First, collate the returned questionnaires and determine which of the items have been checked most often. These should determine the major topics for seminar discussion. Next, see if any of the other needs expressed, particularly those write-in comments, can be subsumed under major categories. Finally, build in a Q-and-A time to deal with the expressed needs that do not fit into other categories. One parent educator has developed a technique for dealing efficiently with a number of parents' questions that also involves the whole group rather than just himself as responder. The parent (or the group leader) poses the question, and then the group is asked to provide individual responses, preferably from their own experiences. The responses are not evaluated or discussed but are simply recorded on a sheet of newsprint. The leader can of course add her own comments as well, but the ground rules state that there not be a discussion of the suggestions. The questioner is encouraged to take the suggestions, consider them, and see if any can be adapted to his or her situation. This structured-response Q-and-A time allows the group to have an opportunity for input while dealing with several issues rather than getting bogged down on just one or two.

Finally, when dealing with a long list of needs and interests, the leader can provide books, articles, and brochures that address some of the issues, particularly those that fall outside the parameters of the time and topic coverage of the seminar. It is always good to include in your introductory remarks a statement of appreciation for all of the input. Explain that many issues were checked as being of interest to members of the group and that there was only time enough to cover a few of these. Outline your basic seminar plan and topic coverage and invite the participants to review the books and pamphlets you have available. Another idea would be to plan a second seminar to deal with a major topic of expressed concern, such as "Protecting my child from sexual abuse."

OTHER CREATIVE TECHNIQUES   Your constant challenge as an educator is to design creative ways to do the three needs assessment tasks: ask, study, and observe. You may be visiting in a home, office, or classroom. You may be calling on the phone or handing out questionnaires or polling participants. Or you may be doing something even more innovative, such as posing a "three wishes" question to children about their family life or asking a group of pregnant teens to draw their greatest fears about becoming a mother. It may be asking a group of new parents to take a pretest about infant development during the first hour of a seminar. This is a wonderful method, incidentally, because it gives the leader a chance to note knowledge gaps and also to provide accurate information while involving the group in a "kinetic" activity. The point of all of this is to form warm, caring connections with the participants so that you become an informed friend instead of the "sage on the stage."

LISTENING EFFECTIVELY

Reuel Howe (1963) in his book *The Miracle of Dialogue* tells the story of an architect who was hired to build a house. The owner met with him to discuss the particular features she wanted in this new home, but when the architect returned with the plans, none of the special features had been included. "Why have you not included the things I told you about?" queried the homeowner. "Well, I didn't think they were that important, and you probably would regret spending the extra money. After all, I'm the one with experience in building houses," the architect replied. The architect was fired, and a new one hired. This new architect listened carefully to the owner and took her wishes seriously, while offering feedback and suggestions that would make the features less costly. Together, they built a house that was of outstanding design, better than either could have done alone.

Keys and Barriers to Effective Listening

Howe (1963) emphasizes that one of the biggest obstacles to communication is the tendency to carry on both sides of a dialogue. We draw conclusions in advance or make assumptions about the other person's response. Such communication then becomes a calculated monologue, which robs the other person of his freedom to be heard. Learning to really listen to another person involves a conscious decision to put aside one's personal agenda and assumptions. Virginia Satir (1988) explains that to listen fully means to:

- Give full attention to the speaker and be fully present
- Put aside any preconceived ideas of what the speaker is going to say
- Interpret what is said descriptively, not judgmentally
- Be alert for any confusion in the message received and be ready to reflect or ask questions to get clarity
- Let the speaker know that she or he has been heard and also the content of what was communicated

To effectively combine all of the elements of active listening takes concentration and practice, because a number of barriers can block the pathways. Howe (1963) lists four major barriers: language, image, anxiety and defensiveness, and contrary purposes. Language barriers are not limited to two people speaking in different tongues. Even people speaking the same language can be confused because of the various connotations and hidden meanings each person attaches to particular words and phrases.

Satir (1988, p. 71) illustrates with this simple exchange:

"I think it's hot in here."
"Do you mean that you're uncomfortable?"
"Yes."
"Do you mean that you want me to bring you a glass of water?"
"No."
"Do you mean that you want me to know that you are uncomfortable?"
"Yes."
"Do you want me to do something about it?"
"Yes."

There was certainly more being communicated in that one sentence than was readily apparent.

The barrier of image involves one's prejudices and preconceived ideas about the other person. Whether the images are negative or positive, they block out the possibility of true dialogue and understanding. The speaker and listener respond to ghosts and shadows, always holding something back, failing to hear and understand the other's needs and concerns.

The barrier of anxiety and defensiveness follows naturally on the heels of image. I (Powell) decided many years ago to take each person's comments at their best interpretation rather than their worst. I have been amazed at how often I was more on target with my better interpretation and have found that the hurtful remark was seldom really caused by dissatisfaction with me but rather arose out of the other person's history of past hurts or current stress.

Finally, the barrier of contrary purposes arises to block communication effectiveness. The speaker and listener must both be honest with themselves about their agenda. If the educator is doing a needs assessment in order to fulfill a requirement rather than to truly find out what the learner thinks, wants, and needs, then there will be no dialogue—only two people talking. Have you ever had to make a complaint to a store manager or supervisor? Typically, the manager starts explaining or making excuses before the customer finishes speaking. There is very little real attention to the customer's concerns. Rather than seeing this as an opportunity to improve customer service now and in the future, the manager tends to see his or her purpose as a defensive one. So the "conversation" of contrary purposes usually ends in frustration for both parties, one of whom will probably not patronize that business again.

Counselor and author Robert Doyle (1992) states that the primary role in establishing a trusting relationship is being able to communicate the message *I am interested in what you have to say and I am available to you.* Once that attitude is genuinely felt by the listener, there are some verbal and nonverbal listening techniques that will help to get the message across.

Types of Listening Skills

VERBAL CUES   The simple minimal verbal statement is a primary way to convey the message that the listener is tuned in to what is being said. "I see," "umhumm," "go on", and so forth are the verbal equivalents of a head nod and encourage the speaker to continue without interruption of their train of thought.

REFLECTIVE STATEMENTS   In this kind of "feedback," the listener acts as a mirror for the speaker's words. No interpretation should be done. The listener simply repeats a phrase or sentence or summarizes what the speaker has been saying. Here are some examples:

Speaker: I really get uptight when my children start fighting. It makes me want to just run away and never come back.

Listener: So their fighting makes you want to run away.

Speaker: What I really need to know is how to get my children to go to bed and stay there after I put them there.

Listener: Getting the kids to stay put!

Speaker: I don't really care about all that information on nutrition and exercise that our teacher keeps talking about. I want to know how to earn a living for myself and my baby!

Listener: Nutrition and exercise are not that important to you. You just want to know how to earn a good living.

Note the lack of judgment or advice giving. The reflective statement requires a neutral listener stance. Amazingly, a speaker will often rethink or qualify an opinion when it is repeated in this way.

ACCENT   This listening technique is especially helpful when getting feedback from a focus group or directing a class discussion. The listener accents—picks up on—some part of what the speaker has said and encourages the listener, or the group, to elaborate on that point. Not only does this demonstrate attentive listening, but it also validates the contribution of the speaker. For instance, the listener/facilitator may say, "Mary, I'm really interested in your comment on the difficulty you have in knowing how to discipline Mandy without spanking. Could you say some more about that?" Or, "Do others of you have the same

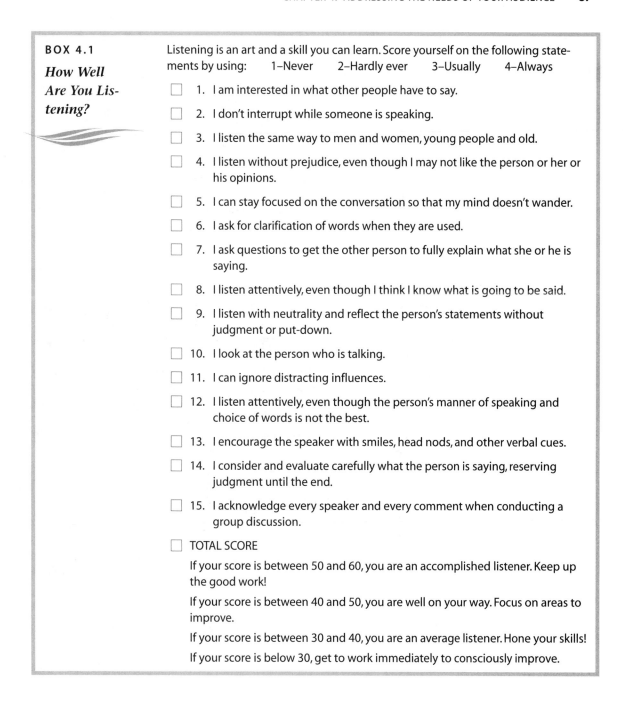

BOX 4.1

How Well Are You Listening?

Listening is an art and a skill you can learn. Score yourself on the following statements by using: 1–Never   2–Hardly ever   3–Usually   4–Always

☐   1. I am interested in what other people have to say.

☐   2. I don't interrupt while someone is speaking.

☐   3. I listen the same way to men and women, young people and old.

☐   4. I listen without prejudice, even though I may not like the person or her or his opinions.

☐   5. I can stay focused on the conversation so that my mind doesn't wander.

☐   6. I ask for clarification of words when they are used.

☐   7. I ask questions to get the other person to fully explain what she or he is saying.

☐   8. I listen attentively, even though I think I know what is going to be said.

☐   9. I listen with neutrality and reflect the person's statements without judgment or put-down.

☐   10. I look at the person who is talking.

☐   11. I can ignore distracting influences.

☐   12. I listen attentively, even though the person's manner of speaking and choice of words is not the best.

☐   13. I encourage the speaker with smiles, head nods, and other verbal cues.

☐   14. I consider and evaluate carefully what the person is saying, reserving judgment until the end.

☐   15. I acknowledge every speaker and every comment when conducting a group discussion.

☐   TOTAL SCORE

If your score is between 50 and 60, you are an accomplished listener. Keep up the good work!

If your score is between 40 and 50, you are well on your way. Focus on areas to improve.

If your score is between 30 and 40, you are an average listener. Hone your skills!

If your score is below 30, get to work immediately to consciously improve.

problem?" Or, "Sara, I'm glad you mentioned the issue of decision making between you and your husband. You know, this is one of the major reported stressors among new parents. What do you think causes it to be so stressful?"

PARAPHRASING   Here the listener restates the elements of the conversation, using different words that go beyond the speaker's words and include underlying meanings. Unless you are in a counseling setting, psychological interpretations of the speaker's statements should be avoided.

To further examine your listening skills level, score yourself on the "How well are you listening?" assessment (Box 4.1). After determining your strengths and weaknesses, choose one or two areas at a time to focus on improving. Empathic, active listening is an art and a skill that can be learned.

SUMMARY

This chapter addressed the issue of assessing needs of the program participants through a process and an understanding of developmental needs and abilities. Techniques for conducting needs assessments were reviewed and the role and skills of empathic, active listening emphasized.

The importance of timing was also stressed. To address a future need too soon or a felt need too late will sabotage a program's effectiveness. Thorough knowledge of developmental tasks at each age level, as well as acquaintance with the cultural and social contexts of the learners, keeps the program on target and the learners' life themes in focus.

QUESTIONS/PROBLEMS FOR DISCUSSION AND REVIEW

Class Discussion

1. Look again at the introductory example of expressed needs in regard to a sexuality education program. Which ones would be categorized as felt, ascribed, and future needs? Is one type more important to address than another in a program for adolescents? Explain your answer.

2. Persons have many different ways of processing information, and they are at many different stages. In light of this, how do you go about designing an effective program that takes this variability into account?

3. Think of a time when you worked together with someone of another culture or age group. What things did you or they do that helped you to work well together?

Research Problems/Activities

1. Choose an ethnic group from your community to research in the library and on the Internet, looking particularly at marriage and family experiences and customs. Then set up interviews with three or four persons from that ethnic group. Using the Life Span Family Life Education Framework (Appendix A, this volume), choose one of the categories (e.g., interpersonal relationships or families in society). Formulate a set of interview questions about the category across the life span that will help you examine how the developmental tasks articulated under that category are experienced by the chosen ethnic group.

2. If possible, audiotape your interviews from the previous activity so that you may critique your listening skills. How often did you make reflective statements or ask open-ended questions? What verbal cues and other attending behavior (smiles, nods, eye contact) did you use? What areas do you want to improve?

Case Study Design

1. If you are developing a program for a specific group, now is the time to conduct a needs assessment. Determine the type of assessment technique you want to use. Preferably, the class should divide into several groups, and each group should conduct a different type of assessment (focus group, questionnaire, interview, creative idea) to share with the class.

2. When the needs assessment is being conducted, assign two people as observers to evaluate the interviewers' listening skills. Have them note strengths and areas for improvement to share later with the group.

3. Review your experience with the class. What generally did you learn about the participants (about their developmental needs and abilities, their learning styles and unique characteristics) through the process of "ask, study, observe"? How would you evaluate your rapport with the group? Observers should share, without identifying specific people, what strengths and weaknesses in listening skills they observed.

4. Discuss the felt needs that were identified through the assessment process. What other needs (ascribed, future, developmental) should also be addressed in the program?

Understanding Group Process

AUTHOR ANNA QUINDLEN, in her book *Thinking Out Loud* (1993), cites a fortune cookie message as having had a major impact on her life. The cookie read: "To remember is to understand." "I have never forgotten it," said Quindlen. "A good judge remembers what it is like to be a lawyer. A good editor remembers being a writer. A good parent remembers what it was like to be a child" (p. 222). And a good group leader remembers what it was like to be a part of a group or a class directed by someone who knew the secrets of effective leadership. Stop reading now, and think for a moment about the best teachers or group leaders you ever had. What made them so effective? List the qualities in the margin of your book or on a separate sheet of paper. How did being a part of that class or group make you feel? Record that, too. Then remember and refer to these experiences as you consider your own potential for group leadership.

The capability to lead groups is listed by Gross (1993) as one of the main tasks of an effective family life educator. In this capacity, the educator is expected to:

- Provide learning experiences and activities that will help participants develop their own skills to more effective levels
- Maintain a balance between the presentation of information and the personalizing of the information through group discussion
- Cope with interpersonal problems that inevitably arise in groups
- Have an understanding of life-cycle development
- Have a good grasp of group development theory

Gross doesn't list *leap tall buildings in a single bound,* but it may seem like an unspoken expectation. Does a group leader have to be superhuman? No. Effective leadership skills can be learned. But most of all, a group leader must continually *remember* what it was like to be in a group that worked well. And by putting yourself in the place of the participants, you will develop empathy with them and understand more clearly what to do.

DEFINING A GROUP

As a family life educator, you will be called on to address all types of groups: from the civic group who gather for lunch and a 20-minute speaker to the stepparent support group that will meet together monthly for the next year. Some of these experiences will be purely presentational, whereas others will involve long-term, interactive small-group facilitation. It is the latter that we discuss in this chapter.

Although definitions of small groups differ, Shaw (1981) offers what might be termed the most generic definition of a small group: "Two or more people who are interacting with one another in such a manner that each person influences, or is influenced by, each other person" (p. 8). Shaw lists several essential elements of a small group: (1) 5 to 7 participants ideally, certainly not more than 20; (2) interaction between group members and with the facilitator; (3) a common purpose; and (4) mutual influence by talking and listening to each other, sharing values, expectations, and resources, thereby becoming interdependent.

It is important to note that small groups are formed for a variety of reasons. Bertcher and Maple (1996) enumerate several basic types. *Treatment groups* have as their primary purpose changing significant psychosocial problems that affect the group members' personal functioning and well-being. Leadership is by highly trained human service professionals, and the intensity of interaction is high. *Support groups* consist of individuals who strive to cope with similar issues and who support and encourage one another. Examples include alcohol or divorce recovery or parent support groups. Intensity of interaction would be considered moderate. Leadership can be provided by a group member who may have been informally trained or by human service professionals, or by representatives of both categories. *Educational groups* are designed to increase knowledge, teach skills, consider value issues, or all three. No assumptions are made of personal involvement or that the material will be difficult to grasp. It is assumed that the learning will affect behavior. There is little selectivity about who will participate, and intensity is low to moderate, depending on the topic and the amount of time allotted for the group to interact. *Task groups* assume no personal involvement with an issue and no change in the participant's daily life. A task group is formed to address a specific task. Leadership is usually elected or appointed from within the group, or it may be supplied by an administrator who needs input and group problem solving. An educational or support group can sometimes take on a task-group role, to carry out a specific project, for example. A *residential group* can be considered a subgroup of one of the other groups. The main difference is that participation in a residential group (e.g., at a prison or hospital) often may not be voluntary and could pose a particular challenge for the group leader. *Groups on the Internet* are a relatively new phenomenon by which groups form to discuss a variety of topics, including family relations and services. For example, potential adoptive parents may join an online group to discuss adoption issues. Anonymity can prompt some persons to share deeply with other anonymous persons. Bertcher and Maple (1996) see such groups as having "amazing potential" for dealing with personal issues, particularly for persons who would be hesitant to join a face-to-face group.

Shaw (1981) and Bowman (1990–1996) emphasize that having a common purpose does not imply that all group members think alike or that they come together with the same expectations or levels of need. Other personal and societal factors also influence receptivity or response. The recognition of this point is seen as one of the many signs of growing sophistication in the family resource movement. More attention is now being given to the impact of differences in life circumstance, learning style, and history of the participants. In the not-too-distant past, participating in a group was the only choice that many agencies had to offer to parents, regardless of their distinctive differences. According to Bowman (1990–1996), "Frequently, the primary distinctions in program choices were in ages of children, not parental circumstance, need, or tradition. . . . There was little recognition that stress, grief, gender, race, age, life circumstance or education could make a significant difference in the ways people might be able to learn (p. 1)."

Today, many more options for education and intervention are available to family case managers, such as peer helping, home-based services, video checkouts, and telephone "warm lines," call-in lines for parents in crisis or who need parenting information. Family life educators are now much more aware of certain life realities of the community members they seek to serve.

THE VALUE OF GROUP PARTICIPATION

Eric Berne (1963) proposed that *survival needs* are the basic reason that people join groups. He explained that as social beings, the motivation to join together with others actually fulfills four basic human needs: (1) a biological need for stimulation of the physical senses, especially touch, sight, and hearing; (2) a psychological need for time structuring—talking, working, playing together; (3) a social need for intimacy—being close, sharing thoughts and feelings; and (4) a physiological need for safety—the protection and support of others. Schultz (1989) described the appeal of the group to human needs in different terms: (1) the need for inclusion—to be wanted, to belong, to be recognized as a person of worth; (2) the need for control—over one's personal choices and over the environment in which one lives; (3) the need for affection—to both give and receive personal warmth and esteem, to get close to others.

All of these needs are powerful forces in human life. To provide a context in which such basic needs hopefully can be met is indeed a worthy endeavor. But groups are valuable for other reasons as well. Schultz (1989) points out the power of the group to effect change and to accomplish tasks that the individual might find impossible or at least much more difficult to achieve. The term *synergy* describes the concept of the whole being greater than the sum of its parts. The group, as well as its members, is stronger when individuals bring a variety of backgrounds and perspectives to bear on a problem:

> The hallmark of effective group process is mutuality, reciprocity, give and take. When it occurs in a group, power is unleashed. . . . Some give something they have. Others receive. And like popcorn popping, mutual help moves from person to person. At its best, reciprocity is energizing, empowering, and enduring. (Bowman, 1990–1996, p. 58)

THE FACILITATOR ROLE

Although the titles *leader* and *facilitator* denote basically the same role, the term *facilitator* is preferable because one who facilitates is less likely to be seen by the group as the expert with all the answers. Falling into the answer trap can short-circuit the group interaction process, and personal involvement with the issue ceases.

This is not meant to imply that groups work better without leadership. According to Schultz (1989), group leadership is necessary because groups need direction. They do not progress naturally in an organized fashion but tend to alternate between task needs and social needs. Issues also need clarification, and the impact of social-emotional relationships must be understood. An effective leader-facilitator helps to keep the group on track and functioning efficiently.

Napier and Gershenfeld (1983) point out a fundamental difference between the role of group facilitator and the role of teacher. The facilitator is not in charge, as is the teacher in a typical classroom. The group is in control of their learning and use of materials. Although the facilitator definitely must plan beforehand and have a goal in mind, it is the interaction of the group, which is not always predictable, that makes the group experience work.

Attributes of Effective Group Leaders

A classic study by Leiberman, Yalom, and Miles (1973) identified several important attributes of effective group leaders. *Caring* conveys friendship, protection, affection, and the invitation for members to receive feedback, support, and encouragement. This caring must be more than warm regard. It involves action that demonstrates the leaders' commitment to support families. This type of support aids them in building on their strengths in their neighborhoods and communities. But caring alone is not sufficient to sustain a lasting positive outcome. *Meaning attribution* helps the members to understand the plan, the purpose, and the importance of the group. Tasks include clarifying, interpreting, and providing frameworks for change. The leader understands that people learn by instruction as well as by doing. *Emotional stimulation* encourages but does not force emotional involvement of group members. Moderate-level sharing of the facilitator's personal feelings and life story is also received positively by group members. The *executive function* includes the ability to set goals, direct the flow of the meeting, and set necessary limits and structure. This function involves inviting, questioning, suggesting procedures, and decision-making functions.

But a group leader is not a perfect person, and mistakes in tactics or judgment will happen. In order to continually check one's congruency of motive and behavior, Bowman (1990–1996) suggests that facilitators regularly ask themselves the following questions:

☐ *Do I see the group members as clients, registrants, students, or partners?* A vision of collaborative learning and problem solving that does away with hierarchical roles will create the environment and results we desire. Collaboration doesn't mean that the facilitator discards skills, training, or the facilitator role. It does mean an attitude change and the ability to see persons as people with resources, ideas, new thoughts, and experiences that can be combined with yours to bring about learning and growth.

☐ *Do I see problems, weaknesses, and blame, or strengths and resiliency?* It is hard to move past prejudices and stereotypes, whether of homeless people or unwed mothers, and a litany of shoulds and oughts, to a point of encouragement for small strengths and possibilities of new directions. Because we all bring to the group our own beliefs and values, it is difficult to lay judgment aside; but effectiveness for meaningful group participation will be curtailed otherwise.

☐ *Am I exploring options, or giving answers and solutions?* When the leader assumes the role of fixer, the individual takes no ownership or lasting interest in the solution provided. It is important to resist the temptation to provide answers and instead to encourage the group members to explore possibilities.

Leadership Can Be Learned

Wood (1977) and Napier and Gershenfeld (1983) stress the fact that leadership behaviors can be learned. The primary requirement of anyone who wishes to learn to lead groups is adaptability. Effective leaders know how to adapt their contributions to the needs and expectations of the group. In other words, they have learned to diagnose and respond to what is going on in that particular group. They remain open to change and growth (Wood, 1977). Bertcher and Maple (1996) point out that some people work better with certain populations—for example, senior citizens, children, the terminally ill. Generally, a person who matches the demographics of the group (gender, race, age) is most likely to be accepted quickly. But this is not always the case. Deliberately mixed groups would probably fare better with cofacilitators who represent the major diversity factors.

Although the task of group leadership may seem daunting, fledgling leaders can cope with anxiety and build confidence by being thoroughly prepared and practicing activities beforehand. Starting small and building up, working with a co-leader, and getting experience as a group participant under an experienced group leader are also advisable (Napier & Gershenfeld, 1983). Finally, it is absolutely vital to be genuine and available and willing to ask for feedback from the group. Bowman (1990–1996) stresses the importance of leader self-care throughout the course of one's career as a group facilitator. Failure to care for one's own needs will result in burnout and fractured personal relationships. Establishing a mentor relationship with a colleague and interspersing group times with periods of relaxation can provide important self-care. Other stress reducers might include a standing lunch date with a good friend following a stressful group time or blocking out preparation time before a group time.

DEVELOPING A CLIMATE FOR PARTICIPATION

Getting Started

RECRUITING GROUP MEMBERS   Not everyone is totally comfortable being part of a group, particularly at first. If the group membership is required, rather than voluntary, anxiety and reluctance to participate will definitely be heightened.

Bertcher and Maple (1996) note that recruiting members may be the most difficult part, because people often have preconceived notions about what the group will be like. They may have had a previous bad experience with a group that has left them uneasy and afraid. They may simply be overwhelmed with other obligations and see this as just one more thing to add to a very busy schedule rather than as something that could help them manage other stress. It is very important to provide information to potential participants about the nature of the group, a statement of purpose that clearly states how this group will meet the needs of the individual, what time and how often the group will meet, and who to call if there are other questions.

Recruitment can be done directly through personal contact by the group facilitator (the person creating the group) or indirectly through referral resources. Either way, do not assume that one contact or announcement about the planned group will yield enough participants. Follow-up with referral resources and repeated announcements about the planned group are often necessary. Direct contact is preferable because it allows the group facilitator to determine personal roadblocks by asking if the person has ever participated in a group before and, if so, what the experience was like. If it was bad, the leader can then point out how this group will differ from his or her past experience. Getting personally acquainted with participants so that they have a chance to voice any reluctance can greatly enhance willingness to participate. Groups that are time limited (four sessions or one weekend, for example) may get greater participation, because the person is not obligated for an extended period of time. A group can always be extended for those who want to continue.

CHOOSING A MEETING SITE   In choosing a meeting location, it is essential to have privacy, audibility, comfort, and an absence of distractions. A meeting site that is close to the participants' neighborhoods or workplaces and therefore convenient is another important factor.

It is also important to choose a room size that matches the size of the group (Bertcher & Maple, 1996). Six people meeting in a banquet hall does not invite intimacy! Room arrangement also is a major consideration for enhancing group participation. Chairs in a circle or around a table (if this is a task-oriented group), rather than in rows, is always preferable. Bowman (1990–1996) points out that even the placement of the facilitator's chair—whether it is set apart or included as part of the circle—sends a message about the group climate.

SIZE OF THE GROUP   The size of the group also affects the amount and quality of communication within the group. With only six members and one facilitator, for example, each person has to manage 21 different relationships (Bertcher & Maple, 1996). The relational complexity increases exponentially with each addition to the group. Size also affects group members' motivation to get involved in group work. There appear to be higher satisfaction and cohesiveness in smaller groups and an increase in disagreement and antagonism as size increases. Although a large group has more resources to call on (knowledge, skills, and abilities), people often feel intimidated and unable to participate in a large group. The dominant members become more talkative, and their ideas tend to dominate decision making and the overall group climate. Research has shown that the more each member actively participates in the group, the more he or she will be affected by the group experience. If the group must be larger than six to eight people, the facilitator should divide the group into smaller units to discuss topics and have the large group reconvene at the end to reconnect with each other.

The First Meeting

INTRODUCTIONS   The first session sets the tone and direction the group experience will take. It is important to get acquainted and to address needs, expectations, and fears that group members might have. Napier and Gershenfeld (1983) note the importance of the first hour of the first session as a "grace period" during which the group reserves judgment and is cooperative and friendly. This is the time to establish yourself as an effective facilitator. There should be some review of your experience and an indication of your openness and humor. Let them know you have a plan and are well prepared. Convey a sense of confidence that you can handle any situation that arises because you believe in the competency of the group members to assist in working out the kinks in the plan. Be responsive to questions and comments, and learn their names.

GROUND RULES   Addressing ground rules and expectations for participation is another important topic to cover in the first session. This helps group members to feel safe as participants. Bowman (1990–1996) also emphasizes the value of group rituals, such as expected ways of beginning and ending the group and of ending relationships when members leave the group. Rituals are important because they establish needed boundaries and remove distractions to full participation. They aid in handling expressions of conflict or grief and give comfort. Gross (1993) summarizes some basic ground rules, which should be reviewed and posted at the first session: (1) everyone is encouraged to participate, but participation is voluntary; (2) we share our experiences, not our opinions; (3) every contribution is valuable and should not be judged or criticized; (4) you are free to ask questions and express concerns as we go along; (5) confidentiality and respect for each other is expected.

THE IMPORTANCE OF VARIETY   Bowman (1990–1996) emphasizes the value of variety in fostering group vitality: variety of methods, of tasks and groupings, and of follow-up questions. Sharing the discussion center, managing and encouraging input from everyone, and checking back after someone has received input are other ways to show appreciation for a wide range of feedback and participation.

Levels of Self-Disclosure

Sharing in a group setting is a new experience for many people. It is important for them to see the group as a safe place for taking the risk of self-disclosure. If the experience is rushed, some people may be scared off. The first session should structure opportunities for each person to share personal information without feeling exposed. In most cases, your modeling of appropriate levels of openness will encourage others to be open. Writing the answer to a question and then sharing it with a partner or a small group is one way of encouraging participation by everyone. One caution about pairing people, learned from personal experience, is that you may have people in your group who dislike each other. Forced pairing can cause friction to erupt. If a person seems especially reluctant to pair off, you might ask him or her to be your partner. Another way to handle this is to ask the group members to pick someone they don't know very well to be their partner.

John Powell (1969) enumerates five levels of self-disclosure, with Level 5 being the least disclosing and Level 1 the most. Level 5 is called "cliche communication." It acknowledges the other's presence: "Nice day, isn't it?" "Hi, how are you?" "Fine, how are you?" Level 4 consists of facts and biographical information about self: name, occupation, marital status, number of children. Level 3 moves to personal attitudes and ideas. This involves more risk of rejection or disapproval. Level 2 shares personal feelings, particularly those considered "negative" (anger, guilt, sadness, hurt). Level 1 is considered by Powell to be peak communication. The person shares private truths about him- or herself: Fears, behaviors, and thoughts that could bring rejection or disapproval are revealed. This level of sharing involves the most risk but also the most possibility for intimacy and close relationships. It is usually reached only when there is a high level of trust between people.

The European American cultural assumption that sharing personal stories and feelings is beneficial is not an assumption shared by every culture, or even every European American (Bowman, 1990–1996). The concept of saving or losing face is very important to personal esteem in many cultures. "Saving face" can range from not admitting weakness under any circumstance to a sense of personal privacy that does not allow discussion of personal issues in public. As we relate to more diverse groups, techniques that allow for discussion of personal matters without personal exposure need to be developed. Indirect methods, such as case studies, stories, or hypothetical situations, can allow group members to examine personal issues without the risk of "losing face." If you are working with a culture different from your own, it is very important to find out ahead of time about the particular cultural norms. The best resource is talking with representative members of the culture group, who can share their perspective with you.

The Time Factor

One of the major tasks of a group facilitator is to structure and set parameters for the group's time together. To start and end the group promptly at the time arranged, right from the first day, lets the members know they can trust you to control the boundaries of the group. This trust will carry over to other issues as the group develops. Some structure and a predictable routine create a safe space for risk, change, creativity, and handling of stress. Responsibility for the process lies with the group leader (Bowman, 1990–1996).

Napier and Gershenfeld (1983) emphasize the importance of taking breaks and not overloading a session or a program:

> Often what the group needs is less, not more: less information, fewer experiences and fewer lectures. The one ingredient participants need more of is time: time to regenerate their own energy and interest, time to think and integrate, time for psychological and physical rest, time for a change of pace, time to be reflective about the questions, and time to let go and have fun. (pp. 101–102)

THE GROUP PROCESS

Effective group process can be compared to a dance in which persons are acting and reacting in response to other persons: synchronized and in touch (Bowman, 1990–1996). As studies of learning have shown us, the higher the level of engagement and involvement by the learner, the greater the impact and retention. Group members also learn more when they feel respected and when the new learning is related to their life experience and has some immediate usefulness to them.

Theories of Group Dynamics

Whereas some theorists (Bion, 1961; Lewin, Lippitt, & White, 1939; Moreno, 1953) have focused on the individual's role and responses within the group, Bales (1950) turned his attention to the interaction within the group itself. Bales's work was accomplished through the use of an observational scheme that came to be known as IPA (Interactional Process Analysis) and a later version, called Systematic Multiple Level Observation of Groups (SYMLOG). Using this schematic, Bales and Cohen were able to chart the tasks and socioemotional activities of a group, phases in group development, and the types of roles group members assume. A major finding was the important role that communication plays in producing effective or ineffective groups. The research also confirmed that the most effective groups were those in which all members were essentially positive in their interactions with each other and in which power was shared rather than being in the hands of the leader or a few dominant members. The effective group was also fairly task oriented: There was direction and active work on individual or group goals. An effective facilitator recognizes that he or she must operate two domains of leadership: administrative (group management and task orientation) and affective (person-centered, feelings focus and "climate control"; Bowman, 1990–1996). Leaders who are aware of these needs and value them will see their role in several areas: tension and release of feelings and differences of opinion, "gatekeeping" during complex communication interactions, and encouraging and mediating so that all people can make their views known and no one dominates or is nonparticipative (Beebe & Masterson, 1990).

Systems theory has also been used to analyze group interactions and understand outcomes of group experience (Fisher, 1975). Just as a family operates as a system, with each member functioning in relation to all others and forming a whole unit, so it is with groups that become interdependent and cohesive. Input, process, and output variables can be identified; roles can be established; and the group can operate as an open or closed system.

In studying the developmental process in groups, Tuckman (1965) developed a set of descriptors that define a four-stage process: (1) forming, (2) storming, (3) norming, and (4) performing. Each of the four stages is discussed as it applies particularly to educational and support groups.

AWARENESS OF ETHICAL CHOICE   If your beliefs and values run counter to those of the group that has invited you to present, you must make a choice: to refuse the offer or to hold your own views in abeyance, which is actually impossible to do. Just as judges disqualify themselves from certain cases, facilitators should be aware that working with certain systems that are contrary to their beliefs can cause ethical problems.

AWARENESS OF ONE'S OWN POWER   The facilitator is often viewed as the expert on everything. You must resist the temptation to dominate or manipulate. Playing favorites is also unwise and tends to cause jealousy and antagonism among other group members. Ask for feedback (anonymous and written) from the group regarding how they see your role in order to provide a safeguard against falling into the "power trip trap."

TRUTH IN PACKAGING   Avoid false advertising about what this group experience will accomplish or what the possible risks are. Accept and acknowledge your limitations and those of the group.

VOLUNTARY PARTICIPATION   When a group member is forced to do anything, it can build resistance to future involvement. Ground rules that stress this point can emphasize the importance of this concept for you and them.

PRIVACY AND CONFIDENTIALITY   This is expected of leaders and group members. You should not obligate yourself to any sort of written report that reveals personal

Forming

A number of aspects of group formation were discussed earlier in the chapter. This section focuses on the leader's role in facilitating the formation process. There is always a tension between being well prepared and organized and being flexible and open to the group's ideas.

Recently, I (Powell) was asked to lead a four-session program on interpersonal relationships for women who were victims of domestic violence. The staff counselor had arranged the experience and given me some idea about the things she saw as topics that needed to be discussed. However, I had had no prior contact with the group before the evening of the first session. I definitely wanted to get their ideas and involve them in setting the agenda, but I could not go in empty-handed. By sketching out a four-session program beforehand, with a major topic assigned for each night, I had some feeling of preparedness. I also planned several get-acquainted exercises that involved low-level sharing of personal feelings and thoughts. But the main item on the first night's agenda was to ask them what they wanted to talk about in regard to personal relationships during the next four weeks. They were brimming with ideas. Their focus was not always the same as mine. It was easy, however, to incorporate their concerns into my basic outline confidences. If group participation is required by court, you may have to write a general statement about a person's involvement in the group. This should be noted at the outset.

COMPETENCE   The leader is expected to have the training and certification he or she claims to have. It is one thing to feel new and apprehensive, to know the material but be fearful about having the ability to work with the population. It is quite another thing to be so overwhelmed with an assignment that prayer and the fact that you are a good person are all that sustain you. Going beyond your level of competence is dangerous. It is not taking a risk; it is inviting disaster.

VALUE AND BEHAVIOR CONGRUENCE   The leader who advocates a certain value but whose behavior contradicts that value is acting incongruently. Examples include incongruent values/behavior in managing conflict, self-disclosure, or confidentiality.

AVOIDANCE OF HARM   The member's right to pass on any exercise should be stressed. Goading, sarcasm, or scapegoating can cause psychological harm to a person and to program effectiveness.

Source: *Learning to Work with Groups,* by M. B. Miles, 1981, New York: Columbia University, Teacher's College Press.

(which I gave to them the following week, with their topic suggestions included). The result was an enjoyable experience of interchange and new awareness, most of which I drew from their own comments as we focused on various topics.

One aspect often overlooked by group facilitators in the process of group formation is the ethical dimension of leadership. Miles (1981) developed a set of rules of thumb that can guide thinking about ethical decisions in groups. As facilitators, we have various styles, but these guidelines should undergird all our efforts (see Box 5.1)

Storming

As group members become comfortable with each other and with the leader, the "honeymoon" period of social niceness wanes, and people begin to express a genuine range of personal responses, including disagreement, slight, and frustration. Everyone has a personal investment in what she or he believes. If an idea seems to challenge those beliefs, we tend to reject it, as a way of upholding our self-worth (Schultz, 1989). This need to defend oneself is just one of the reasons group members may get into conflict. Opposition to new ideas and insufficient time to process an idea or task may also cause friction and discomfort. An ineffective group tends to focus on the flaws of any proposal being made. Also, many group members may not be actively participating and may even be sabotaging the group's work if their own needs are not being met (Schultz, 1989). When a group member is expressing strong emotions, either verbally or nonverbally, it is good to ask, "How can the group be helpful to you right now?" (Bowman, 1990–1996). Then name some of the types of support: listening, giving suggestions, sharing similar experiences, telling the member that we understand. This produces a thoughtful pause and emphasizes personal needs and awareness.

Gibb (1961) determined that small groups were more effective in managing conflict when conditions were supportive rather than defensive. Such a climate of support is possible when people (1) listen and respond in nonjudgmental terms; (2) participate actively and show an understanding of each other's views; (3) are willing to experiment with new ideas; and (4) recognize their interdependence, as well as their dependence. Defensive climates occur when (1) attempts are made to control the behavior of others; (2) people fail to understand the other's feelings; (3) communication is self-serving and competitive; (4) criticism is directed at persons, not at ideas; and (5) statements are delivered with such certainty and dominance that a negative climate results. Conflict is not necessarily a bad thing to happen in group interaction. Schultz (1989) points out that healthy conflict can foster consideration of diverse ideas and perspectives. It encourages participation by more people and fosters more intense involvement with the task or subject. Conflict can also clarify the problem.

The leader's task, when conflict occurs, is not to squash it, but instead to manage it. Gross (1993) suggests that leaders discourage labeling an approach as right or wrong, good or bad. General statements, such as "Some of us feel strongly about. . . . Let's hear/explore other viewpoints," will keep the discussion from getting out of hand or being dominated by one or two persons with very strong opinions. The leader may have to keep emphasizing that within the group individual differences, values, and attitudes are respected.

Beebe and Masterson (1990) identified three types of common interpersonal conflict: pseudoconflict; simple conflict; and ego conflict. Pseudoconflict, as its name implies, is not really conflict but more likely a misunderstanding in communication or a misperception of the problem. Simple conflict arises when individuals disagree over which course of action to pursue. Ego conflict involves a person's sense of "losing face" or being personally attacked by another. Each type of conflict is best managed when it is identified and dealt with in a specific way. Table 5.1 summarizes the suggested approaches to each type of conflict.

Norming

If conflict situations are managed forthrightly and calmly, the group will move to a new level of working together. Ground rules established at the beginning now have more meaning, and the group may even decide to adopt

TABLE 5.1 Managing Different Types of Conflict

	Pseudoconflict	*Simple Conflict*	*Ego Conflict*
Source of conflict	Misunderstanding individuals' perceptions of the problem.	Individual disagreement over which course of action to pursue.	Defense of ego: Individual believes he or she is being attacked personally.
Suggestions for managing conflict	1. Ask for clarification of perceptions. 2. Establish a supportive rather than a defensive climate. 3. Employ active listening: *Stop* *Look* *Listen* *Question* *Paraphrase content* *Paraphrase feelings*	1. Listen and clarify perceptions. 2. Make sure issues are clear to all group members. 3. Use a problem-solving approach to manage differences of opinion. 4. Keep discussion focused on the issues. 5. Use facts rather than opinions for evidence. 6. Look for alternatives or compromise positions. 7. Make the conflict a group concern rather than an individual concern. 8. Determine which conflicts are the most important to resolve. 9. If possible, postpone the decision so additional research can be conducted. This delay also helps relieve tensions.	1. Let members express their concerns but do not permit personal attacks. 2. Employ active listening. 3. Call for a cooling-off period. 4. Try to keep discussion focused on issues (simple conflict). 5. Encourage parties to be descriptive rather than evaluative and judgmental. 6. Use a problem-solving approach to manage differences of opinion. 7. Speak slowly and calmly. 8. Develop rules or procedures that create a relationship that allows for the personality difference.

From *Commuicating in Small Groups*, 3rd ed., by Steven A. Beebe and John T. Masterson, 1990, Glenview, IL: Scott, Foresman. Copyright 1990, 1986, 1982 by Scott, Foresman and Company. Reprinted by permission of Addison-Wesley Educational Publishers.

others. But norming does not ensure that the unpredictable will never happen. The unexpected crisis will inevitably come. It may be a crisis in the community or a disclosure of personal hurt or discomfort. Sherwood and Scherer (1975) label this a *pinch,* which can be managed more effectively if it is expected and if certain norms are followed. First, address the disruption directly and kindly. If it is a personal issue, deal with it empathetically (put yourself in that person's place and space). Second, invite shared group responsibility and affirm the ability of the group to deal with the issue and move on. The tendency is to gloss over or avoid pinches instead of dealing with them. Then they become crunches that can seriously disrupt group effectiveness (Bowman, 1990–1996).

Other group norms should include periodic feedback or evaluation from the group and the setting of limits by the group facilitator. Setting limits is often viewed negatively, but it is really a positive. It helps the group to focus attention and move toward a goal.

Performing

Because this aspect of group process constitutes the majority of time spent in a group, it is discussed in the following section.

EFFECTIVE GROUP WORK

Basic Design

Gross (1993) suggests a basic design for facilitating a group session. At the beginning of the session, the facilitator should announce the topic and plan for the day. Be prepared to ask open-ended questions to invite group participation and discussion. Do not be surprised if you are met with silence (as often happens). Be ready to rephrase the question or ask another one after waiting an appropriate time for a response. Facilitators are often uncomfortable with silence and may fill up the silence too quickly after a question is asked. But silence can be a rich time for personal reflection, tension release, and collecting one's thoughts. Give the participants time to think and perhaps to get a little uncomfortable with the silence. Otherwise, you will undermine the possibility of group response. They will get in the habit of letting you "fill up the space." Asking members to first write their response encourages group participation and gives everyone a chance and a reason to really think about the question. I would not use this method exclusively, but it can be a good way to begin group discussion.

When a person does share a response, acknowledge it appreciatively by reflecting back what has been said or by writing the answer on a chart or board. Then ask for other responses, but do not pressure anyone. Dividing into dyads or small groups of three to five also encourages more personal responses and involvement.

The Minilecture

Family life education implies group interaction rather than a classroom lecture format. Research confirms that lecture has the poorest rate of effective retention. Knowles's (1989) research, discussed earlier, stated that we retain 20% of what we hear versus 80% of what we see and do. Nevertheless, there are times when information and input are needed. The minilecture allows for input and group interaction. The goal is to keep the lecture time at 10 minutes or under, interspersed with response or a kinetic activity related to the topic.

Praxis

Praxis is defined by Vella (1994) as "action with reflection" or "learning by doing" (p. 4). The best type of action is not contrived but drawn from the life experience of group members. The next best is involving the group in a project or group task that illustrates your learning points and then reflecting together on the process and the outcome.

Good Communication Skills

Gross (1993) stresses the importance of teaching good communication skills and personal sharing by modeling these skills when appropriate. It is important not to monopolize or redirect a group member's concerns. Stay with a topic as long as it seems important to the person or the group to continue the discussion. Again, just because the group is silent for a little while does not necessarily indicate that they are ready to move to a different topic. Often, asking a second question related to the first will help gauge whether there is more to be said on the topic.

The use of active listening skills by the facilitator will provide an important model for group members who may have poor listening skills, a common deficiency in our society. But active and effective listening skills can be learned by everyone in the group. The main requirements are good modeling and lots of practice.

The largest part of human communication is nonverbal rather than verbal. Many gestures, such as smiles, frowns, yawns, clenched fists, movement of legs or body, raised eyebrows, and eye contact (or the lack of it), are subtle and ambiguous pieces of communication. We cannot immediately conclude that the restless person is bored or that a raised eyebrow means disapproval of what is being said. It is up to the leader to take notice and move to a kinetic application of the topic or to ask the group if they are ready for a break. Again, do not put an individual on the spot. Instead of, "John, I see you are yawning. What's up?" you might comment, "Well, I'm noticing some restlessness and signs of boredom. Is it time for a break?" The raised eyebrow could prompt you to ask, "Joe, do you have something to add?" Then allow time for response.

A leader's own nonverbal communication is also very important. Smiles beget smiles. Eye contact conveys that you are confident and can decrease the psychological distance between you and the group members. Directness and warmth, a sense of humor, and a relaxed stance can reduce tension and encourage relaxation among members.

BOX 5.2

Checklist for an Effective Group

☐ Does everyone have a chance to talk?

☐ Are comments understood? Is everyone given feedback?

☐ Are group members open-minded about ideas and opinions? Do they allow arguments to surface?

☐ Does each person get recognition even if his or her idea was not accepted?

☐ Does the group avoid "win-lose" situations?

☐ Do members help the group to examine the process of exploring problems and making decisions?

☐ Do members urge others to confront their differences rather than simply agreeing to disagree?

☐ Do members assist the group in working toward the group's goal?

From *Communicating in the Small Group: Theory and Practice* (p. 215), by Beatrice Schultz, 1989, New York: Harper & Row. Copyright 1989 by Harper & Row. Reprinted by permission of Addison-Wesley Educational Publishers.

Follow-Up

Follow-up of unfinished business or a recapitulation of what went on in the last group meeting allows for continual correction of misconceptions and reinforces concepts taught. Another type of follow-up may occur after the program is completed and can be built into the original plan or contract. For example, the group will be asked to assemble again in a month or so to see how they are doing with their newfound insights or skills. Box 5.2 lists questions for reflection that can assist the facilitator in determining if the group is functioning effectively.

PROBLEMS FREQUENTLY ENCOUNTERED

Experienced group leaders are often asked to comment on a number of topics that seem to be common challenges to group facilitation. The following problems and responses are a few that may help the reader in the future.

- *What do you do when the group depends on you to be "the expert"?* It is flattering to have persons asking your opinion, but it is very costly, because they come to depend on you for every decision or administrative detail. They become like children instead of collaborators or colleagues. There is definitely a balance that must be struck between "taking over" and being "out of it." When should you give answers and when should you not? When a question is asked by a group member, always return it to the group if possible. Or give several options and ask the group to evaluate. Continually remember your role as that of facilitator and a resource, but not the "answer person."

- *How do you deal with discussion dominators?* Some people are by nature more verbal than others. You don't want to squelch, just manage. Ideas for doing this include dividing into small groups for discussion or task assignment, having everyone write a response before asking for verbal response, or specifically asking for others to comment. The "fish bowl" discussion method is another good technique. Have the group divide themselves into two categories: the Mostly Talkers and the Mostly Listeners. Then have the Mostly Talkers sit in an outside ring to observe the Mostly Listeners discuss a topic. Then switch observers and discussants. Finally, have each group share what they noticed about what happened in the group they were observing and the group they were participating in. This is good example of praxis.

- *How do you deal with frequent interruptions?* Again, the goal is not to squelch, but to manage. It is important to acknowledge the person's statement or question and to eventually deal with the topic at a more appropriate time. A quick way to acknowledge is to ask the person to hold the question until you finish the current discussion. You might also comment, "That's a good question, but one we can't answer quickly. Let's get back to it." Then don't forget to do it. If the interruption has to do with a question about a task assignment, you probably need to halt everyone, go over the instructions to clarify them for everyone, and ask for further questions.

- *How do you handle a disruptive member?* This is not an easy or a pleasant task, but if the problem is not attended to, the group's effectiveness will be gravely diminished. It is also a caring thing to do, because it is a matter of courtesy, it is respectful of all group members, it is excellent modeling, and it is crucial to group morale. Disruptions can include crying, put-downs of other people, personal disclosure in a way that others have not done, getting angry with someone in the group, interrupting with inappropriate laughter, or other behaviors that control or disrupt conversation between the facilitator and the other members. There are several ways to address this problem. First, make an effort to hear what the person is saying by reflecting back his or her comments or general concern. Then have the person respond. You might offer to meet after group to discuss it further. There might be a need to refer the person for counseling. The facilitator can also set limits with firmness and remind the group about the ground rules if someone begins to overstep them. Or, for the constant talker, "I'm going to have to call time here so we can move on to hear from others in the group."

Disclosing a painful experience can be especially disruptive if the news is shocking to the group or if it's the first time a person has become extremely emotional. It is not unkind to interrupt the speaker and acknowledge the difficulty of his or her situation and the group's concern with listening carefully and being supportive. In rare instances, a person may start to divulge a serious secret about himself or herself, one that could be inappropriate for a support or education group. Often people in distress may be unaware of the level of disclosure they are making. If this is not a therapy situation, it is a kindness to offer them a time to pause to reconsider their words.

- *How do you deal with a person in crisis?* Assess the immediacy of the crisis. Often group time is well spent in supporting a hurting member. If needs are vast and chronic, then referral to other resources would be best. In private, provide names and phone numbers, and affirm the person's worthiness to get the resources he or she needs.

- *What about the person dealing with deep emotions of grief and loss?* Grief is better handled when it is recognized and shared, but group facilitators are still sometimes uncomfortable with its expression. Most life transitions incorporate some type of loss. It is a predictable and legitimate component of group work (Bowman, 1990–1996). The primary task of the facilitator is to encourage the grieving person to "put words to their tears" so as to bring understanding and a sense of being heard and comforted. There is no one right order or manner of handling grief. Don't push or judge the person. Sometimes denial or distraction is a healthy response. You are not here to confront or evaluate but to provide empathy and acceptance. Don't expect him or her to "get over it" in a hurry. Stay clear about the purpose of the group and gently return to the topic.

  Another major problem can arise when deep grief is shared in the group. Some members will rush in to express similar experiences and draw the focus away from the one who has brought up the issue. Also, a member may compare her or his coping mechanism to that of the grieving person and imply that it is superior. As a result, the other person may come away from the group feeling inferior rather than supported. It is up to the leader to bring the focus of attention back to the original speaker and affirm his or her unique perspective.

ENDINGS

Whether it is the closing of one session or the ending of the group experience, the time of closing is often neglected or rushed through. Yet what happens during this period either completes or fragments the effectiveness of the session

(Bowman, 1990–1996). If you start your planning by thinking about closure, it directs the flow of the meeting. Think first of where you want the group to be when the session or program is over. Be very aware of the time your closing will take and be willing to stop discussion and move to closing when it is time. A good closing includes recapping what has been said and concluded, checking about hurt feelings or disgruntled members, and pointing ahead to the next meeting. Take time after closing to reflect on and note lessons learned, new insights, and other needs to attend to. Then give yourself credit for what you were able to accomplish and move on.

If this is the final session of a group experience, it is better not to introduce new topics but to use this as a time of closure and tying up loose ends. Always include time for group members to comment about the group and to ask any lingering questions, time to say good-byes and affirmations to one another, and time to fill out an evaluation questionnaire. Where to go from here is also an important topic for the last session. Suggestions of available community resources and other ways of sustaining growth should be offered. Family resource centers are a good example of community support. Bowman (1990–1996) notes that family therapy gurus Carl Rogers and Virginia Satir were asked in 1970 (independent of each other) what they projected as a base of support for families in the twenty-first century. Both described the family resource center concept, to which people in all stages of life could come for assistance in dealing with a variety of family issues, from child care and parent education to literacy and job skills training to anger management classes to having coffee and conversation with friends. Just knowing such resources are available is all many people need to cope with life's challenges.

SUMMARY

This chapter looked at the various elements and dynamics that make up effective group processes. The definition of a group and the individual perspectives that members bring to a group were discussed. The value of group participation and the hesitancy of some persons to join a group were examined in light of human needs and human fears.

The setting, the room arrangement, the introductions, the time factor: All of these contribute to whether the group climate is chilly or warm and inviting. In order to provide a climate of safety so that persons are willing to risk sharing with others, the facilitator must be able to balance the maintenance of boundaries with openness to the interests and ideas of the group.

Theories of group dynamics point to the value of positive regard and individual involvement as keys to learning within a group. But effective group process does not proceed along a constantly smooth track. Generally, a working group can be expected to travel through stages of forming, storming, norming, and performing. The facilitator's ability to handle the various stages with calmness and respect for all the members will certainly influence the rate at which a group arrives at the performing stage, or if they arrive at all.

Aspects of effective group strategies, from the basic design to the value of good communication skills and the use of praxis, were discussed. Suggestions about how to address specific problems the facilitator may encounter should provide assistance to new and veteran group facilitators.

It is obvious that the facilitator has the major role in establishing a climate for full participation and in guiding and inspiring the group members to discover new resources within themselves. Leadership is a skill that can be learned if the person is honest and flexible and genuinely cares for the group members. That caring must go beyond sympathy to a willingness to set aside preconceived ideas about certain groups of people and to the ability to empathize with each individual as he or she strives to grow at his or her own pace.

"There is considerable agreement in the literature to support the claim that the educator's personal qualities are potentially as important as any specific technique he or she employs in facilitating the group process" (Gross, 1993, p. 25). Each educator-facilitator's preparation must start with his or her own personal awareness and comfort with the leadership function and with expressions of feelings, conflict, and criticism. Remembering your own experience as a group member in a well-led group—and getting feedback from mentors and colleagues—will work to help you develop the skills you need to do successful and effective group work.

QUESTIONS/PROBLEMS FOR DISCUSSION AND REVIEW

Class Discussion

1. Review the questions asked in the first paragraph of this chapter. Share your answer with others in a small group. Choose what you consider to be the top three attributes of an effective teacher or group facilitator.

2. How are the roles and the tasks of a classroom teacher different from those of a group facilitator?

3. Consider again the definition of praxis. Give an example of praxis in your own life. Why is this such a powerful learning tool?

Research Problem

A great deal of research on group dynamics and group process was done during the 1960s and 1970s, a time when encounter and sensitivity groups were popular. Choose a text on small-group process from that time period and one from the 1990s to compare in terms of emphasis and methodology. What is different? What is the same?

Case Study Design

Consider carefully the known characteristics of a group you will be facil-itating. Determine a plan for recruitment and assess the quality of the location and the anticipated size of the group. What can you alter to improve the anticipated group climate?

Consider also your personal readiness for leadership, based on the ethical guidelines in Box 5.1. Discuss with your group how comfortable you are in a conflict situation or a boundary-setting situation. How might you develop more comfort?

CHAPTER 6

Evaluation of Family Programs

INTRODUCTION

Imagine that you are the director of the Southwest Family Center, a neighborhood resource center located in a large metropolitan city. Funded by the United Way, the Southwest Family Center serves residents with children from before birth to age 6 living in the nine neighborhoods that make up the southwest section of the city.

The overall goal of the Southwest Family Center is to increase learning readiness in children entering kindergarten. It was developed through the efforts of professionals at a lead agency and the input of community residents and business and service providers. The developers of the program have determined that one way to increase learning readiness is to provide families with formal and informal support systems.

The Southwest Family Center provides formal and informal support through a number of activities, events, resources, and services. Activities and events include an Indoor Playground, a Family Fun Night, numerous baby and toddler classes, and parenting education and support groups. They also offer a resource and toy library, make home visits, and produce a monthly newsletter and calendar of events for families with small children. The Southwest Family Center has been operating for 5 years.

Overall, things seem to be going well. But how do you know for sure? How do you and your staff know if you are meeting your goals? How do you know if you are making the best use of your limited staff and resources? How do those funding your program know if the program is effective and if it is making a difference?

A family agency or organization can spend a great deal of time and money promoting and carrying out programs designed to meet the various needs of families. But without conscious, systematic evaluation efforts, it might be time and money misspent. This chapter provides an introduction to the evaluation of family programs. The intent is not to make you an evaluator but rather to familiarize you with the concepts and steps that make up this sometimes complicated, but always important, aspect of family life education. Throughout this chapter we use the Southwest Family Center as an example to help you to understand and apply the concepts discussed.

The number and scope of family education programs has increased substantially in the past decade. However, efforts at evaluating these programs are relatively new, and debate over terminology, techniques, and approaches is ongoing. Greater evidence of the effectiveness of family programs is needed, as is increased understanding and knowledge of how to evaluate programs.

> Few issues present a greater challenge to parenting education and family support than those surrounding evaluation and accountability. There may be thousands of programs nationwide and in many of them important things seem to be happening. But, except for a few pilot programs and focused research on individual dimensions of parenting, we haven't provided the conclusive evidence. Nowhere is the "adolescence" of this field more apparent than here: the maturity, clarity and confidence that comes with measured accomplishment and proven effectiveness is still ahead of us. (Carter, 1996, p. 58)

A number of national parenting education models have been studied over the past 25 years. These important studies have served as benchmarks in helping us examine the effectiveness of parent education and family support programs. Studies examining the effectiveness of such programs as Parents as Teachers, Parent Effectiveness Training, Home Instruction Program for Preschool Youngsters (HIPPY), Minnesota Early Learning Design (now known as MELD), and Minnesota's Early Childhood Family Education (ECFE) have provided important groundwork for replicating and understanding program effectiveness in the broader context of family education as well. The combination of small- and large-scale studies has shown us that "there is solid evidence on the critical role parents play in raising healthy children and that well-designed, controlled programs can have positive impacts on parenting outcomes" (Carter, 1996, p. 59). Family life educators must continue to carry out thoughtful and careful evaluation to ensure that family programs reach their goals in the most efficient manner possible.

In recent years, the political climate in the United States has become more accepting and supportive of preventative efforts as opposed to the service and intervention approaches of the past. In light of this, we need to design evaluations to record individual program effectiveness, as well as to collectively address questions on the minds of policy makers about which family support and education programs work, for whom, how, when, where, and why (Weiss & Jacobs, 1988). The development and recognition of effective prevention programs could serve to restructure the delivery of human services in this country. Although great strides have been made in recent years to increase the thoroughness and effectiveness of family program evaluation, there is still much to learn.

DEFINITIONS

We begin the discussion by looking at the definition of evaluation as articulated by several contributors to the literature on program evaluation. Patton (1982) defines evaluation as "the systematic collection of information about the activities, characteristics and outcomes of programs, personnel, and products for use by specific people to reduce uncertainties, improve effectiveness, and make decisions with regard to what those programs, personnel, or products are doing and affecting."

Littell (1986, p. 17) considers program evaluation to be "the systematic collection, analysis, and interpretation of information designed for use in program planning and decision-making. It is concerned with the types of interventions used, by whom, toward what ends, under what conditions, for whom, at what costs and with what benefits."

Finally, evaluation is defined by Weiss and Jacobs (1988, p. 49) as: "the systematic collection and analysis of program-related data that can be used to understand how a program delivers services and/or what the consequences of its services are for participants. . . . It is both descriptive and 'judgmental' of program merit, with the emphasis on designing an evaluation that fits the program."

Though the definitions vary, they contain similar concepts, namely, that evaluation is a systematic collection of various types of information and that the results of the collection and analysis of information are used to modify programs, increase effectiveness, and aid in decision making.

It is important to note that evaluation is different from research. Evaluation is used to determine the value, quality, or effectiveness of a program. It is judgmental, and the results are usually program specific. It is usually motivated by the program's needs. Information gathered can be subjective. The major reasons for conducting evaluation are for planning, improving, or justification. The goal of evaluation is to come to some sort of recommendation.

Research, on the other hand, looks more at the relationships among variables and cause and effect. It is nonjudgmental and conclusion oriented. Information gathered should be objective rather than subjective. The intent is to have information that can be generalized rather than specific to any one particular program. Evaluation answers the question of *what*, whereas research answers the question of *why*. (See Box 6.1.)

CHALLENGES OF EVALUATION

For many family life educators, evaluation provides quite a challenge. Thorough evaluation takes planning, time, and money, often beyond the capabilities and resources of the average family education program and the technical expertise of the staff. And there can be resistance to evaluation. Program directors and staff may be concerned that evaluation will divert resources away from the pro-

BOX 6.1	The staff of the Southwest Family Center wants to know if babies who attend a program like the Indoor Playground (which includes opportunities for climbing and exercise on playground equipment) on a regular basis show more advanced motor skills than babies who do not attend such a program. This type of study would be considered *research*.
Evaluation or Research?	The staff of the Southwest Family Center wants to know how the parents who attend the Indoor Playground feel about the program and if they find it to be a good opportunity to connect with other parents in their community. This type of study would be considered *evaluation*.

gram's activities, that it will increase the burden for program staff, or that it is too complicated. Some fear that it may produce negative results, which will jeopardize the funding of the program.

So why should evaluations be conducted? The reality is that evaluation is imperative to the success of a program. "Program providers are becoming increasingly aware of the need for program evaluation and for practical program evaluation strategies that will: (1) yield information of use to them for program improvement and (2) answer questions about program effectiveness" (Cooke, 1991, p. 13). Through evaluation you can find out what is and isn't working with your program. You can improve the efficiency and effectiveness of your staff's efforts by identifying strengths and weaknesses. You can increase the likelihood that resources are used effectively and goals are reached. Evaluation can show those who fund your program, as well as community members, how your program is benefiting its intended audience. And when results are shared with others running similar programs, it can contribute to knowledge in the field. If consciously incorporated into the design and ongoing operation of a program, evaluation does not need to be overly complicated or time-consuming.

TYPES OF EVALUATION

Assessing Needs and Assets

Perhaps one of the most important concepts about evaluation is the need to incorporate an evaluation plan into the development and initial planning stages of a program. A well-developed program begins with a ministudy (sometimes referred to as a needs assessment, a feasibility study, or an assets inventory). These ministudies (part of the research and evaluation continuum) often include examining the current situation, that is, why or to what degree is this program justified? Who is the target audience for this program? What resources are available? What are the strengths or assets of this community? Do similar programs exist in this community? Will the community support our efforts?

What benefits are likely to be produced through our program? It is important to be clear about the need for and goals of your program. If you don't have a clear picture of what your program is trying to accomplish, you won't know how to tell if you've been successful! Think seriously about what it is you want to learn from the evaluation, and integrate the evaluation into the ongoing activities of your program. Always remember that evaluation is a process, not an event. Consider its place in the ongoing implementation of your program.

Formative Evaluation

Evaluation efforts can have different goals and can be conducted at different points throughout the development and implementation of a program. Historically, many evaluations have been considered to be formative or summative in nature. Formative evaluations generate information for the purposes of planning, monitoring, and improving programs. Formative evaluations describe a program and provide feedback on how it is doing while the program is still in progress, often prompting changes in timing, approaches, and so forth. Formative evaluation might include surveying participants midway through a scheduled program to see if the program is meeting their expectations.

For example, imagine that your agency holds a monthly meeting to provide education on infant development to mothers of newborns. You notice that although the participants seem very enthusiastic about the meetings, attendance has been sporadic. By surveying the participants, you find that the availability of transportation is a defining factor in whether or not they are able to attend. You arrange a car pool that provides rides for everyone who wants to attend the meeting. Attendance increases dramatically. Had you waited until the end of the program to survey participants, it would have been too late to implement the car pool, and a number of possible program participants would have missed out on the program. The use of formative evaluation throughout the program allows you to make changes that will increase the likelihood that you will effectively implement your program and reach your goal.

Box 6.2 gives an example of a formative evaluation of the Indoor Playground program. With this information the staff can determine if the Indoor Playground is meeting the needs of the participants. They can make changes in scheduling and format. They can also determine which marketing efforts are working best. This formative evaluation has provided them with information that they can use to modify the program while it is still in progress.

Summative Evaluation

Summative evaluations are concerned with the end results of a program. How did it affect the people it served? Were the program goals met? Summative evaluations can be used to determine if a program should be replicated, expanded, or

---

BOX 6.2

Formative Evaluation

The Indoor Playground is held each Friday at the Southwest Family Center. Once each month staff distributes a survey to the attendees. The survey includes questions such as:

- [ ] How many times have you attended the Indoor Playground?
- [ ] What is your main reason for attending?
- [ ] Is this a convenient day for you to attend?
- [ ] Is this a convenient time for you to attend?
- [ ] If not, when would be better?
- [ ] What changes would you like to see in the Indoor Playground?
- [ ] How did you hear about the Indoor Playground?
- [ ] Do you attend any other Southwest Family Center events?

BOX 6.3

Summative Evaluation

The Southwest Family Center sponsors a New Parents support group for parents of newborns. The meetings are facilitated by parents in the community who have completed a 16-hour small-group-facilitation training program. Parents enter the program before their babies are born or just after. The program meets twice a month for 2 hours for a 2-year period. A *summative evaluation* of the New Parents program would be carried out at the end of the 2-year period. Participants might be interviewed or asked to complete a questionnaire. The intent of the survey or questionnaire would be to determine how the parents benefited from the program. Did they learn new skills regarding parenting? How about new knowledge about child development? Did their participation help them to feel more confident about their abilities as parents? Did they feel less alone and isolated? Do they feel more connected to their community, having met other families in a similar situation? Results of this summative evaluation will help the staff of the Southwest Family Center know if their goals have been met. The results may determine if the program will be replicated.

---

perhaps discontinued. In the example given in Box 6.3, a summative evaluation carried out at the end of the program cycle could determine if participants in the New Parents program had increased their knowledge of infant development.

COMMONLY USED TERMS IN EVALUATION

Although the specific terminology varies, some common terms and concepts are used in the literature on evaluation. The United Way publication *Measuring Program Outcomes: A Practical Approach* (United Way of America, 1996) provides

BOX 6.4

Inputs

Inputs at the Southwest Family Center would include financial support provided by the sponsoring agency, staff members and staff time, and members of the community who volunteer their time to various programs and services offered through the Southwest Family Center. The site at which the Southwest Family Center is located, including meeting space, materials, supplies, playground equipment, and toys available through the Indoor Playground would also be considered input.

a helpful conceptual framework for understanding evaluation. It defines the following measurement terms.

Logic Models

Programs can be developed and outcomes identified with a *logic model* (United Way, 1996), or an "if-then" method of looking at a situation. Logic models can help you think through the progression of steps taken by program participants and can give you a more realistic view of what you can expect of your program. Logic models also help you identify key components that must be kept track of in order to determine if the program is effective. Logic models include inputs, activities, outputs, and outcomes. An example of a logic model might be: *if* classes (activities) can teach about child development and parenting skills (output), *then* parents can acquire knowledge, gain skills, and change their attitudes about how to care for their children (initial outcomes). *If* they learn new approaches in dealing with their children, *then* they will change their behavior to reflect these new methods (intermediate outcomes). *If* they change their behavior, *then* they will increase the likelihood of positive results. Applying this method can help you to identify the steps needed to reach your goals and link your activities to program outcomes.

INPUTS   *Inputs* include resources dedicated to or consumed by the program. Examples are money, staff and staff time, volunteers and volunteer time, facilities, and equipment and supplies (see Box 6.4).

ACTIVITIES   The program uses its inputs to fulfill its mission through *activities*. Activities include the strategies, techniques, and types of treatment that make up the program's service methodology. In our example of the Southwest Family Center, activities would center on providing education and support to families with small children. These activities would include the Family Fun Night, the Indoor Playground, the community calendar, and other events and services intended to provide education and support to parents of small children.

BOX 6.5

Outputs

How many people attended the Indoor Playground? How many sessions of Family Fun Night were held? How many people used the toy library? How many brochures or flyers about the Southwest Family Center were distributed at neighborhood festivals and community events? These questions attempt to gather information about *outputs*—the direct product of programs and activities carried out by the Southwest Family Center.

BOX 6.6

Outcomes

Parents attending a monthly class, "Discipline and Your Child," learn new techniques for directing the behavior of their toddlers. The staff hopes that providing comprehensive information about child development and discipline alternatives will expand parents' understanding of these topics. By increasing parents' knowledge, the staff hopes that parents will make better choices about strategies when disciplining their child. Because making better choices about discipline strategies includes approaches to preventing misbehavior, the staff believes that parents will use less punitive means and employ more appropriate choices with their children. By preventing misbehavior, the staff hopes that parents will have a more positive attitude about discipline, feel more confident about being able to prevent misbehavior, feel more successful as parents, and enjoy their child more. These are all examples of *outcomes*—the benefits and changes experienced by the participants of the parenting class.

OUTPUTS   *Outputs* are the direct products of program activities and usually are measured in terms of the volume of work accomplished—for example, the number of classes held, brochures distributed, and participants served (see Box 6.5).

OUTCOMES   *Outcomes* are the benefits or changes to individuals or groups that come during or after participation in program activities. Outcomes are influenced by outputs. Outcomes are reflected through modified behavior, increased skills, new knowledge, changed attitudes or values, improved conditions, and other attributes. They represent the changes in the participants from the time they started the program to the time they completed it. For example, outcomes of the program described in Box 6.6 would be a better understanding of infant development and a resulting change in parenting behavior, such as the use of more appropriate discipline strategies.

BOX 6.7 *Indicators*	One of the goals of the Indoor Playground is to provide opportunities for parents in the community to connect with each other. Staff at the Indoor Playground events might observe parents to see if they are interacting with each other and if relationships are forming. This interaction between the parents, especially if the same parents sit together and talk to each other at subsequent events, could be considered an *indicator* that the parents are connecting with each other. Staff might observe other Southwest Family Center events to see if some of the same parents attend and if they interact with other families. An overall goal of the Southwest Family Center is to increase learning readiness of children entering kindergarten. One indicator of learning readiness is having received all recommended shots before entering kindergarten. Another indicator might be that children have been screened for hearing, vision, or speech problems and have received the appropriate intervention. These problems have been identified early enough for actions to be taken so that the children are ready to learn by the time they enter kindergarten.

Indicators

An *indicator* identifies the factors that are being measured as a way of tracking the program's success on an outcome. An indicator is observable and measurable (see Box 6.7).

Qualitative Data

Qualitative data refers to the types of data and the methods used to collect them or to describe the nature of the study. Qualitative data are verbal or narrative and can be collected by observing participant behavior or by interviewing participants, for example. Qualitative data describe and interpret happenings or emotions. Methods for collecting qualitative data include focus groups, interviews, case studies, and direct observation. Although qualitative data are hard to measure, they address the kinds of effects that influence positive human behavior and that family programs hope to affect. Qualitative data might include descriptions of how parents teach children to play with a new toy; stories about how a support group changed a parent's perception of a crisis situation; or a series of excerpts from a parent's journal that describe what was learned during a year of being involved in a home visiting program (see Box 6.8).

Quantitative Data

Information gathered through quantitative methods is typically reported numerically and is easier to measure. *Quantitative data* are typically, although not

BOX 6.8 *Qualitative Data/ Evaluation*	If the staff of the Southwest Family Center wanted to gather *qualitative data* or carry out a qualitative evaluation, they could interview or survey the participants of the programs to collect information on how they feel about the programs and how they think they have benefited. Another option would be to observe parents at various activities and record information about their interaction with their children or other parents. Or they might hold a focus group of parents of 4-year-olds to determine what issues are of most concern for them at this stage in their children's lives. This information could be used to help them design future classes or determine what resources might be most helpful.

BOX 6.9 *Quantitative Data/ Evaluation*	At each event held by the Southwest Family Center, a sign-in sheet for the participant's name and address is provided. Staff uses this information, in addition to attendance, to monitor how many people are attending each event. They may collect information on how many kindergartners had received all their shots when entering first grade in 1993 and compare that number with the number of kindergartners inoculated in 1998. This would be considered *quantitative data*.

always, objective. Age, education level, and attendance counts for various events would all be considered to be quantitative data. Quantitative data can be gathered through questionnaires, forms, tests, and surveys and sometimes simply by counting the number of participants in the program (see Box 6.9).

Although evaluators with different educational backgrounds are likely to continue to debate the best approach to evaluation design and data collection methods (i.e., qualitative vs. quantitative), many evaluators believe that the questions that focus the evaluation study should lead to a discussion about which types of approaches are used. It is also important to note that many studies employ a mixed-methods approach, that is, a design using both qualitative and quantitative methods. The needs and interests of the stakeholders in your program may influence the evaluation design and methodology as well. Stakeholders are those people who are affected by the program's existence, that is, staff, funders, program participants, policy makers, academics, professionals in the field, and so forth.

LEVELS OF OUTCOMES

In some instances there is just one desired outcome for a program. But in many cases there is a series of outcomes, each of which can contribute to the accomplishment of another and, ultimately, to the final outcome goals of the program. Different programs use different terms to describe these same levels. The important concept to consider is that there are varying levels of outcomes.

Initial Outcomes

Initial outcomes are the first changes or benefits that a participant experiences as a result of the program. It may be a change in attitude, knowledge, skills, or all of these. In most programs these initial outcomes would not be ends in themselves but important steps toward reaching the desired ends.

Intermediate Outcomes

Intermediate outcomes connect a program's initial outcomes to the longer term outcomes intended for its participants. Intermediate outcomes are often exemplified by changes in behavior as a result of the new knowledge, skill, or attitude.

Longer-Term Outcomes

Longer-term outcomes are the ultimate outcomes that a program wants to achieve. These are usually meaningful changes that are often related to condition or status. An example of a longer term outcome might be that parents who participate in the program no longer spank their children as a form of discipline but instead use positive discipline techniques such as logical consequences. The change in behavior comes as a result of increased knowledge regarding alternative parenting techniques and skill in using these techniques, which results in a new understanding of the goal of discipline as an opportunity to teach rather than as a form of punishment. (See Box 6.10.)

Unfortunately, many programs have the resources to measure only initial outcomes. The cost of carrying out evaluations to include intermediate and longer-term outcomes is sometimes prohibitive for organizations operating on limited budgets.

STEPS IN CONDUCTING AN EVALUATION

A number of steps are involved in the evaluation process. Cooke (1991) adapted the following steps from the work of several leading contributors to the literature on family evaluation, including Michael Patton (as cited in Cooke, 1991):

- Identify and organize the intended users of the evaluation: Who is the audience? Who are the stakeholders?

BOX 6.10

Levels of Outcomes

INITIAL OUTCOMES   By attending the "Single Parenting" class, Mary learns of the importance of taking time for herself in order to more effectively care for her two boys. This new knowledge would be considered an *initial outcome* of the "Single Parenting" class.

INTERMEDIATE OUTCOMES   Because she understands the importance of caring for herself, Mary no longer feels guilty for wanting to get away by herself once in a while. She arranges to have her parents watch her boys one night each week so that she can go out to a movie or dinner with her friends. This action, or change in behavior, would be an *intermediate outcome*.

LONGER-TERM OUTCOMES   Because Mary is able to get away one night a week, her stress level drops. She is calmer and happier around the boys. She yells at them less and finds that she has more energy to devote to them. The boys in turn act out less often. The environment in the family home improves. This resulting positive home environment would be considered a *longer-term outcome*.

- Identify and focus the evaluation questions: What do we need to know about the program?
- Make design, methods, and measurement decisions: How will we carry out the evaluation?
- Collect, analyze, and interpret data: How will we understand what the information means?
- Disseminate and use the results: How will we use the evaluation results?

The first two steps look at conceptual issues regarding program evaluation. The remaining three steps focus more on the specific design of the evaluation. Numerous models that identify the steps involved in the evaluation process are available, though most go beyond the scope of this chapter. Francine Jacobs's (1988) five-tiered approach to program evaluation is frequently cited in the evaluation literature.

CULTURAL CONSIDERATIONS IN EVALUATION

Regardless of the method of evaluation chosen, it is important to keep cultural contexts in mind. Most standardized instruments were designed for White, middle-class populations. These instruments are often not appropriate when English is not the primary language of the individuals who will complete them or if Western cultural concepts would not be well understood or do not carry the same value. The issue of language is complex. For example, not everyone from a particular ethnic group can read and write in their native language. Dialects and regional language differences exist. Abilities to communicate differ among generations, across socioeconomic groups, and among people with different educational histories.

Some Western concepts are difficult to translate and require elaboration by data collectors for study participants. For example, self-esteem is not only a concept that is challenging for U.S. researchers to define and measure but also a concept unfamiliar to new or recently arrived Southeast Asian Hmong people. Carrying out pretesting interviews and surveys or setting up advisory group review committees would be two ways to determine the best approach for examining questionable words or concepts. This procedure is sometimes referred to as pilot testing.

It is also important to be aware of the possibility of cultural response sets. In some cultures, asking for help or appearing needful is inappropriate. Participants from such cultures may not feel comfortable revealing what they consider to be weaknesses. There may also be cultural taboos against revealing too much personal information.

Other things to be considered within varying cultures might be gender, age, and socioeconomic status. Are family programs experienced differently by men than by women or by people at different economic levels? Awareness and sensitivity to such factors will increase the effectiveness of your information-gathering strategies.

STANDARDS FOR EVALUATION

Although the scope of this chapter does not allow a thorough discussion of standards for evaluation, it is important to mention briefly the *Standards for Evaluations of Educational Programs, Projects, and Materials,* developed by the Joint Committee on Standards for Educational Evaluation (1981). The committee was guided by the assumption that sound evaluation can promote the understanding and improvement of education. They believed that a set of professional standards could play a vital role in upgrading the practice of educational evaluation. The standards do not promote a particular view of what constitutes good education, nor do they present specific criteria by which to judge. However, they do contain advice for dealing with these issues. In general, the standards are guiding principles for evaluation, and they address issues of utility, feasibility, propriety, and accuracy.

The purpose of *utility* standards is to ensure that an evaluation will provide practical information. *Feasibility* refers to the need for the evaluation to be realistic, prudent, diplomatic, and frugal. Standards of *propriety* are intended to ensure that the evaluation is conducted legally and ethically, with regard and concern for those involved in the evaluation and affected by the results. Finally, standards for *accuracy* were established to ensure that an evaluation will reveal adequate information regarding the program being evaluated. More detailed information regarding these standards for evaluation is available through the Joint Committee on Standards for Educational Evaluation.

SUMMARY

As you have no doubt surmised after reading this chapter, evaluation can be a complicated issue. But its value and importance cannot be underestimated. If you find yourself involved in family programming in any way, you will be directly or indirectly involved in evaluation. Take the time to assess the needs and strengths of your audience. Identify existing resources. Consider stakeholders and their expectations. Develop a logic model that thoughtfully considers the relationship between actions and results. Build formative evaluation into the design of your program. Identify your activities, inputs, outcomes, and indicators. Carry out a summative evaluation at the end of your program or class to help you determine what worked and what could be improved.

By following these important steps and considering the multiple aspects of evaluation, you will increase the likelihood that your program will improve and enhance the lives of its participants.

QUESTIONS/PROBLEMS FOR DISCUSSION AND REVIEW

Class Discussion

1. Describe how you would do a needs assessment, a formative evaluation, and a summative evaluation for a one-night, 3-hour workshop on "Balancing Work and Family."

2. Identify possible inputs, activities, outputs, outcomes, and indicators for the same program.

3. How would you gather qualitative data in the above situation? Quantitative data?

4. Describe possible initial, intermediate, and long-term outcomes that may occur as a result of attending the "Balancing Work and Family" workshop. Could all be carried out at the end of the workshop, that is, at the end of that same day?

Research Problems

1. Locate one or more of the evaluation studies cited on page 113. What were the results regarding program effectiveness? Is there a common characteristic of successful programs?

2. Identify a large federal grant opportunity that focuses on prevention rather than intervention. How would evaluation be different for a program that focuses on prevention?

3. Read Chapter 2, "The Five-Tiered Approach to Evaluation: Context and Implementation" by F. H. Jacobs, in *Evaluating Family Programs* by H. B. Weiss and F. H. Jacobs (1988). Provide examples of evaluations performed at each tier.

Case Study Design

1. Your 6-week workshop, "Sexuality and Your Teen," has not been going as well as you had hoped. Attendance has been dropping. Attendees seem distracted, and it has been difficult to engage them in group discussion. How would you best go about finding out what the problem is?
2. What are some of the possible reasons for their discontent?

PART III

Contexts for Family Life Education

CHAPTER 7

Foundations of Sexuality Education

HISTORY

Sexuality education is a relatively new field for family life educators. In 1984, as part of the 20th anniversary of the founding of the Sex Information and Education Council of the United States (SIECUS), cofounder Lester Kirkendall (1984) recalled his own personal history of "sex education":

> In my boyhood, [if] there had been an organization such as SIECUS, it might have helped me with some of my sexual problems. Mainly I was distressed over my inability to cease masturbating. This was around 1914 or 1915 and I had discovered hidden away in an attic an old book published in 1897, *What a Young Boy Ought to Know* by Sylvanus Stall. It was intended to help males "avoid vice and deliver them from solitary and social sins." After I had read the pages on the "abuse of the reproductive organs," I realized that I was on my way to having a "sallow face, glassy eye, drooping form, [lacking in] energy, force or purpose, [being] a laggard in school, shy, avoiding the society of others, disliking good books, avoiding the Sunday-School, and desiring to escape from every elevating Christian influence." I was unsuccessful in stopping my "solitary sinning," but I did watch fearfully for these terrifying symptoms. (p. 1)

Kirkendall's subsequent tenure as a public school teacher, from 1927 to 1933, and as a resource for male students who had sexual concerns, further convinced him that "much of what had been taught [to them] was erroneous and that there was a need for organizations that could promote and direct sex education" (Kirkendall, 1984, p. 2). Kirkendall wrote several books, including *Sex Education as Human Relations* (New York, 1950), which proposed the unique idea that sex education should be considered an integral aspect of complete and satisfying living. "I became totally aware that the methods we use in relating to others, sexually and otherwise, are of highest importance. I knew then that the rest of my life would be devoted to helping people learn how to build relationships" (Kirkendall, 1984, p. 3). In 1960, he initiated one of the first university courses in human sexuality for undergraduates, at Oregon State University. In 1961, he met physician Mary Calderone, and the two shared their visions of an organization to promote sexuality education in the schools. As a result of their leadership, SIECUS was established in 1964. During the first 18 months of active promotion of materials and information, from January 1965 to August 1966, SIECUS received 3,930 requests from schools, the medical profession, religious groups, Parent-Teacher Associations and individuals from every state in the United States.

The decade of the 1960s was a time of revolutionary change in attitudes and public interest in education about healthy sexuality. It contrasted greatly with the reception of William Masters's initial medical school research on the basic physiology and psychology of sexual functioning. In 1954, after more than a year of deliberation, the Washington University Board of Trustees reluctantly approved Masters's research proposal "on the basis of academic freedom" (Allgeier, 1984, p. 16). When Masters, then an associate professor in the medical school, went to the library to begin his research, he found that only full professors could check out the sexual anatomy texts. Eventually he began a collaboration with Virginia Johnson to interview populations of women, including prostitutes, who were willing to be research participants in the physiology lab and who would talk openly about physiological sexual response. In 1960, Masters and Johnson submitted the first article on their research to the obstetrics and gynecology (OB-GYN) and psychiatric journals. "Psychiatry rejected the material outright as pornographic, and OB-GYN banned me for life in both [its] journals. That ban has since been rescinded voluntarily" (Masters, cited in Allgeier, 1984, p. 18). His medical school course on reproductive biology, which included information on female sexual physiology, also was not well received in 1960. More than 20% of the medical students asked the dean to discontinue the lectures, as did three of the executive faculty. Masters's and Johnson's laboratory equipment was repeatedly sabotaged and their families verbally attacked and socially ostracized.

Adults who were adolescents in the 1950s recall a sexual climate filled with "major doses of silence, embarrassment, ignorance, and fear. For many, parent-child talks were nonexistent, and sex was seen as an activity to which women submitted in order to satisfy their husbands" (Selverstone, 1989, p. 7). Girls who got pregnant before marriage were seen as shameful, "bad girls." They usually dropped out of sight (visiting a "relative") during the pregnancy and placed the baby for adoption, often keeping the dark secret to themselves for the rest of their lives.

Although these children of the 1950s speak gratefully of the current openness about sexuality and the access to good information, they express concern about the increased sexual involvement of their children and grandchildren and the subsequent rise in teen pregnancies and sexually transmitted diseases.

They observe that the old double standard still exists, with girls who have many sexual partners being labeled "sluts," whereas boys who show identical behavior are considered "studs" (Selverstone, 1989). They also support sex education in the public schools by a consistent majority of 85% or better (Harris, 1988). Support for HIV/AIDS education is even higher, with 94% of parents surveyed supporting the teaching of their children about safer sex as a way of preventing AIDS (SIECUS, 1998).

Yet it was not until 1965 that it became legal everywhere in the United States to purchase, sell, or use contraceptives. And as late as 1972, it took both houses of the Connecticut legislature to rescind a state law that made it illegal to have intercourse on Sunday (Selverstone, 1989). Box 7.1 (see pp. 132–133) recounts a timeline of significant events in the "sexual revolution."

THE CURRENT SITUATION

Currently, most states support some type of sexuality education in the local schools, although the types vary greatly from state to state and they are rarely comprehensive or long term (Engel, Saracino, & Bergen, 1993). The majority of school systems offer short programs—10 hours or less—that are embedded in health or physical education courses. Less than 10% of the sexuality education that students receive is given in a separate course, according to a 1989 survey of more than 4,000 junior and senior high school teachers of health- or science-related courses (Forrest & Silverman, 1989). And although most of the teachers believed that sexuality education should include topics of sexual decision making, abstinence, and birth control methods, as well as pregnancy and AIDS prevention, they reported having less than 6.5 hours of total time devoted to sexuality education topics. They also believed that sex education should be provided at least by the time young people reach junior high school, yet most schools did not address the topics until Grade 9 or 10. A survey of high school students (SIECUS, 1994) supported this conclusion. Fifty-eight percent of those who had received some type of sexuality education in school reported having had it at the junior high level. Only 5% indicated that they had received sexuality education every year while in school. The topics most frequently covered were AIDS, abstinence, and contraception.

A 50-state survey taken in 1998 confirms the earlier findings (Wertheimer & Moore). Whereas states have been aggressive in mandating HIV/AIDS education (42 now require such education), they have been much slower in adopting similar policies that encourage pregnancy prevention programs. Only 19 states mandate these programs. And teens continue to take risks: Less than half of sexually experienced teen boys and only 38% of teen girls report having used birth control every time they have had intercourse (Kaiser Family Foundation, 1998).

BOX 7.1

Timeline of Significant Events in the "Sexual Revolution," 1948–1999

1948	*Sexual Behavior in the Human Male* (Kinsey, Pomeroy, & Martin) published by W. B. Saunders
1950	*Sex Education as Human Relations* (Kirkendall) published by Inor Press
1953	*Sexual Behavior in the Human Female* (Kinsey and colleagues) published by the Institute for Sex Research
1960	The "pill" first marketed in the United States
1964	Sex Information and Education Council of the United States is founded
1965	*Griswold v. Connecticut.* The Supreme Court establishes the right to privacy and married women's right to contraception
1966	*Human Sexual Response* (Masters and Johnson) published by Little, Brown
	National Organization for Women is founded
1968	Feminists protest at Miss America pageant
1969	*The Sensuous Woman* (by "J") published by Dell
	Stonewall riots in Greenwich Village help launch gay rights movement
	Woodstock festival celebrates era of free love, drug culture, and antiwar protests
1970	Title X Family Planning Program established
1972	*The Joy of Sex* (Comfort) published by Crown. Selling more than 5 million copies, it is on the *New York Times* bestseller list for 8 years, longer than any other book in the history of the list
	Title IX establishes sex equity in education
	U.S. Commission on Population and the American Future established
	Open Marriage (G. and N. O'Neill) published by M. Evans
1973	*Roe v. Wade.* The Supreme Court establishes women's right to choose abortion
	Our Bodies, Our Selves (Boston Women's Health Book Collective) published by Simon & Schuster
1974	American Psychiatric Association removes homosexuality from list of mental illnesses

Engel et al. (1993) said, in summary:

> Pre- and posttest research on the effectiveness of school-based curricula usually report evidence of increased knowledge but little or less evidence of changed attitudes or behaviors. Thus it appears that, while school-based curricula may be effective in accomplishing the traditional educational goals of schools (i.e., to increase

1978   Louise Brown, first test-tube baby, born

1979   Moral Majority founded

1980   Ronald Reagan elected president

1981   First cases of AIDS diagnosed

1982   Reagan administration proposes "squeal rule" to require clinics to notify parents of teens who have received contraception

1985   U.S. Attorney General appoints Commission on Pornography

1986   *Bowers v. Hardwick.* The Supreme Court sustains constitutionality of sodomy laws

Surgeon General C. Everett Koop publicly advocates that sex education, including AIDS education, be directed toward preadolescents and adolescents

1990   *The Kinsey Institute New Report on Sex* (Reinisch & Beasley) published by St. Martin's Press, based on national statistically representative sample research conducted in 1989

Title X of the Health Service Act and the Adolescent Family Life Act mandates that sex education content that promotes abstinence as the primary sexual value for adolescents be required for the agencies receiving federal funds to do sex education

1995   The National Coalition to Support Sexuality Education established (see Appendix D, this volume)

1998   AIDS education now mandated in 42 states; 23 states and District of Columbia mandate sexuality education programs in public schools

1999   Nationwide randomized study reports that 70% of parents surveyed support the teaching of age-appropriate, comprehensive sexuality education in schools

Surveys report a 20-year low in the teen birth rate and a significant drop in the abortion rate. Researchers say fewer teens are having sex and that those who are are more likely to use contraceptives. United States still leads all industrialized nations in the highest rate of teen pregnancies, more than 1 million per year

knowledge), other interventions may be necessary to accomplish social and health-related goals (i.e., behavior change and problem prevention). (p. 67)

Fortunately, sexuality education programs are not limited to public school education. A number of youth-serving organizations, such as the Boys and Girls Clubs of America, the American Red Cross, and others have developed sexuality education programs. So have many religious groups and organizations. Although the goals and length of programs vary widely (from 5 to 30 hours, for example), the content usually is more comprehensive than in public schools. Topics typically include family relationships, drugs and alcohol, consequences of adolescent pregnancy, dating relationships, and myths and stereotypes. Skills such as values clarification, communication, and assertiveness are also frequently covered. Frequently excluded from objective discussion are the more "controversial" topics, such as homosexuality, abortion, masturbation, and contraception, as well as skills in listening, employment, and knowledge of health care systems (Engel et al., 1993). Yet these are the very areas in which youth are making choices every day.

Even in the "free speech" arena of media coverage (television, radio, music CDs, movies), many aspects of sexuality—particularly those aspects that call for responsibility and that look at the consequences of risk-taking behavior—are rarely covered. The late 1970s saw a vast increase in the number of media references to seductive behavior and implied acts of sexual intercourse. Verbal references to intercourse increased from 2 to 53 per week during this time (Haffner & Kelly, 1987). A national analysis of sexual content on prime-time television conducted in 1978–1979 (Sprafkin & Silverman, 1981) determined that more than 20,000 scenes of suggested sexual intercourse and behavior, sexual comments, and innuendos appeared in one year of evening television broadcasting. Yet it was not until the mid-1980s that birth control or particular types of contraception were mentioned on network television, even in advertisements (Haffner & Kelly, 1987).

Are teens "educated" by the media? In 1982, teens ranked media in the top three most important influences on their values and behaviors (National Institute of Mental Health, 1982). More than 40% of youth believe that TV gives a realistic picture of sexually transmitted diseases, pregnancy, and the consequences of sexual activity (Harris, 1986). With teens watching some 24 hours of television and listening to more than 18 hours of radio per week, the "sexuality education" they receive in school or community or church programs, over a year or over a lifetime, hardly weighs in at all (Haffner & Kelly, 1987).

In light of the rapid sexualization of society over the past 40 years, a National Coalition to Support Sexuality Education was formed in the mid-1990s. Composed of more than 100 national nonprofit organizations concerned with health education and social concerns of families and individuals, the coalition sees its mission as assuring that comprehensive sexuality education will be provided for all children and youth in the United States (SIECUS, 1997). See Appendix D, this volume, for the list of participating organizations.

This chapter explores definitions of sexuality education, including comprehensive sexuality education; the need and contexts for sexuality education; and theories and methodologies that have proven to be helpful in understanding and designing effective programs. Chapter 8 continues the discussion of sexuality education with a look at types of programs, a discussion of cultural-specific concerns, and suggestions for evaluating program effectiveness.

DEFINITIONS

Terms are often defined by the specific concerns of the program planners. This is particularly true in the area of sexuality education. Because of the critical health risks of premature sexual involvement, sexuality education is often "defined" by program planners as that type of education that will reduce and prevent unanticipated teen pregnancy and sexually transmitted diseases, HIV and AIDS most particularly.

As Douglas Nelson, president of the Annie E. Casey Foundation (1998) observed:

> We as Americans are finally coming to terms with the gravity, magnitude, and tragedy of unprepared parenthood. Over the past decade, there have been increased efforts—on the part of parents, teachers, community leaders, and service providers—to talk with and to inform young people about the challenges and hazards of adolescent sex. (p. 5)

There is wide consensus among politicians, health educators, parents, and professionals about what is sexually unhealthy: premature and unprotected sexual intercourse, exposure to sexually transmitted diseases, sexual abuse, and date rape. Yet there is wide disparity about what is sexually "healthy" for children and youth. The public debate about adolescent sexuality has often focused on which sexual behaviors are appropriate or inappropriate for adolescents and ignored the complex dimensions of healthy sexuality (Haffner 1995).

In 1994, the National Commission on Adolescent Sexual Health was convened to focus attention on the development of healthy values, attitudes, and skills, as well as the avoidance of unhealthy decisions and behaviors (Haffner, 1995). The commission adopted a consensus statement that defined sexual health and reproductive health as encompassing "sexual development and reproductive health as characterized by . . . the ability to develop and maintain meaningful interpersonal relationships; appreciate one's own body; interact with both genders in respectful and appropriate ways; and express affection, love, and intimacy in ways consistent with one's own values" (National Commission on Adolescent Sexual Health, cited in Haffner, 1995, p. 3).

Are these concepts of sexual health appropriate for adolescents only? Gradually, the realization is dawning that sexual health, as a part of sexuality education, is appropriate and needed by people of all ages. Hence the move to describe sexuality education as "a lifelong process of acquiring information and forming attitudes, beliefs, and values about identity, relationships, and intimacy . . . encompassing sexual development, reproductive health, interpersonal relationships, affection, intimacy, body image, and gender roles" (National Coalition to Support Sexuality Education, 1997). Such a definition confirms the role of parents as the primary sexuality educators of their children and reinforces the idea that responsibility and obligation for sexuality education are shared on a community-wide basis. Sexuality education does not, and should not, occur just within the classroom or home. It is most effective when each arena (home, school, religious setting, community group, media) accepts its unique role in teaching and reinforcing concepts of sexual health and responsibility.

Research has shown that comprehensive programs of sexuality education are effective in sexually transmitted disease (STD) prevention and in helping young people to postpone intercourse and use contraception. An international study of programs (Grunseit & Kippax, 1993) concluded that the best outcomes were obtained when education was provided prior to the onset of sexual activity and when information about both abstinence and contraception and STD prevention were included. Such programs were shown not to encourage sexual activity or experimentation.

Not everyone agrees with the value of comprehensive sexuality education, however. In the 1990s, a vocal minority stepped up opposition to specific subject matter and content in public school courses (Ross & Kantor, 1995). Insisting on abstinence-only education has been one way of narrowing the discussion. Other controversies have centered around removing lessons on puberty from elementary school health programs, eliminating elective sexual health-related courses from high school curricula, and separating classes by gender. Securing parental permission on an "opt-in" (parents must sign a permission form in order for their child or adolescent to participate) rather than an "opt-out" (parents must write only if they do not want their child to participate) has also been a confounding tactic in some school districts.

THE NEED FOR AND CONTEXTS OF SEXUALITY EDUCATION

In spite of the organized protests in school districts and states that continue to occur, national surveys consistently indicate that the vast majority (more than 80%) of parents and of adolescents in the United States desire sexuality education that is more comprehensive in scope and age range and that they support it being offered in a variety of settings. Parents also express the desire to know how to communicate better with their children and teens about all aspects of sexual health and values. And, despite myths to the contrary, teens also want to be able to talk to their parents. This then is the first aspect of "need" for comprehensive sexuality education: the need to be better informed and comfortable with one's sexuality.

A second aspect of need revolves around concern over the unhealthy consequences of premature, unprotected, or inappropriate or unwanted sexual activity. Although pregnancy rates in the United States have actually declined since their peak of 117 per 1,000 young women in 1990, unintended teen pregnancy still occurs far more often in the United States than in any other developed nation. Among U.S. teenagers, 85% of all pregnancies are unintended. Teen pregnancy rates are twice as high as those in England, Wales, or Canada, and nine times as high as in the Netherlands or Japan (Alan Guttmacher Insti-

TABLE 7.1 Real Facts: The Most Common STDs*

STD	Annual Estimated Incidence	Curable
Chlamydia	4 million	yes
Trichomoniasis	3 million	yes
Pelvic Inflammatory Disease	1 million	yes
Gonorrhea	800,000	yes
Human Papillomavirus or Genital Warts	500,000–1 million	no
Genital Herpes	200,000–500,000	no
Syphilis	101,000	yes
HIV/AIDS	80,000	no

From "Fact Sheet: Sexually Transmitted Diseases in the United States," 1997, *SIECUS Report, 25* (3). Copyright 1997 by the Sexuality Information and Education Council of the U.S. Reprinted with permission of the Sexuality Information and Education Council of the U.S.

tute, 1996). Poverty is another condition that exacerbates teen pregnancy and affects both mother and child. Among teens 15 to 17 years old, 46% of those with family incomes below the poverty line are at risk for unintended pregnancy, compared with one third of teens with family incomes 2.5 times or more above the poverty level. Only 70% of teen mothers complete high school, and 25% are on public assistance by their early 20s (Kaiser Family Foundation, 1996, 1998). Thirty-five percent of all pregnancies among women 19 years of age or younger are terminated by abortion. Young age and low income are the reasons most often cited for the abortion decision (Alan Guttmacher Institute, 1994).

Sexually transmitted diseases are also a major concern to be addressed by sexuality education. Some 12 million new cases of curable STDs are reported annually in the United States, the highest rate of curable STDs in the developed world (SIECUS, 1997a). Additionally, as many as 56 million American adults and adolescents may have an incurable STD other than HIV (see Table 7.1). Contraction of HIV/AIDs adds another 80,000 persons annually to this number. The public and private costs of STD infection are tremendous: over $10 billion annually ($17 billion when HIV/AIDS is included) in the United States alone. Complications of STDs include various cancers, infertility, ectopic pregnancy, spontaneous abortion, and possible infection of the newborn baby. STD infections also increase susceptibility to HIV, a fact that less than half of Americans under age 65 are aware of. Although chlamydia is the most common bacterial STD, only 23% of American adults under 65 who were surveyed even cited chlamydia when asked to name kinds of sexually transmitted disease (SIECUS, 1997a). There is great need for more information.

A third aspect of need involves the need to protect persons of all ages, but particularly children, from sexual abuse. Although many sexual abuse prevention programs were introduced in the 1980s, there is still great uncertainty regarding both the positive and the potentially negative outcomes of such programs (Engel et al., 1993). If this is the only sexuality education that children receive (as it is in some school districts), it may engender unwarranted attitudes of fearfulness or interfere with appropriate expressions of affection with significant adults (Krivacska, 1991). "To avoid this, abuse intervention programs should be offered in the context of (or as a component of) comprehensive health-focused sexuality education" (Engel et al., 1993, p. 75). On the other hand, even a one-time classroom presentation about sexual abuse has helped many children to recognize that their situations are harmful, and they have finally been able to tell someone about it. The value of the intervention aspect of sexual abuse programs should not be overlooked. Nor should the program occur only once in a child's 12 years of public education.

TEACHER EDUCATION

Providing clear and positive sexuality education across the life span requires well-trained, competent professional educators. This obvious need was stated as far back as 1912, when sexuality education consisted mainly of information about "venereal" diseases. The National Education Association passed a resolution favoring special training for sexuality education teachers (Krueger, 1991). Margaret Mead echoed the concern for special training of teachers in 1968:

> We're faced with a serious problem in the whole sex education field. This problem is the tremendous shortage of people who by their background and training and experience are able to stand up in front of a mixed group of people—a diverse set of parents, a bunch of adolescents—and talk simply and clearly, without embarrassment *and with emotion* [italics in original], about sex relationships, those relationships which we split off so badly from the rest of life. (Mead, 1985)

So how has this need been addressed in the ensuing years? A recent research survey study (Rodriquez, Young, Renfro, Asencio, & Haffner, 1996) determined that very few college and university teacher education programs (14% of the 169 surveyed) require a health education course for all new teachers, and no schools require a sexuality education course. This is true in spite of the fact that most states now mandate at least HIV/AIDS prevention education for all students in public school (Daley, 1996). As a result, most of the sexuality education offered in public schools is given by persons with little or no training in sexuality education. Physical education teachers most often have the responsibility, followed by health educators, biology teachers, family and consumer sciences teachers, and school nurses (Forrest & Silverman, 1989).

The good news is that 94% of the institutions surveyed do offer at least one sexuality course, and 87% at least one health education course. With courses already available, many new teachers could have at least minimal training in sexual health education if state certification requirements mandated such training.

Although the emphasis of this discussion has focused on public school teachers, the need for adequate and comprehensive training for community family life educators is just as acute. If programs are offered by an organization, such as the Boys or Girls Clubs, or by a religious denomination, there is usually a teacher-training component included, although the training may vary widely in length and coverage. Many programs for parents are one-shot or short-term programs in which no curriculum guide is used, and the presenter may or may not be trained or well versed in the components of effective sexuality education.

USING THEORY TO DEVELOP PROGRAMS

In listing the attributes of effective sexuality education programs, longtime researcher Douglas Kirby (1994) emphasized the importance of theory-based program designs and needs assessments. Three levels of theory are particularly appropriate.

General Sexual Development Theory

General sexual development theory can provide a foundational philosophy for all program designs. Such theory proposes that experiencing one's sexuality is appropriate at every age and stage of life and that sexual learning can enhance healthy, sexually positive attitudes (Engel et al., 1993). Sexually positive attitudes are described as attitudes that promote experiences that are noncoercive, nonexploitative, risk-free, and mutually pleasurable (Haffner, 1990).

This is contrasted with sexually negative attitudes, which promote fear, guilt, manipulation, avoidance of discussion, and denial of sexual feelings and which often result in participation in risky behaviors. These attitudes have also resulted, over the years and centuries, in lack of enjoyment of sexual lovemaking, particularly for females, who were expected to be passive and disgusted by the whole business. David Mace (1970) recounted an experience that happened to a physician colleague in 1943 at the first Marriage Guidance Center that opened in London. The physician was conducting an intake interview with a middle-aged woman. When he asked the woman if she enjoyed sex with her husband, she hung her head shamefully and replied, "I'm afraid I do."

Another example of sexually negative attitudes comes from my (Powell) own experience: as a preteen in the 1950s I received a harsh scolding from my mother for using a dirty word: *passion*. Later, when passion became an experience instead of just a word, I had no basis for analyzing my rush of conflicting feelings or for talking with my boyfriend about how we should handle a potentially risky situation. So, as a college student in the early 1960s, I decided I needed more information. I was afraid to be seen looking up such a subject in the library (I was at a church-sponsored college), so I ordered a sex "encyclopedia" by mail in a plain brown wrapper. The publishers sent the book to me, but for some reason they sent the bill to my mother! When she mailed the bill to me (with no word of encouragement for wanting to know more), I was so embarrassed at getting "caught" that I sent the book back! My sexually negative education put me at high risk at a time when the normal feelings of sexual excitement yearned to be expressed. I didn't know what to do except either to try to resist and risk losing the person I cared about so much or to give in and keep my fingers crossed that nothing "bad" would happen. He too was torn between the pleasurable sensations of natural desire and the guilt of even having these new feelings. Neither of us could talk to the other one about it. We had little sexual vocabulary and no experience at discussing sexual issues. So there we were, trying to cross a minefield with no map.

Haffner (1990) lists eight concepts of a sexually positive developmental paradigm:

1. Begin sexuality education at birth.
2. Promote the development of a healthy self-concept.
3. Acknowledge a wide range of values and experiences.
4. Talk honestly and openly about sexual questions and issues.
5. Prepare for realistic long-term relationships.
6. Value the future: career achievement, personal fulfillment, and personal health.
7. Focus on shared responsibility: home, school, community, religious organizations.
8. Address the political implications of change.

Engel et al. (1993) stress the importance of providing more sexuality education for neglected audiences and clienteles. This includes adults of all ages—young adults, parents, and older adults, to name a few—and of all circumstances. Gay and lesbian couples and persons with physical disabilities are examples. Where sexual dysfunction is present, because of ignorance or prior traumatic experiences, counseling or therapy should also be available.

Many times it is assumed that adults do not need or are not interested in sexual education and enrichment. My personal involvement as a leader with my husband in marriage enrichment conferences says otherwise. As one of very few couples who are willing to talk openly in front of a group about our own sexual experiences, we have found our conferences to be always well attended and appreciated.

Social Learning Theory

Social learning theory examines how people learn and incorporate behaviors and attitudes through societal interaction and influences. Learning takes place through a series of steps. *Knowledge* is the first step, whether it be accurate or inaccurate, comprehensive or sketchy. I often remind parents who are attending a meeting prior to the beginning of a church-sponsored sexuality education program that their children are getting sexuality education from the time they turn the radio on in the morning until they turn the television off at night. The questions are whether that is all the sex education they need and if it is the kind of sex education the parents want them to have. *Motivation,* the desire to act on the knowledge received, is the second step in social learning. Both internal and external motivations can be present: from curiosity to fantasy to the desire to please a favored one to wanting to fit in with the group or to prove something to oneself or to stay true to one's values. *Outcome expectancy* is a powerful determinant of behavior that also relates to cognitive development theory. When one can think rationally about the consequences of certain behaviors and whether these consequences are deemed to be good and pleasurable or harmful and risky, better decisions can be made. Social influence theory focuses on the social pressures that may override rational thinking about outcomes and how persons act. Brown (1995) and others (Bearinger, 1990; Bryant & Jennings, 1994) have looked particularly at media influences on adolescent sexual attitudes and behaviors.

The final step in social learning is *self-efficacy:* the belief that one has the power to learn new attitudes and behaviors and to control one's choices. Self-efficacy does not come quickly, nor just by hearing "you can do it," nor by other positive messages, encouraging as they are. Self-efficacy takes practice and support, from a peer group, a mentor, a therapist. Self-efficacy also has a cognitive component, for one must be able to "self-talk" in encouraging and rational ways and to be self-forgiving when mistakes are made in the effort to claim personal power and achieve goals.

Kirby (1994) has determined through his review of sexuality education programs that effective programs are designed on a solid theoretical base of social learning and behavioral theories. In other words, just giving children and teens the "facts" and expecting them to make their own decisions about behaviors and attitudes is not taking into account the higher steps in social learning theory. Programs must send a very clear message about the role of sexuality and sexual behavior in the lives of adolescents, and this message must be reinforced by the other experiential, interactive elements of the program. Kirby articulates the message very simply: kids should be abstinent, but, if they do have sex, they should always use condoms; or kids should always use condoms but should keep in mind that abstinence is the only means of preventing pregnancy and sexually transmitted diseases that is 100% effective (Kirby, 1994, as cited in Settles, 1998). Because too much information can be confusing for teens when they are struggling with difficult choices, discussion of comprehensive issues, such as gender roles, dating, and parenthood, were not included in the programs that Kirby studied.

Kirby (1994) identified other elements of adolescent sexuality programs that were shown to be effective in delaying the onset of sexual activity among participants and/or that increased the use of contraceptives among participants who initiated sex after being in the program. In addition to a strong learning theory basis and a clear message, the other common elements were (1) teaching of resistance skills through role playing and group discussion; (2) instruction on social influences and pressures; (3) setting peer norms and challenging normative myths (such as "everybody is doing it"); and (4) using activities that increase relevant skills or confidence in those skills.

Settles (1998) observed:

> It is important to note that these expectations do deviate from the typical sex education program which teaches only biological facts or decision-making skills in a value-neutral environment. Sex educators are now concluding what advertisers have known for years: too much information obfuscates. It's possible to sell ideas to people, but you can sell only one primary idea at a time. (p. 5)

Kirby (1994) and Settles (1998) also stressed the importance of tailoring the message to the target audience. If the audience is teenage girls who are at high risk for pregnancy and sexually transmitted diseases, the emphasis on how to protect oneself and how to say "no" is critical. On the other hand, a strong focus on abstinence, with information about avoiding pregnancy and STD risks, would be effective for young audiences or for high school groups in which most of the youth are not already engaged in sexually risky behavior. But if the school has a high rate of sexual activity, then the primary focus should be on protection from pregnancy and disease, with the option of abstinence also encouraged.

Moral Development Theory

If programs designed to influence behaviors have any hope of succeeding, they must also address the underlying values and moral decision-making thought patterns of the learners. An understanding of the stages of moral development as proposed by Kohlberg (1984) and enhanced by Gilligan (Brown & Gilligan, 1992; Gilligan, Taylor, & Ward, 1988) is helpful. Based to some degree on the cognitive development theory of Piaget, Kohlberg proposed three levels of moral development. The first level, preconventional, is consistently practiced by young children. Obedience and other "right" actions are governed by fear of punishment and self-preservation. The second level, conventional morality, is seen more often in older children and adolescents. Moral decisions are based on good interpersonal relationships and good motives, which help to maintain the social order. There is more concern for society as a whole and for the importance of laws, social responsibility, and values such as love, empathy, and trust. Kohlberg saw a higher, third, level of morality, one which very few people attain and which he called postconventional morality. People who live and operate at this level may value but also challenge the views of conventional society. They are less willing to accept a "law" at face value if they think a higher good is being jeopardized. They also consider the living conditions and rights of other people to be equally as valid as their own. Gilligan (Gilligan et al., 1988) added new moral considerations to Kohlberg's stages based on her studies with girls and women as they responded to moral dilemmas. She contended that men and women may have alternative moral frameworks from which to base their decisions. A deep concern for making and maintaining relationships determines the actions of many female adolescents and adults. In close relationships, this concern may override other interests, such as self-preservation or societal norms, particularly if these have not been clearly discussed or supported.

Although one's cognitive development stage does influence one's moral development stage to some extent, persons do not necessarily advance in their moral thinking as they grow older. Clarity in moral thinking and decision making requires the opportunity to discuss, with some guidance, dilemmas and options and the moral high ground. Such guidance is not meant to be an exercise in authoritarian judgment by an outside "expert," however. Learners must be respected and their differing views acknowledged and accepted even as they are considered in the light of high moral standards. Settles (1998) points to Robert Coles's interviews with children and adolescents about moral issues. Coles (1997) observed that the young people raised various ethical questions that showed their concern about not only how they should behave but also why, in accordance with a larger scheme of things. Coles marveled at their "tenacious moral seriousness," even though most had no idea where to go from there.

Kohlberg maintained that moral development was not a product of socialization but of one's own serious consideration of ethical questions and behaviors (Crain, 2000). However, social experiences do promote development by encouraging each person to articulate his or her position and then to consider other viewpoints in a nonjudgmental context. Kohlberg also saw role-taking opportunities as a very effective way to consider others' viewpoints. But whatever the context, the interactions should be open and democratic. Gilligan et al. (1988) emphasize the importance of mentors who have clear values and a moral philosophy that is not hypocritical or condemning but that demonstrates caring and genuine interest. She points out that adolescents are keen discerners of contradiction and sham. Settles (1998) summarized a discussion of sexuality and moral development theory: "The clearest lessons learned are that we, as educators, must be clear about our students' needs and knowledge, we must be clear about our own values and goals and we must take a stand that incorporates both concerns in order to most clearly benefit the healthy growth of the adolescents in our charge" (p. 17).

THE PRAXIS PRINCIPLE

In all of this, it is important to see the learner as an active, not a passive, participant. When learners begin to interact with the subject and with each other and to practice *praxis*—action with reflection—amazing change in attitudes and behaviors can occur. "If we follow what we know about learning, we would 'teach' in a way that activates the learner because we know that people 'learn best by doing,'" observed an experienced sexuality educator (Rudrauff, 1999):

> The droning lecture needs to end forever for any group of people including adults. Replace it with activity and skills-based exercises such as simulation games, role plays, performing arts experiences, game shows, demonstrations, student-led discussions, small group projects, service learning in the community, experiments, interviews of interesting people, and a myriad of other teaching and learning events. . . . When we mobilize the "student as leader" in their own learning process, we hook their emotional selves for internalization of the messages so behavior change might occur. (p. 4)

Evaluation of programs in which praxis occurs shows positive change in learners' attitudes, increased family communication, behavior changes in relation to relationships, and lower risk-taking behavior, as well as an increase in knowledge.

SUMMARY

Clear, comprehensive, positive sexuality education continues to be an urgent need for people of all ages and cultures in our society. The life-changing—and life-threatening—consequences of premature and unprotected sexual involvement have motivated much of the focus on sexuality education thus far. Yet it is obvious that developing children and older youth long for opportunities to learn about their bodies and their feelings in a context that is not threatening or embarrassing. Discussion of moral and ethical issues and decision making, with mentors who can offer guidance and acceptance, should also be included. Surveys continually confirm that parents want this type of education for their children and that children value what their parents have to say. Yet most parents and teachers express anxiety at the thought of actually doing the education. Teacher training and parent education are both elements of sexuality education that must be addressed by teacher-training institutions, teacher-certification bodies, and community and religious organizations. Many resources are now available for information and education; the challenge is getting them all connected. Chapter 8 elaborates on how that is being done in a variety of settings and with emphasis on valid evaluation of effectiveness.

QUESTIONS/PROBLEMS FOR DISCUSSION AND REVIEW

Class Discussion

1. Looking at the 50 years of history of sexuality education and the "sexual revolution," what have been the benefits and the detriments of this societal movement? Could education have had a greater positive impact? In what ways?

2. If teacher education certification should require a course in health education, what teachers should be required to take it? Is a general course in health education sufficient to teach sexuality education? Why or why not?

3. If the majority of parents desire sexuality education in the public schools, do you think that a vocal minority who oppose it should be allowed to control the decisions of school administrators? Why is sexuality education such a hot topic?

Research Problems

1. Review the theories presented in this chapter as bases for sexuality education. Then search the current scholarly journals for program design reviews. Identify at least one program that exemplifies each theory, and give examples to support your answer.

2. Take a random sample survey of students at your university regarding their level of sexuality education and its perceived effectiveness. Develop a phone survey or questionnaire that will allow you to define which type of education experience they had and how they would evaluate it.

Case Study Design

Using the contexts of sexuality education discussed in the chapter, divide the class into small groups to design educational programs that would be appropriate for different ages and societal contexts. Be sure to include programs for adults and for persons with disabilities. How would you address the issues of sexual orientation and sexual abuse?

CHAPTER 8

Approaches to
Sexuality Education

ALTHOUGH IT IS USUALLY ASSUMED that sexuality education takes place in the public school classroom with adolescents, this is not the only setting in which it occurs or is needed. This chapter discusses the focus of various program types and the audiences they address. A review of the elements of effective programs and concepts of evaluation concludes the chapter.

TYPES OF PROGRAMS

For Education

Programs designed primarily to educate have at least five major objectives: (1) to promote sexual health in persons of all ages and sexual orientations; (2) to reduce teen pregnancy and sexually transmitted disease; (3) to prevent child sexual abuse; (4) to assist parents in talking with their children and youth; and (5) to assist teachers in preparing to teach sexuality education courses.

PROMOTING SEXUAL HEALTH   The desire to promote sexual health in persons of all ages and sexual orientations acknowledges that all persons are sexual beings but that all sexual experiences are not alike. The Life Span Family Life Education Poster (Appendix A, this volume), developed by the National Council on Family Relations (1997), addresses the content of human sexuality education programs for children, adolescents, adults, and older adults. Obviously, developmental capabilities and needs determine the content presented; however, a sexual health perspective begins with the assumption that one's sexuality involves far more than sexual arousal and sexual intercourse. A model by Dennis Dailey (Figure 8.1) presents a holistic view of the elements that compose understanding of one's sexuality. Set within the context of sociocultural and family relationship settings, the areas of sexuality, sensuality, reproduction, in-

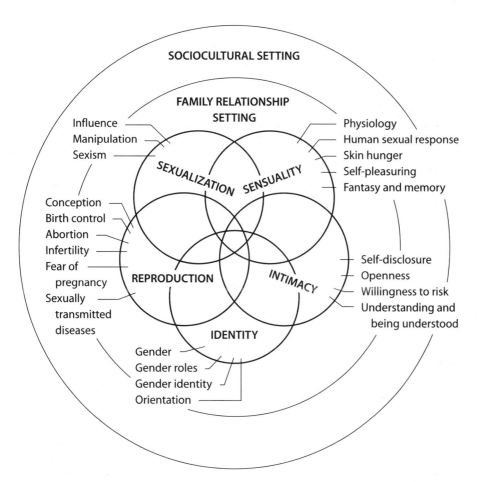

FIGURE 8.1

A Model for Understanding Human Sexuality.

Developed by Dennis Dailey, University of Kansas School of Social Welfare. Based on "The Components of Sexuality," by H. L. Gochros, J. S. Gochros, and J. Fischer, in *Helping the Sexually Oppressed*, edited by H. L. Gochros, J. S. Gochros, and J. Fischer, 1986. Englewood Cliffs, NJ: Prentice-Hall. Reprinted with permission of Dennis Dailey.

timacy, and identity overlap and influence one another. Certain aspects of one's sexuality come more into focus at various times of life, and depending on the sociocultural and family relationship settings, these aspects develop in either positive or negative ways. For example, research has determined that uncertainty about sexual orientation declines with age as students move through adolescence: about one fourth of 12-year-old students report uncertainty about sexual orientation, but only about 5% of 17-year-old students (Remafedi, 1992). At the same time, the sociocultural setting for many gay and lesbian students is certainly less than positive. One in five school health teachers said that students in their classes often used abusive language when describing homosexuals. In a 14-city survey of lesbian and gay youth, 46% said they lost a friend after disclosing their sexual identity to them, and less than 20% of the adolescents said they could identify someone who was very supportive of them (Telljohann & Price, 1993).

Persons with disabilities or chronic illnesses should also be affirmed as sexual beings who have the same feelings and desires as all other persons. "All

> **BOX 8.1**
>
> *Common Values Concerning Sexuality Education in a Pluralistic Society**
>
> - Sexuality is a natural and healthy part of living.
> - All persons are sexual.
> - Sexuality includes physical, ethical, social, spiritual, psychological, and emotional dimensions.
> - Every person has dignity and self-worth.
> - Young people should view themselves as unique and worthwhile individuals within the context of their cultural heritage.
> - Individuals express their sexuality in varied ways.
> - Parents should be the primary sexuality educators.
> - Families provide a child's first education about sexuality.
> - Families share their values about sexuality.
> - In a pluralistic society, people should respect and accept the diversity of values and beliefs about sexuality that exist in a community.
> - Sexual relationships should never be coercive or exploitative.
> - All children should be loved and cared for.
> - All sexual decisions have effects or consequences.
> - All persons have the right and the obligation to make responsible sexual choices.

too often adolescents [and adults] with developmental disabilities or chronic illnesses are viewed as nonsexual beings by professionals, peers, and parents" (Heighway, 1989, p. 4). Education about healthy sexual development for students with disabilities should include all of the elements of a typical comprehensive sexuality education program, as well as opportunities to learn and develop social skills and the teaching of appropriate touch.

Family context certainly has a great influence on one's sexual health. From the way a child's simple questions about body parts are answered to attitudes toward nudity to the roles of men and women in the family and society: All provide a foundation for positive or negative attitudes about one's sexuality. When incest and other inappropriate sexual behaviors are present in the family, a child's self-image and sense of control over her or his life can be so seriously affected that it may take a lifetime of therapy to overcome the negative messages.

Sexual health addresses the aspects and context of one's sexual development in ways that are affirming and teach respect for one's own body and the rights of others. Sexual health acknowledges the pleasurable aspects of sensuality but resists the sexualization of society that treats persons as objects for drawing attention and making money. Sexual health looks at health risks, as well as at ways to avoid the risks. The *Guidelines for Comprehensive Sexuality Education*, (SIECUS, 1997c), developed by a task force of SIECUS in 1990, articulated four primary areas for sexuality education that focus on the promotion of adult sexual health: (1) information, (2) attitudes, values, and insights, (3) relationships and interpersonal skills, and (4) responsibility. These goals are based on a set of specific values that relate to human sexuality and that reflect the beliefs of most communities in a pluralistic society (SIECUS, 1997c). Box 8.1 lists the values articulated by the task force.

- Individuals, families, and society benefit when children are able to discuss sexuality with their parents and/or other trusted adults.
- Young people develop their values about sexuality as part of becoming adults.
- Young people explore their sexuality as a natural process of achieving sexual maturity.
- Premature involvement in sexual behaviors poses risks.
- Abstaining from sexual intercourse is the most effective method of preventing pregnancy and STD/HIV.
- Young people who are involved in sexual relationships need access to information about health care services.

---

*Developed in 1990 by the National Guidelines Task Force, which consisted of 20 professionals in the fields of medicine, education, sexuality, and youth services. The guidelines were updated in 1996 to reflect societal and technological changes that had occurred during the subsequent 5 years. From "Fact Sheet: Guidelines for Comprehensive Sexuality Education: Kindergarten–12th Grade," 1997, *SIECUS Report, 25*(6). Copyright 1997 by the Sexuality Information and Education Council of the United States. Reprinted with permission of the Sexuality Information and Education Council of the U.S.

PREVENTING HEALTH RISKS   Adolescents are especially vulnerable to the two biggest health risks of sexual activity: pregnancy and sexually transmitted diseases. Thus it is not surprising that the focus of most sexuality education programs is preventative rather than comprehensive. Among teenagers, 85% of pregnancies are unintended (Alan Guttmacher Institute, 1996). Three million of the more than 12 million Americans infected each year with an STD are adolescents, a fact that shows the need for education of adolescents as well as adults. Although consistent use of condoms by sexually active adolescents and adults can significantly reduce both health risks, only 10 states allow clear contraceptive messages to be included in sexuality education at the high school level. Only five states have HIV/AIDS prevention curricula that include practical information about condom use, and only 33% of HIV educators in schools teach correct condom use. It is the topic least likely to be covered (Gambrell & Haffner, 1993).

PREVENTING CHILD SEXUAL ABUSE   Child sexual abuse prevention programs vary widely in content, length and number of sessions, age of students, methodology, and context. According to Engel et al. (1993), most programs focus on delivering the following messages: (1) children have a right to control their own bodies; (2) there are different kinds of touch, good and bad, and not all kinds need to be tolerated; (3) children can trust their feelings and recognize inappropriate touching; (4) children can learn to say "no" to touching that makes them feel uncomfortable or afraid and can run away; (5) children should tell an adult they trust about confusing or inappropriate touching; (6) the abuser may be someone the child knows, not a stranger; (7) "secrets" about touching need not be kept; and (8) any abuse that occurs is not the child's fault.

Teaching methods usually go beyond traditional classroom instruction and include booklets that children and parents can read together, comic books, video and theater performances, puppets, role playing, and coaching sessions (Engel et al., 1993). Another reason that education must go beyond the classroom is that child victimization occurs at a very young age, usually before age 7 (Finkelhor, 1984). It happens to young males, as well as females, at about a 1:3 ratio. Although there are no conclusive studies on the effectiveness of such child abuse prevention programs, preliminary research indicates that the learners do gain knowledge; but the knowledge may be short-lived and needs to be reinforced (Graham & Harris-Hart, 1988). In order to enhance retention and desired protective behavior, children need to have opportunities to practice and interact with the teacher and the materials. This type of learning tends to increase desired behaviors in the face of potential danger, such as responding to strangers' playground requests (Graham & Harris-Hart, 1989). Also, as previously mentioned, sexual abuse programs tend to have an intervention function also, with children being offered the opportunity to confide their "secret" and their fears to someone. Although current programs tend to focus on education for the child only, it is thought that education for parents and other caregiving adults might enhance effectiveness. Other potential program areas could focus on the offender, who is rarely considered in educational programming (Gilgun & Gordon, 1985).

The need for education in sexual abuse prevention certainly does not end with puberty. Programs for adolescents and for developmentally disabled youth and adults should also be considered. Ryerson (1984, p. 6) defines sexual abuse as "rape, attempted rape, incest and indecent exposure," although legal definitions vary from state to state:

> We cannot wait . . . to respond to the educational needs of developmentally disabled individuals in regard to self-protection. Nor can we shy away from the issue because it is a sensitive one, difficult to approach with children. . . . Regardless of their disability, these people can learn reporting and self-protective practices, both of which should be a critical part of every disabled student's basic education. (Ryerson, 1984, p. 7)

ASSISTING PARENT/CHILD/ADOLESCENT CONVERSATION   The largest study of adolescent behavior conducted to date (Kids Count Special Report, 1998) confirms the findings of other major studies over the past 2 decades: Parents are the earliest and most important influence in their children's decision making about risk-taking behaviors. Over 90,000 adolescents participated in a study sponsored by the Institute for Youth Development and the National Teen Pregnancy Prevention Research Center. The study found that teens who know their parents strongly disapprove of risky adolescent sexual behavior are much more likely to abstain from that behavior. Miller (1998), in reviewing 2 decades of research on parent-child relationships and influence, added that teens who are relationally close to their parents are also more likely to remain abstinent or to postpone sexual intercourse. And they are more likely to use contraception if they do have intercourse. Evidence also indicates that strong parental attitudes and values that disapprove of adolescent sexual intercourse and pregnancy and that caution about the dangers of unprotected intercourse are related to lower adolescent pregnancy risk.

Teens have stated consistently that they prefer to talk to parents about sex and health and rank that source of information as the most reliable. Only 1 in 10 said a friend was most reliable. And when teen mothers were asked about the reasons they had participated in risky sexual behavior, 75% cited lack of communication with their parents as a primary reason (Kids Count Special Report, 1998).

At the same time, numerous studies confirm that parents are uncomfortable discussing sexual issues with their children and welcome help from more formal programs and from other sources. Educational seminars that target parents as the primary sexuality educators of their children are usually well attended and appreciated. The Zero Adolescent Pregnancy (ZAP) program in Cortland, New York, is a good example. A series of workplace lunchtime seminars focus on improving communication between parents and children of all ages on all kinds of subjects, including sexuality and relationships. A needs assessment, administered before the program starts, helps the facilitator to tailor the program to the particular parent audience. Parents who attend the seminars report that they are "mobbed" after each session by coworkers who were unable to attend asking for advice and information. So the program has a definite spillover effect (National Campaign to Prevent Teen Pregnancy, 1998).

Sources of material for parents also abound. These include books, booklets, videos, and age-appropriate books for parents and children to read together. Yet many parents admit being at a loss when it comes to finding information. Appendix E (this volume) lists selected clearinghouses of resources that are continually updated.

It is important to note and to emphasize in parent education seminars that the most important factor in influencing children and adolescents is not being a "sex information expert." Rather, it is the cultivation of an ongoing, positive relationship with the child (which includes focused attention and listening skills) and an ability to state one's opinions and values on many subjects, including sexual behavior, clearly and succinctly.

EDUCATING TEACHERS OF SEXUALITY EDUCATION   Hickman-Brown Research, Inc., conducted a national poll in 1999, which revealed that a distinct majority of parents, 70% or better, support age-appropriate sexuality education in the public schools (Figueroa & Hanock-Jasie, 1999). Ninety percent believe that abstinence should be taught as the best sexual decision, but 70% oppose an abstinence-only education and want both abstinence and contraception to be taught, as well as other age-appropriate topics.

Although there is no federal law or policy requiring sexuality or HIV education, currently 23 states and the District of Columbia require that schools provide sexuality education. Forty-two states and the District of Columbia require schools to provide STD/HIV/AIDS education. Topics covered vary widely depending on the community and the age level of students in the program. The most commonly covered topics (in order of frequency) are body image, reproductive anatomy, puberty, decision-making skills, families, abstinence, STDs and HIV/AIDS, sexual abuse, and gender roles (Gambrell & Haffner, 1993).

Engel et al. (1993) listed three essential qualifications for sexuality educators at all levels of public education: (1) comfort with sexual communication; (2) the ability to listen, understand questions, and assess needs; (3) appropriate education and knowledge about human sexuality.

Rodriquez et al. (1996) identified six key concepts of a comprehensive sexuality education program: human development, relationships, personal skills, sexual behavior, sexual health, and society and culture. When teacher education courses available at colleges and universities were evaluated for inclusion of these concepts, the researchers concluded that 93% of the teacher education majors would not receive training in all six areas, even if they took every related course available.

In their recommendations, Rodriquez et al. (1996) urged colleges and universities to ensure that human sexuality courses are comprehensive in scope, covering all six of the key concepts. For current teachers, in-service and continuing education programs are vital. "Whether the explanation is lack of funds, lack of time, or lack of thorough understanding, the states which have mandated sexuality education are, with few exceptions, neglecting their teachers' cries for guidance, training, and professional preparation" (Krueger, 1991, p. 3). In addition to joining the Sex Information and Education Council of the United States, teachers may seek certification through the AASECT and through the CFLE program of the NCFR. New Internet technologies also offer opportunities for sharing resources, training opportunities, and program guides.

Service and Youth Development Programs

Service programs typically combine education with access to health services. School and neighborhood clinics often provide basic health care and, in some high-risk areas, contraceptive information and access. Some programs are designed to assist pregnant teens with basic child development education, infant care, and parenting skills. These programs may also have school-hour child-care services, usually on a time-limited basis, for young mothers who might otherwise drop out of school for lack of child care. Sara McDonald Rohar directs the Young Mother's Program in Birmingham, Alabama, and has been involved in services to pregnant teens for more than 13 years. She believes that such services are highly effective as education and prevention tools:

> This critical time in an adolescent's life is also a period of intense interest in sexuality education and family life education. We have a window of opportunity to reach and teach young mothers about contraception and risk prevention, positive parenting and self-sufficiency. The self-sufficiency component is vital to avoiding

poor decision making in the future. It involves learning to manage their personal lives and finances and developing employment skills. It is this combination of services and education, presented in ways that relate to the teen's current environment, that has made our program work. A strong comprehensive program has the potential to help young parents become high school graduates who are responsible nurturing parents, able to support themselves and their families. The payoff is certainly worth the effort. (personal communication, April 5, 1999).

Parent and Child/Adolescent Programs

Recognizing the importance of parent-teen communication, many pregnancy prevention programs have developed components that involve both parent and child. The National Campaign to Prevent Teen Pregnancy (1998) gives several successful examples:

In rural Missouri, the Family Planning Department of the Family Guidance Center for Behavioral Health Care created "Parents and Kids Learn Together," a comprehensive family life education program for parents and their teens and preteens. Working with parent groups, youth organizations, local religious institutions, and area educators, the Family Guidance Center designed a six-class curriculum for both mothers and fathers with youth aged 9–12 and 13–17. The first class in each series is for parents only, in which they place anonymous questions in a "question box" for group discussion. The remaining classes bring parents and kids back together for learning that is active and fun. (p. 2)

Girls Incorporated, a national youth development program, developed "Growing Together," a four- to five-session curriculum that seeks to delay the onset of teen sexual activity by fostering mother-daughter communication. Mothers and daughters who attended the program in Cobb County, Georgia, say the safe, supportive environment helped them build stronger relationships. Planned Parenthood of Los Angeles has trained their lay health workers to conduct "growing together" workshops in Spanish. (p. 2)

In Fayetteville, North Carolina, the "Steel Magnolias" program, part of the Support Our Students (SOS) initiative, has served sixth-, seventh-, and eighth-grade girls and their mothers over the past four years. This collaboration of middle schools, the community, and Fayetteville State College provides six weeks of structured workshops in which mothers and daughters interact. After "graduating," they move to an "alumni group" with ongoing opportunities to learn and practice new skills. Many of the "Steel Magnolias" women are single mothers or guardians who welcome the support. The program was so successful and popular that boys at the middle schools wanted a similar opportunity. "Brother's Keeper," stressing self-confidence, spirituality, and knowledge, now offers activities for boys three nights a week. On the fourth night, the boys and their parents discuss healthy human growth and development and sexuality issues. (p. 3)

Culturally Specific Program Designs

As with other types of family life education programs, no generic program of sexuality education will "fit" all or appeal to all cultural groups. Because of cultural distinctives in norms and behaviors, an intervention that is effective with one culture group may fall flat with another.

> *In McAllen, Texas, the Planned Parenthood Association of Hidalgo County, which serves a low-income Latino community near the Mexican border, has trained a cadre of Spanish-speaking lay health workers (promotoras) who go door to door to reach underserved women with a "friend and neighbor" approach. "Entre Nosotros" ("Just Between Us") is a ten-year-old peer education program run by 12 women, four men, four teens, and one mother-daughter pair who offer reproductive health education, family planning techniques, and information on how to avoid sexually transmitted diseases and AIDS to their friends, family and neighbors. The peer leaders attend monthly training sessions. Promotoras are also available at clinic sites to welcome people referred by the projects, help with paper work, answer questions, and provide emotional support. Promotoras serve 25,000 people a year. (National Campaign to Prevent Teen Pregnancy, 1998, p. 9)*

It is important for educators who design and present programs to become well acquainted with the cultural distinctives of the various groups with which they are working. The following discussion is not meant to be exhaustive or to provide all the information that the program designer needs, but it is meant to heighten awareness of the multicultural nature of our work.

A second important variable that must be considered is the economic status of differing cultural groups. More than 70% of children in "communities of color" live in extreme poverty (Columbia School of Public Health, 1996). Research studies show a direct correlation between poverty and parental education levels and pregnancy rates. The birthrate for Latina and African American teens is 108 per 1,000 females aged 15–19, compared with 40 births per 1,000 for Caucasian females of the same age, who have a youth poverty rate of only 14% (Child Trends, 1996).

> Growing numbers of adolescent voices [in poverty communities] are now saying, "There is no hope. There is no one who values me. There is no one who cares." Under such conditions, it is no wonder that some young people, instead of becoming industrious and hopeful, become sexually intimate for a short-term sense of comfort, and ultimately become profoundly fatalistic. In such cases, intercourse is used as a coping mechanism. Youth workers, teachers, and counselors must replace the use of that coping mechanism with concrete and hopeful (not rhetorical) alternatives such as decent employment, a bank account, improvement in school, a place in college, or a meaningful career or vocational track. These are the elements that produce desirable outcomes in young people and reduce teen pregnancy, teen violence, and teen substance abuse. (Carrera, 1995, p. 16)

A researcher and sexuality education specialist, Carrera assisted in design-ing a long-term, holistic, multidimensional pilot program with young people, parents, and adults in the Harlem community. The program, sponsored by the Children's Aid Society of New York, addressed sexuality education within a con-text of cultural and poverty awareness. It was highly effective and is now being replicated in several states. According to Carrera, the most well-attended mod-ule in the program was the one on employment, with an attendance rate of 89%. This even exceeded the attendance rate for the program's sporting events!

Added to the poverty factor are the cultural norms, customs, and mores that various culture groups value and adhere to. Latinos, Native Americans, Asian and Pacific Islanders, and African Americans all operate as distinct culture groups within American society, and yet it is risky to generalize any particular characteristics to all persons within that larger group. One major point made by all the writers on cultural distinctives is that within each group are small groups with which individuals identify. For example, the Latino population, which is the fastest growing minority in the United States at an estimate of more than 20 million people, includes individuals who speak many different languages and come from very different regions, races, classes, and cultures of the Ameri-cas and Europe (de la Vega, 1990). The same is true for the other major culture groups. Yet there are some points of distinctiveness that generally apply to each major group. The reader is urged to refer to primary sources for more in-depth discussion of the cultures presented here.

LATINO CULTURE GROUPS   "We must become sensitive to the differences that ex-ist among Latino groups, respond appropriately to nuances of Latino behavior, and most importantly, become aware of perceptions Latinos have about human sexuality and their own sexuality" (Medina, 1987, p. 1). Medina lists several ar-eas of special importance in working with Latino groups:

1. The educator must be bilingual. Even Latinos who are quite proficient in English will choose to address sensitive subjects in their native tongue and usually in private, if at all. Sexual topics are especially sensitive, and the establishment of *confianza* (trust and breaking down of barriers) will rarely be achieved if the language barrier is not crossed.

2. Religion and family are primary values. Some 85% of all Latinos profess the Catholic faith, and religious experiences are deeply embedded in their culture. Family loyalty that extends to several generations and relation-ships is also a major value. Child-rearing responsibilities are often shared, lifting some of the parental burden from single parents especially. *Com-padres,* or godparents, are also considered to be family and have an inter-est in the children's welfare. Living in an Americanized culture raises fears for parents about the corruption of their children by drugs or violence or by learning different sexual mores, values, and customs. They often shy away from public school sexuality education programs because of this.

School-based comprehensive health care programs, which include sexual health, must invest time to sensitize Latino parents and their children to the meaning of preventive health care and health maintenance. Anything that may threaten traditional family stability and challenge parental authority will be rejected by Latino parents (Medina, 1987). Programs that address child safety, rather than child abuse prevention, for example, will be more positively received and attended.

3. Gender roles, usually traditional and male-dominant, are an important factor to be considered in educational interventions with Latino adolescents or adults. The best intervention involves both the males and females, engaged educationally at the same time, even if they are in different rooms (de la Vega, 1990).

Culturally sensitive programs conducted by persons who have gained the trust and respect of the community have a good chance of success.

NATIVE AMERICAN CULTURE GROUPS   Because of stereotyping, Native American people have not been considered to be sexual in the same way as the rest of humanity (i.e., including persons who are homosexual or bisexual), so AIDS/HIV prevention programs were slow in coming (Rowell, 1990). Another misconception that has hampered sex education interventions is the idea that the federal Indian Health Service takes care of the health needs of Indian people and that they receive generous health benefits from the government. Actually, the Indian Health Service is a small, poorly funded agency that is unable to provide health services for even half of the Indian population. The result is that Native Americans have a poorer health status than the general U.S. population on almost every health indicator. Infant mortality rates have improved since the mid-1950s, but they are still higher than for all other races in the U.S. (U.S. Congress, 1986).

Prompted by the rising number of HIV/AIDS cases among their people, the Native Americans took the initiative to develop educational strategies that would work in their communities. The skills of traditional Native American healers, many of which are preventive in nature, have been used, as well as Western medicine. Indian artists and musicians were also invited to bring their talents to bear on the problem. As a result, a number of Native American–targeted materials have been produced, capitalizing on the culture's common values: respect for elders, teaching children survival skills, focusing on the extended family, strong spiritual traditions, storytelling, and humor (Rowell, 1990). An award-winning health education publication and video, *We Owe It to Ourselves and to Our Children* (National Native American AIDS Prevention Center, 1990) brought together traditional poetry, Native American stories, and artistic images, to present the message about STD prevention and treatment in a subtle and beautiful way. Focus groups have shown that Native Americans feel embarrassed to discuss most materials on STDs. Culture-sensitive resources are available from the National Native American AIDS Prevention Center (www.nnaapc.org).

ASIAN AND PACIFIC ISLANDER CULTURE GROUPS   Making up more than 15% of the nation's total population growth since 1990, Asian and Pacific Islanders represent a vast diversity of languages and traditions from more than 40 countries and territories, speaking 100 different languages and dialects (Lee & Fong, 1990). Recognizing and understanding the distinctions among the different groups is especially important when attempting to address their needs and to reach them with appropriate information and education programs. Differences between American-born and foreign-born, young and old, and new immigrant or refugee status and English proficiency among these groups are also nuances that must be considered.

At the same time, some basic similarities characterize most Asian and Pacific Islander subgroups: a strong sense of priority of family and community over individual rights; a taboo on sexual discussions; unacceptability of homosexuality by either the family or the community; and avoidance of discussion of illness and death. The reason for the latter is that discussion of such topics is considered a self-fulfilling prophecy.

So how might sexuality education be presented in an acceptable way? Lee and Fong (1990) urge more involvement by Asian and Pacific Islander health professionals, researchers, and community activists in one-on-one encounters, realizing that acceptance of new ideas comes slowly and depends on trust relationships. Television media educational campaigns also have high potential for effective communication, because this is the most popular source of information for many new citizens who may not be able to read or even have a written language, such as the Mien and the Hmong. But programming must be culturally sensitive and linguistically specific. Media educators must engage the concerns of Asian and Pacific Islander communities and not just use a "token" Asian representative. They must also go beyond the "model Asian" myth of the family who is highly self-sufficient and skilled and understand that many families are struggling with limited resources, a very different language and way of life, and possibly a traumatic past that would make them afraid to trust "outsiders."

AFRICAN AMERICAN CULTURE GROUPS   In a 1997 national survey of high school students, approximately 61% of all high school seniors reported having engaged in sexual intercourse at least once. This is a drop of 9% from 1990 survey figures. Yet among African American youth, the percentages did not drop and actually increased by 1%, to 73% (Annie E. Casey Foundation, 1998). The risk factor for this culture's youth is further increased by the number who live in poverty situations: some 41.9% of all African American families, as compared with a rate of 35.2% for Latino families and 14% for Caucasians (Columbia School of Public Health, 1996). The National Adolescent Sexuality Training Center and the Children's Aid Society of New York surveyed 200 Harlem youth who were involved in their comprehensive sexuality education program. Three-fourths did not live with both their mother and father, and one fifth did not live with either parent. Twenty-two percent have been homeless. Thirty percent were born to teen mothers (Carrera, 1995).

Programs designed for African American youth must take into account the high-risk contexts and the hopelessness that results, as well as the cultural norms and values. Consider the example of AIDS prevention programs. Currently, the incidence of AIDS and the death rate among African Americans is 10 times that of Whites. Smith (1999) notes that part of the problem has been misinformation: The disease was originally seen as a White gay disease, so Black communities took few precautions. This was especially true in heterosexual relationships. Furthermore, many young African American males still view condoms as a challenge to their manhood (Smith, 1999).

Several recent program designs have addressed these issues and have statistically monitored the immediate and long-term effects. The Harlem project model is a unique, intensive, and comprehensive preventive model approach. Program participants are involved in the program's activities for years on a regular, daily basis. Components include the Job Club and Career Awareness; Family Life and Sex Education; Medical and Health Services, Mental Health Services, Academic Services and Homework Help; Self-Esteem Through the Performing Arts; and the Lifetime Individual Sports. Most participants record 20 or more contacts with the program per month. Outcomes on measures of educational achievement and aspiration, substance abuse, parental involvement, and rates of sexual activity and contraceptive use indicate significantly higher achievements and much lower rates of high-risk behavior for program participants.

"Although abstinence is emphasized throughout all program activities as the most desirable behavior for young people, some make the personal choice to have intercourse, especially as they get older. Therefore, this program cannot accurately be called abstinence-based; rather it is based on the realities of the young people we serve" (Carrera, 1995).

The effectiveness of abstinence-based sexuality education versus a "safer-sex" condom education program for African American youth was compared recently, using a randomized controlled trial study with middle school students in Philadelphia, Pennsylvania. (Jemmott, Jemmott, & Fong, 1998). This study used a vastly different approach: a short-term, one-day program, focusing on cognitive-behavioral intervention. The researchers compared the short- and long-term results of an abstinence approach that stressed delaying sexual intercourse or reducing its frequency and that was not fear based (a definite turnoff for this culture group) with those of a safer-sex intervention that emphasized sexual responsibility and condom use. A control group intervention concerned health issues unrelated to sexual behavior. Both adults and peers were used as cofacilitators to test leadership model effectiveness. Learning activities were designed to be educational but also entertaining and culture sensitive. Many had been previously tested for successful response with other inner-city African American adolescents. Each intervention incorporated the "Be proud! Be responsible!" theme that emphasized personal and community esteem and considerations of future goals and consequences. After surveying the program participants at 3-, 6-, and 12-month intervals, the researchers concluded that the safer-sex strategy may hold the most promise, particularly with those adolescents who are already sexually experienced (Jemmott et al., 1998).

Samuels (1995) also noted that educational models that place emphasis on social norms and commitment to social responsibilities are more appealing to African American students and encourage responsible sexual behaviors. This contrasts with models that emphasize individualistic rational reasoning and/or a health belief model. For many African Americans who grow up in contexts of severely limited resources, sexual expression becomes a source of power that leads to a more positive sense of self and a bond to the community at large (Samuels, 1995). Therefore, the typical educational models that emphasize individualistic, direct, and rational behavioral decisions do not work well with African American youth. The evaluation results of the innovative models presented here seem to bear that out. McAdoo (1993) reiterated the impact that economic inequality has had on African American families. This poverty factor has contributed to an unfavorable depiction of the culture that fails to recognize the strong resilience and cooperative nature of African American communities. When middle-class Black and White families are compared, many of the stereotypical differences fall away.

EVALUATING EFFECTIVENESS

Whereas the effectiveness of most educational programs is proven by learners' scores on written tests, family life education programs are typically designed with the hope that they will alter behaviors and attitudes, as well as increase knowledge of facts and consequences. The vast majority of well-designed programs do indeed show significant knowledge increase by the learners. They have also been found to clarify values, increase parent-child communication, and help young people delay the initiation of sexual intercourse. Additionally, they may increase the use of contraception and condoms by sexually active participants while not encouraging young people to begin intercourse or to increase the frequency of sexual activity (Frost & Forrest, 1995; Grunseit & Kippax, 1993; Kirby et al., 1994; Moore, 1995; Powell & Jorgensen, 1985).

Behavior and attitude changes are more difficult and elusive goals to attain. They are also much harder to assess. Self-reporting by participants is often unreliable, because many persons will report the socially desirable answers to questions about their attitudes and behaviors. This is particularly true in the area of sexuality education evaluation, in which topics are often very personal and embarrassing for some participants. Many schools and communities do not want personal behavior questions included on assessments. And yet the great majority of sexuality education programs have been designed with the hope that they will change attitudes and prevent high-risk behaviors that lead to early pregnancy or sexually transmitted diseases.

Another major problem with evaluating effectiveness of sexuality education programs is how to statistically control for outside influences such as peer values and the media, which are especially pervasive in the area of sexual behavior and decision making. And because the act of conception involves two people, the ultimate outcome of a pregnancy prevention program will be affected by the attitudes and behavior of the program participant's partner, often a nonparticipant in the program.

Additionally, the level of rigor that constitutes valid scientific research is very expensive, time-consuming, and difficult to implement. Kirby (1997) lists the key components of rigorous evaluation:

- A sufficient number of participants
- Random assignment to experimental and control groups
- Long-term follow-up
- Appropriate statistical analyses
- Use of independent evaluators
- Replication of successful programs
- Reporting of both positive and negative results

Because very few programs have had the resources to conduct such rigorous evaluation, definite conclusions about program effectiveness cannot be made. Nevertheless, enough programs have now been conducted with some level of valid evaluation and published information that sexuality education researchers can draw conclusions based on reasonably strong evidence of effectiveness or ineffectiveness. In the case of some program designs, insufficient evidence exists to make a judgment of effectiveness or ineffectiveness, and further study needs to be done.

Recognizing these constraints, a 1996 symposium of prominent researchers in sexuality education and pregnancy prevention programs identified the following common characteristics of effective programs:

1. Using a theoretical model for behavior change
2. Targeting specific behaviors
3. Providing information about the risks of unprotected sexual intercourse and how to reduce risk
4. Providing opportunities for student input and interaction; practicing communication and negotiation skills and discussing situations that are realistic and meaningful
5. Addressing the influence of media, peers, and culture on teens' sexual behaviors and decisions
6. Developing and reinforcing beliefs and values among students that support their decisions to be abstinent and/or to protect themselves (Haffner & Goldfarb, 1997)

A review of research by Miller (1998) stressed the value of parent involvement in the program design and the importance of reinforcement by community and religious programs and of addressing socioeconomic and cultural factors that may intervene in what would otherwise be a successful program. The "bottom line" is that reducing adolescent pregnancy is possible, but challenging (Kirby, 1997). Programs that focus on only a small number of sexual beliefs or skills or even on access to contraception are not likely to have a dramatic effect on pregnancy rates.

Based on a study of program evaluation designs and constraints, the symposium participants made the following recommendations regarding evaluation (Haffner & Goldfarb, 1997):

- Doing no evaluation is better than doing a bad evaluation
- Rigorous outcome evaluations are appropriate only after a program has been successfully implemented for a period of years
- Evaluations must be consistent with the expressed goals of the program and the course content
- Evaluations of comprehensive sexuality education should go beyond measuring changes in whether young people are having intercourse or whether they are using a contraceptive method
- Evaluations of school-based sexuality education should focus on changes in knowledge, attitudes, and skills. Be cautious about measuring outcomes outside the classroom
- Simple programs should be evaluated by simple measures; complex outcome measures on behavior change should be reserved for multiyear, intensive strategies
- There is a need for new instruments to measure the sexual health objective
- Qualitative methods are an important supplement to quantitative methods

SUMMARY

There is no doubt that more sexuality education is desired by youth, parents, and other adults for a variety of reasons, both personally enhancing and preventative. Yet, although the majority of parents want age-appropriate, comprehensive public school programs for their children, attempts to incorporate new programs face several barriers. Strong opposition from a vocal minority in the community often intimidates school administrators, who would rather ignore the need than risk the public spotlight. The lack of trained teachers also hampers program effectiveness, even though sexuality education is now mandated in four out of five states. Furthermore, most school programs have a very narrow focus, most prominently on AIDS/HIV prevention education or abstinence-only education. Fortunately, other community and religious groups can and do address a wider range of topics and offer programming for parents and for parents and teens. Because parents' attitudes and involvement with their children have proven to be a major factor in curbing high-risk adolescent behavior, these programs hold great promise for community education, a major domain of family life educators.

Increased understanding of the distinctive learning styles and values of various culture groups increases program effectiveness. The results stress the importance of incorporating culturally relevant ideas and educational styles into the program designs and identifying more indigenous leaders to seek training in family life education.

After some 4 decades of research refinement, effective evaluation of programs is now better understood. The ability to draw conclusions about characteristics that effective programs have in common will be a valuable assist to program designers in the future.

QUESTIONS/PROBLEMS FOR DISCUSSION AND REVIEW

Class Discussion

1. In public school programs, how should administrators determine what subjects and value approaches to cover?

2. How can family life educators promote nonschool programs and culturally diverse programs of sexuality education in the community? What can boost your confidence to conduct such programs?

3. Look at Figure 8.1. Are there areas of sexual experience that Dailey has failed to include? Why and how do contexts of the family and society impact each of the overlapping circles of sexual expression?

Research Problems

1. What research has been done on the effectiveness of parent-teen programs? What areas seem to show the most improvement?

2. Using the values articulated in Box 8.1, develop and administer a questionnaire to several diverse audiences to assess their level of agreement with the statements. Write a report of your findings.

Case Study Design

Divide the class into several groups, each representing a board of education. Assign a person in each group to represent one of the following: a member of one of two different ethnic minority groups, a religiously conservative person, a bank vice president, a parent whose child was molested at a school playground, a member of Planned Parenthood, a young teacher in the school system, and a veteran school nurse. Each board has the task of determining the level of comprehensiveness of sex education courses and programs in their school. How do they come to consensus?

CHAPTER 9

Education for Relationships and Marriage

"FOR BETTER OR WORSE, MARRIAGE HITS A LOW." This headline appeared in the July 2, 1999, *Washington Post* (Fletcher, 1999). The article cited a publication from Rutgers University's National Marriage Project (1999) that reported the nation's marriage rate has dropped by 43% since 1960. The 1996 rate of 49.7 marriages per 1,000 unmarried women is the lowest in recorded history.

The National Marriage Project (NMP) report also suggests that the quality of marriage is declining. Married people who report being "very happy" in their marriages fell from 53% in 1973–1976 to 37.8% in 1996. Although Americans still hope for long-term marriages, the researchers report that increasing numbers of young people, particularly women, are pessimistic about finding a lasting marriage partner. Many young people are far more accepting of alternatives to marriage, including cohabitation and single parenthood.

"Young people today want successful marriages, but they are increasingly pessimistic about their chances of achieving that goal," commented Barbara Dafoe Whitehead, codirector of the NMP (Fletcher, 1999). Young people have good reason to be pessimistic about marriage. Although the divorce rate in the United States has declined slightly but steadily since the late 1980s, it has risen more than 30% since 1970 (National Center for Health Statistics, 1996). A young person entering marriage today is projected to have only a 50% chance of avoiding divorce. More disconcerting, Norval Glenn, a sociologist at the University of Texas, estimates that only about 25% of couples in first marriages are still together and happy after the first 10 years (Glenn, 1991).

THE NEED FOR RELATIONSHIP AND MARRIAGE EDUCATION

If we as a society value marriage, and the NMP report suggests that we do, then we must find ways to better prepare people of all ages to build successful relationships that sustain long-term happy marriages. According to the NMP report, "Marriage is weakening but it is too soon to write the obituary" (NMP, 1999, p. 15). One of the reasons for hope offered by the researchers is that a marriage education movement seems to be emerging among marriage therapists, family life educators, schoolteachers, and clergy. An example of this movement is the Smart Marriages: Happy Families conferences sponsored annually by the Coalition for Marriage, Family, and Couples Education. The 1999 conference drew 700 mental health professionals and more than 300 clergy, educators, and government policy makers, as well as a host of reporters from such media outlets as CNN, *USA Today, Time,* and *The Washington Post.* Diane Sollee, founder of the coalition, says the work she and her colleagues are doing represents a marriage and family education movement:

> It's an optimistic, cost-effective approach to reversing the epidemic of divorce and family breakdown. The idea in founding the coalition was to put marriage education on the map. I thought there was a whole body of knowledge that wasn't getting out there. The threatening thing [to some therapists] is that we've known for 20 years that you don't have to be a behavioral health provider to teach marriage education. ("Special report," 1999)

This report points out that Smart Marriages: Happy Families is not antitherapy, but it does explore educational alternatives to therapy. Behind most of these approaches is the basic premise that if couples can master basic skills that are present in good marriages—communicating effectively, resolving conflicts, and being good friends—they can work on building healthy marriages. Howard Markman, a leading marriage researcher and cofounder of the marriage course Prevention and Relationship Enhancement Program (PREP), has found that clergy and laypeople may actually be more successful than therapists in helping troubled couples. Couples struggling with their marriages do not frequently see therapists, but they do see other professionals in the community. Markman found that couples trained by clergy and lay leaders had more positive communication skills after training than did those trained by marriage counselors at the University of Denver (Markman, as cited in "Special report," 1999).

HISTORY OF RELATIONSHIP AND MARRIAGE EDUCATION

Stahmann and Salts (1993) report that historically four approaches have been developed to educate people for marriage: generalized educational programs, premarital counseling, enrichment programs, and marital and premarital therapy. Marriage enrichment and premarital counseling programs in which education is the primary objective are the central focus of this chapter. General marriage preparation programs differ widely due to the varying developmental age levels of the participants and are more academic in nature than are marriage enrichment and premarital counseling. Therapy is not generally considered to be a function of family life education; consequently, marital and premarital therapy are not addressed.

Education for marriage is not a new idea. Stahmann and Salts (1993) report that the first formal marital education program was instituted in the early 1930s, when the Merrill-Palmer Institute established a premarital educational program. Mudd, Freeman, and Rose (1941) report that a premarital counseling program was in existence at the Philadelphia Marriage Council at least as early as 1941. The program was designed to provide education and information about marriage to couples planning to be married and to help them work through interpersonal problems. For more than 50 years general marriage preparation content has been available in high school family life education courses and in colleges through departments of family studies, sociology, and psychology and more recently through community adult education courses and extension programs (Stahmann & Salts, 1993). Although some of the courses are becoming more experiential and skill based, in the past they were primarily didactic. For the most part, they were taken by women and often stressed traditional male and female roles. Most were designed to teach about marriage rather than provide education for marriage.

David and Vera Mace were strong advocates of education for marriage. A pioneer in the development of marriage counseling, David Mace established marriage counseling programs on several continents. After coming to the United States from England in the 1950s, the Maces served as joint executive directors of the American Association of Marriage Counselors, now the American Association of Marriage and Family Therapists (AAMFT). After a long career of trying to rehabilitate relationships through therapy, David Mace in frustration concluded that an army of marriage therapists could not turn back the tide of divorces occurring in the United States in the 1960s and 1970s. He raised the question, "Could not all young people be trained to perform these operations [interpersonal competencies] competently before they marry?" (Mace, 1982, p. 189).

Mace pointed out that young people in our society already spend a major portion of their lives in compulsory education acquiring knowledge intended to make their later lives productive and rewarding. "If it is important that young people be qualified for their future vocations, is it not equally important that they be qualified for their future roles as founders of families?" (Mace, 1982, p. 186).

Mace (1982) recalls an observation by an anthropologist friend who spent many years studying a West African tribe. The anthropologist noted how different the educational system of tribal people is from that of "civilized" societies. Tribal people tend to carefully teach their children about the art of living and cultural traditions and leave them to pick up information about the outside world on their own. By contrast, so-called civilized people spend most of the education time on providing information about the external world and leave children to pick up living skills on their own.

Mace had little confidence in traditional high school and college marriage preparation classes. He argued that the key to better marriage was acquiring "interpersonal competencies," or basic relationship skills, such as communication, anger management, and conflict resolution. Essential relationship skills such as these cannot be developed simply by hearing about them or in two or three easy lessons. Although Mace had spent many years as a classroom lecturer, he reluctantly concluded that the classroom offers limited opportunity for effective marriage and family life education (Mace, 1982). Mace's alternative to the classroom was to teach these interpersonal skills to couples in small groups using experiential learning methods. He called the approach *marriage enrichment.* We look at this approach later in this chapter.

PREVENTIVE VERSUS REMEDIAL APPROACHES

Over the past 25 years there has been a proliferation of programs to prevent the breakdown of marriage relationships (Berger & Hannah, 1999; Mace, 1983; Olson, 1976). Many researchers in the family field have struggled to define the differences between approaches designed to prevent relationship distress and those designed to repair seriously damaged relationships (Berger & Hannah, 1999; Guerney, Brock, & Coufal, 1986; L'Abate, 1981; Mace, 1983; Markman, Floyd, Stanley, & Lewis, 1986). Berger and Hannah (1999) point out that preventive programs for couples, married and unmarried, have appeared under different titles throughout the years. Prominent titles have included "family life education" (Groves & Groves, 1947), "marriage enrichment" (Guerney, 1977; Mace & Mace, 1975), "skills/competence training" (L'Abate, 1986) and "psychoeducational programs" (Leveat, 1986). The common thread in all of these programs is that they are preventive in nature. They are designed for couples who are not in relationship crisis and who want to maximize the potential for relationship wellness in their marriages. *Remedial programs* are therapy programs aimed at dysfunctional couples whose relationship satisfaction has been compromised and the stability of the marriage undermined.

Berger and Hannah (1999) describe *preventive programs* as being based on the strengths of couples rather than on pathology. They employ psychoeducational or skill competency models and are all of the following: cognitive, experiential, structured, programmatic, time limited, affirmative, relatively economical, and primarily small group oriented. In contrast, remedial or therapy models are less structured, nonprogrammatic, minimally didactic, more confrontational, open ended, and much more costly.

During the past decade or two, programs with an educational orientation have been integrated into remedial approaches to couples therapy so that it is now difficult to establish a clear demarcation between prevention, enrichment, and therapy. Berger and Hannah (1999) conclude that the best way to view the commonalities between preventive and remedial programs is to see them as falling at different points along a continuum of interventions.

Levels of Prevention

L'Abate (1983) applied three historical levels of prevention, primary, secondary, and tertiary, to couples programs. Primary prevention programs intervene with couples before they are experiencing difficulties. An example of this level is a program for the parents of entering college freshmen that two certified family life educators have facilitated at Baylor University for the past 20 years. The purpose of the program is to help parents deal with the transition to the empty nest and the resulting changes in parenting and marital interaction. Most premarital counseling programs, such as Prepare/Enrich (Olson & Olson, 1999) and the Saving Your Marriage Before It Starts (SYMBIS) model (Parrott & Parrott, 1999), also fit into this category in that they are designed to identify potential relationship problems and to provide early intervention in the transition to marriage.

Secondary prevention involves interventions with couples "at risk": couples who are already experiencing some degree of relationship distress. Programs at this level are designed to prevent further loss of satisfaction and to increase friendship and intimacy. Gottman and Gottman's (1999) Marriage Survival Kit workshop and the PREP program developed by Stanley, Blumberg, and Markman (1999) are examples of this level of program, although neither program screens couples. Most marriage enrichment programs are aimed at "healthy couples," but many participants actually need secondary prevention.

Tertiary level programs are designed to keep serious relationship problems from getting worse and leading to separation. Such programs are more likely to be carried out by trained therapists and not by family life educators. Most family life education programs address Levels 1 and 2, but identifying which couples are best served by Levels 1, 2, or 3 is beyond the scope of L'Abate's typology.

Berger and Hannah (1999) include 13 preventative approaches in their recent work, none of which claims to be directed toward couples at Level 3. In only 1 of the 13 is it claimed that couples are carefully screened (L'Abate, 1999). The others are open to all couples without screening. Mace (1983) concluded that preventative approaches overlap and cannot be precisely distinguished from one another, and Berger and Hannah (1999) concluded that distinctions are somewhat artificial.

L'Abate (1983) has been one of the strongest advocates of preventive approaches to helping couples avoid marital breakdown. He argues that prevention is cheaper, more innovative, easier, happier, and cleaner, and he has called for prevention and those who practice it to be raised to the same status as practitioners of remedial approaches. Berger and Hannah (1999) document an even stronger rationale for preventive programs. They cite longitudinal studies that demonstrate that early premarital and marital conflict is a major risk factor for future marital dysfunction and that once negative patterns become entrenched it is difficult to eradicate them.

Obstacles to Prevention

If educational approaches to relationship competence have so many advantages, why then are they not more popular? What is it that blocks couples from taking advantage of programs designed to improve their relationship before they begin to experience relationship-threatening problems? Clark Vincent's concept of the *myth of naturalism* (Vincent, 1973) sheds some light on these questions. The myth of naturalism asserts that people are born with all the knowledge and skill necessary to have successful relationships. Successful marital relationships should come naturally and effortlessly to normal adults. Anyone who has difficulty in relationships, then, must be inadequate. Consequently, participating in a communication course or attending a marriage enrichment event is admitting that one is in some way defective. Even if the myth had been true in the past, when marriages were more institutional in nature, it would not be true today, when the marital bond is so clearly dependent on a couple having the interpersonal competencies essential to maintaining a passionate friendship.

Mace coined the term *intermarital taboo* as a further explanation of why couples do not take advantage of preventive programs. The intermarital taboo says, "as a married couple, you shall not reveal to other married couples what is going on inside your marriage" (Mace & Mace, 1976, p. 329). The intermarital taboo is based on the concept of privatism, which refers to cultural attitudes that declare that anything that occurs within the family is too private to be shared outside the family. This belief might have been functional when large extended families were the norm and there were many family members around to discuss issues. Most families today, however, are nuclear and tend to be more isolated. For these couples, practicing privatism is like shutting themselves in a box. It prevents them from seeking marriage preparation or help in figuring out how to relate to each other in mutually satisfying ways. Privatism also fosters the idea that "other couples must be perfect [after all, they look and act perfect in public], so we must be the only ones having a problem with this issue." In designing educational programs for marriage, both the myth of naturalism and the intermarital taboo must be overcome. This is especially true for programs that focus on couples' groups.

Berger and Hannah (1999) have identified an additional barrier to the use of preventive programs: the "if it ain't broke, don't fix it" motto:

> The most obvious and perhaps formidable barrier involves the couple's motivation to change. Attempting to prevent future distress in nondistressed couples creates an inherent paradox: Because preventive programs are geared toward at-risk couples who have not yet developed significant relationship problems, what would motivate such couples to pursue and invest in preventive programs? (p. 9)

Marriage enrichment leaders, in promoting marriage enrichment programs, have frequently heard potential participants comment, "If my marriage was any better, I couldn't stand it." This comment illustrates the motivation problem in recruiting participants to preventive relationship and marriage education programs. One response to such a comment is, "That's great! We need you to come and share your secrets of success with the other couples." Such a comment attacks both the motivation issue and the intermarital taboo.

Another strategy is to link relationship education programs to life cycle transitions or to "teachable moments." The program for parents of entering college freshmen mentioned earlier would be an example of this strategy. The program is offered on move-in day during student orientation. The focus is on parenting the adult child and on the transition to the empty-nest stage. One certified leader couple in the Association for Couples in Marriage Enrichment (ACME) convinced the leaders of a hospital childbirth class to allow them to add three marriage sessions at the end of the usual series of classes. A parenting educator suggests that several marriage enrichment sessions be added to parent education classes and that the participants then be moved into ongoing marriage support groups. In this case, the more threatening marriage education program is being linked to a less threatening and more acceptable family life education program.

PHILOSOPHIES, THEORIES, AND PROCESS

Relationship and marriage education programs vary widely, and to describe the philosophies and theoretical underpinnings of all would be impossible. The purpose of this section is to present the underlying philosophies and theories common to the majority of programs that have been described in the professional literature.

Philosophies

The common philosophical thread among these programs is their educational and preventive nature. Guerney (1977) and Hof and Miller (1981) describe programs based on an educational model as ones that teach attitudes and specific skills in a structured and systematic fashion and that have clear behavioral objectives and appropriate evaluative measures included. Certainly not all relationship programs meet these standards, but all have an educational orientation, with the primary objective to prevent the emergence, development, or recurrence of interpersonal dysfunction (Hof & Miller, 1981).

Because of their educational nature and preventative focus, most marriage and relationship education programs work from the perspective of strength. At their core is a philosophy that is oriented to growth and potential. The strength perspective sees people and relationships as possessing numerous untapped strengths and resources that can be developed. Hof and Miller (1981), describing marriage enrichment programs, elaborate:

> People are viewed as having a natural drive towards growth, health, and personal development. Given the appropriate environment people can learn how to choose and change behaviors and attitudes which will improve their interpersonal relationships, and allow them to experience increased satisfaction in life and in relationships with other people. (p. 8)

Emphasis on strengths or potential does not mean that conflictual issues are ignored. To the contrary, an emphasis on growth affirms that couples can learn to resolve the negatives in their relationship in positive and creative ways.

Mace and Mace (1976) did not use the term *enrichment* to mean the provision of additives from the outside, as in "vitamin-enriched" bread. Enrichment was something that came from within the couple's relationship. They believe the emphasis on growth and potential best communicates the idea that in each marital dyad there exists an inherent capacity for mutual fulfillment and development, which in most instances remains largely untapped. The Maces believe that in many cases marriages end in divorce because couples are unable to access these resources. It follows, then, that marriage education programs designed to help actualize the relationship potential not only prevent some marriages from failing but also improve the quality of many mediocre but stable unions in which interpersonal relationships have never gone beyond a superficial level (Mace & Mace, 1976).

The concept of the "companionship family" has influenced the thinking behind many marriage education programs. In the late 1940s Burgess identified a new form of the family emerging in the United States that he called the *companionship model* of the family (Burgess, Locke, & Thomas, 1971). He contrasted this new model with the traditional model, which he called the "institutional model." The institutional model is seen as rigid and patriarchal, with a hierarchical role structure. The companionship model is relationship driven and characterized by intimacy, equality, democratic decision making, and flexible role structure. The institutional model's unity and strength come from traditional rules and regulations, specified duties and obligations, and community support. Unity in the companionship model depends on the internal cohesiveness of its interpersonal relationships rather than the external coercion of custom and community opinion.

Unfortunately, many of the factors in the companionship marriage that make it appealing also make it less stable and more vulnerable to divorce. Many people in marriages with companionship expectations lack the interpersonal skills necessary to sustain a marriage based primarily on relational characteristics such as mutual affection, sympathetic understanding, comradeship, and mutual respect. As much as a couple may want a marriage based on a loving companionate relationship with a passionate best friend, few actually have the skills to make it work (Dyer & Dyer, 1999). The minimum skills needed are:

- A commitment to individual, relationship, and partner growth
- A means of communication that leads to understanding
- The ability to use conflict to stimulate creative change
- The ability to create and maintain intimacy

Mace (1982) identified the first three of these skills as a couple's primary coping system. The fourth was added by contemporary practitioners in recognition of the importance of intimacy in relationships (Dyer & Dyer, 1989). Most marriage education programs today address one or a combination of these essentials. Hof and Miller (1981) maintain that the ultimate goal and underlying value of most marriage enrichment programs is the attainment and maintenance of an intentional companionship marriage.

The majority of marriage and relationship education programs use a group format. Some, however, are offered to a single couple, and some use both an individual and group format. For example, the Couple Communication Program (Miller & Sherrard, 1999) can be used with a single couple or a group of couples. Prepare/Enrich: Version 2000 (Olson & Olson, 1999), a premarital counseling program for couples, is also offered in a group format called Growing Together (Olson, Dyer, & Dyer, 1998).

Interaction among couples is central to the philosophy of many programs. One way to overcome the intermarital taboo is to provide a safe environment in which couples can share relationship experiences. Interaction occurs at three levels: leader to total group, among couples in the group, and between the partners in the couple. The degree to which this interaction occurs varies among programs. In ACME-style marriage enrichment, couple leaders openly discuss their marriage with the couples in the group and encourage the other couples to do the same (Dyer & Dyer, 1999). By contrast, marriage encounter, another approach to marriage enrichment, limits interaction among couples in the group but encourages a high level of interaction among partners (Elin, 1999). In all cases the hope is that couples will become comfortable communicating positively with each other and will continue the practice at home.

Theories

Stahmann and Salts (1993) stress the importance of basing family life education on a strong scholarly foundation, an approach that requires current theoretical and empirical knowledge and application. Unfortunately, few creators of marriage and relationship education programs have been explicit in documenting their research or theoretical base. Significant exceptions to this general statement include two early programs, Guerney's (1977) Relationship Enhancement (Rogerian, social learning, and interpersonal) and Miller, Nunnally, and Wackman's (1975) Couple Communication Program (communication systems). These programs were exemplary in clearly identifying their theoretical bases.

Three more recent programs with strong scholarly foundations are John Gottman's Marriage Survival Kit (Gottman & Gottman, 1999), based on his 25 years of research at the University of Washington; the PREP program (Markman, Stanley, & Blumberg, 1994; Stanley, Blumberg, & Markman, 1999), based on research at the University of Denver; and the Prepare/Enrich inventory (Olson & Olson, 1999), which also has a strong research base and has been subjected to numerous reliability and validity studies.

Berger and Hannah (1999) compared preventive approaches on seven dimensions, including the theoretical bases. Six of the programs identified their theoretical base as eclectic, including in some form humanistic, systems, and empiricistic theories. Cognitive-behavioral theory was the most frequently cited single theory (seven times), followed closely by learning theory (five times). Others included religious mentoring, religious reflective sacramental, self-psychology, Adlerian, communication systems, Rogerian, Bowenian systems, and object relations theories.

Humanistic psychology and Rogerian psychotherapy have had a strong influence on the development of marriage education and particularly on the marriage enrichment movement (Hof & Miller, 1981). Important concepts in marriage, such as the emphasis on the emotional life and the expression of feelings, the importance of interpersonal relations on personal well-being and the need to create effective relationships, and fulfilling personal and couple potential, are contributions from these theoretical traditions (Guerney, 1977). Marriage education programs generally attempt to create a safe and empathic environment in which participants can freely express feelings, experience acceptance from spouse and others, and acquire new knowledge and skills with a low personal-risk factor. Doing this often employs Rogerian techniques, such as leader congruence and modeling respect and complete acceptance of participants.

Because relationships are the focus of marriage education programs, all the programs owe some debt to systems theory. Bertalanffy (1950) defined a system as any whole with interacting parts. The system concept, that relationships are not static but dynamic living entities that strive to balance stability and change, is central to relationship education programs. "System properties and principles provide a framework for understanding relationship development and dysfunction" (Miller & Sherrard, 1999, p. 127).

The majority of the programs reviewed by Berger and Hannah have an emphasis on communication. Most programs, then, incorporate some form of communication systems theory. Many have relied on the work of Miller, Nunnally, and Wackman (1975), the originators of the Minnesota Couple Communication Program, now known as Couple Communication. Miller and his colleagues, drawing on the earlier works of Virginia Satir, Don Jackson, Paul Watzlawick, and Sidney Jourard, created an integrated, systematic approach to interpersonal communications that is highly teachable.

Attitudinal change and skill development are key objectives in relationship education. To accomplish this, family life educators have drawn on social learning theory, behavior modification theory, and cognitive-behavioral theory.

Marriage educators believe couples can learn new patterns of interaction and correct deficiencies in social learning. New communication and conflict resolution skills can be taught and learned.

"Deficiencies in social learning are thus viewed as important components in relationship discord, and the learning and continued practice of appropriate skills is viewed as an important component in marital and relationship health" (Hof & Miller, 1981, p. 17). Modeling, behavior rehearsal, prompting, and reinforcement are frequently used techniques in marriage education. They reflect behavior modification approaches that incorporate social learning theory. Marriage educators have also recognized the importance of reeducation in the area of attitudes and other cognitive functions. Many programs are based on the cognitive-behavioral tradition of change:

> Therefore, the focus is on ways of thinking (attitudes and expectations) and behaving (communication and conflict management) that are associated with marital success and failure. The skills-oriented approach rests on the assumption that couples can learn new behaviors that can help them prevent the deterioration in relationship quality commonly seen in marriage. (Stanley, Blumberg, & Markman, 1999, p. 280)

Experiential learning models are used extensively in relationship and marriage education programs. Experiential learning is based on the assumption that people learn best by doing. The underlying premise is that experience precedes learning and that involved learning is more potent than vicarious learning. Much of what has been done in the past in family life education has depended on didactic methods and vicarious learning. This kind of information exchange may be effective for some types of knowledge and may change behavior in some areas of life, but it has very limited value in behavioral change in the area of interpersonal relationships. Most therapists long ago gave up on advice giving as an effective means of producing behavior change. Behavior change in interpersonal relations is more likely to occur when learning is a dynamic process in which learners are active participants. This method requires leaders to use techniques that actively involve couples in experiencing new situations, experimenting with new methods, and practicing new skills (Dyer & Dyer, 1989).

Process

The dynamics of group process provide an environment in which experiential learning can take place. Didactic learning is passive; experiential learning is active. Listening to a lecture or watching a film allows learners to remain anonymous and not risk vulnerability. Experiential learning, on the other hand, always requires some risk. Used effectively, group process encourages and supports the learner's ventures into new territory. It is a vehicle of affirmation of new discoveries that provides immediate reinforcement for behavior change. The focus of such programs is on the relationship.

Group process takes on an additional dimension when working with relationship and marriage education programs designed for groups of couples. Leaders must keep in mind that they are dealing with a group of relationships, as well as with individuals. These relationships have a past and a future. The partners are connected to each other in a systemic arrangement that makes it inevitable that change in one partner requires corresponding change in techniques that primarily focus attention on the relationship itself. Maintaining this balance is essential. The relationship cannot grow without corresponding individual growth by both partners, but failing to keep the focus on the relationship risks disrupting the marital system the couple came to improve (Dyer & Dyer, 1989).

APPROACHES TO EDUCATION FOR RELATIONSHIPS AND MARRIAGE

The purpose of this section is to discuss in some depth two of the four types of approaches to education for relationships and marriage: marriage preparation and marriage enrichment. Marriage preparation, or premarital counseling, is designed to help couples before they marry to face marriage realistically and to identify and begin to address specific issues in their own relationships. "Marriage enrichment" is a generic term that refers to preventive programs designed to help couples in functioning marriages increase their relationship satisfaction and avoid marital breakdown.

Marriage Preparation

Marriage preparation, or premarital counseling, has existed in some form for a long time. Mudd and her associates (Mudd, Freeman, & Rose, 1941) at the Philadelphia Marriage Council are generally credited with creating the first program developed by family professionals. Unfortunately, their pioneering efforts did not catch on, and for the most part premarital counseling has been left to pastors and other ministers. Estimates are that in the United States ministers provide approximately 50% of all premarital counseling (Stahmann & Hiebert, 1987). In the past, many ministers were not well prepared for this part of the ministry and had little time to devote to working with couples considering marriage (Olson, 1983). Often preparation for marriage consisted of one or two meetings with the pastor just before the marriage. The content of the meetings focused mostly on planning the wedding and discussing the spiritual and religious aspects of marriage and included little or no education for marriage.

Premarital counseling started to change in the early 1980s, when researchers began to develop scientifically reliable and valid relationship assessment tools for premarital couples (for example, see Olson & Olson, 1999; Markey & Micheletto, 1997). These instruments allowed practitioners to give specific feedback to couples on the strengths and weak areas of their relationships and to focus their efforts on the troubling issues that are likely to create problems later in the marriage. Most of these inventories require some degree of training to be used, and some practitioners have incorporated the assessment tool into structured programs such as Prepare/Enrich 2000 (Olson & Olson, 1999). Increasingly, ministers, family life educators, counselors, and therapists are taking advantage of this training and offering more premarital programs to couples. These programs can be a major intervention to help couples begin their marriages with adequate knowledge and skills to prevent future marital breakdown.

Premarital approaches with couples take many forms. Some are individualized and similar to traditional therapy, some are like classroom courses that depend primarily on lectures about marriage, and others are structured to some degree but focus on strengths and are skill based and experiential in orientation. This section discusses the latter.

Premarital education programs are designed to encourage individuals planning to marry to take a serious look at marriage and at their relationship. The objectives of premarital education differ with various programs; however, all programs are preventative in nature. A primary goal is to enhance the premarital relationship so that the couple might develop a satisfying and stable marriage relationship and avoid marital dysfunction.

Couples seeking premarital education are taught interpersonal skills, such as communication and conflict resolution, to help them in the development of their marriage relationship. Premarital programs should offer an opportunity for couples to assess their strengths and growth areas and to identify potentially disruptive issues. Working together on their relationship may help some couples decide they should delay their marriage or not marry at all.

It is essential for couples to learn effective ways to deal with current issues so that these same skills can be used to attack those issues that occur after marriage. They need to learn that they can resolve issues more easily while they are small rather than allowing them to become major battlefields in their relationship. Premarital programs should attempt to help couples become aware of the potential issues in their relationship and to give them specific skills to resolve these issues.

An important component of premarital education is to alert couples to the idea that good relationships take time and energy (Olson, 1983). Many couples believe that you are just lucky if you have a good relationship. Others think that relationships will be satisfying if they are "in love." Premarital education begins the process of giving attention to the relationship and encourages couples to continue to do so into their marriages.

CONTENT   The topics covered in premarital education vary from program to program, but most give attention to the essentials of a healthy marriage identified earlier in this chapter: (1) a commitment to growth as individuals and as a couple, (2) a communication system that leads to understanding, (3) the ability to resolve conflict creatively, and (4) the ability to create and maintain intimacy (Dyer & Dyer, 1999). Research suggests that couples who have had satisfying, well-adjusted marriages have positive communication patterns that exhibit low levels of anger and resentment. They also have relatively low rates of arguing and communicate positive feelings more often than negative feelings, both before and after marriage (Cate & Lloyd, 1988; Kelly, Huston, & Cate, 1985; Markman, 1979, 1981). Emotional and sexual intimacy is an important component of contemporary companionship marriage and is expected by most couples. Most individuals want to have a "sexy best friend" as their marriage partner. Knowing how to create emotional and physical closeness in a long-term relationship is an important skill for couples anticipating marriage to learn.

Stahmann and Salts (1993) suggest that premarital education should focus on topics that research has connected to marital satisfaction (see Box 9.1). In general, content should focus on education *for* marriage, not education *about* marriage. Skills should be demonstrated, and participants need to have ample opportunity to practice and become proficient in their use. Just talking about skills provides little help.

FORMATS   Couples generally seek marriage preparation during their engagement, many times only a few weeks before their wedding. Couples marrying for the first time, as well as those who have been married previously, participate in premarital programs. In a survey of college students, Silliman and Schumm (1995) found a high interest in brief, high-quality, low-cost voluntary premarital programs led by well-trained professionals.

Some churches require a couple to have premarital preparation in order to be married in the church and by the minister. The Catholic church has such a requirement for all persons marrying in a Catholic church. The couple may choose individual sessions or participate in Engaged Encounter, a program sponsored by the church. In 1998, the state of Florida led the way in a new trend by establishing governmental support for premarital education. Currently, several states are considering similar policies that support premarital education by offering incentives such as reduced marriage license fees to couples who participate in a premarital program.

Programs are offered by a variety of individuals and groups. As noted previously, pastors have historically been the primary providers of marriage preparation, but more recently family life educators, counselors, and therapists have begun to engage in marriage education. Community agencies and organizations such as family service agencies, mental health clinics, community counseling centers, extension service groups, women's clubs, churches, and schools have provided the opportunity for couples to receive premarital education programs. Lay couples with good marriage relationships who are interested in helping other couples are a potential resource for premarital preparation leadership. With training, lay couples can teach relationship skills, as well as share from their marital experience. They may also serve as a useful resource and support for the couples as they enter their first year of marriage (Olson, 1983).

BOX 9.1

Premarital Education Program Topics

The following list includes topics presented in marriage preparation programs that research has connected to marital satisfaction:

- Marriage as a commitment
- Family of origin and individual backgrounds
- Temperaments and personalities of partners
- Communication skills
- Role expectations
- Couple interaction patterns
- Conflict resolution
- Decision-making skills
- Financial resources and financial management skills
- Leisure and recreational interests
- Goals and expectations
- Sexuality and affection
- Children and parenting
- Religious or spiritual values and expectations
- Identifying relationship strengths
- Plans for wedding

Premarital programs are offered in several formats. A number of programs are designed for individual couples. An individual couple may contract with a family life educator, marriage counselor, therapist, or pastor to receive premarital education. The sessions are conducted according to the provider's specifications, which may include a defined number of sessions for a specific amount of time, usually from 1 hour to 1½ hours.

Other programs are designed for groups of couples. The group most often consists of six to eight seriously dating or engaged couples but may also include some newly married couples. Some couples groups meet once a week for 6 to 8 weeks. Other groups may meet in extended sessions for one weekend.

There are advantages to working with individual couples rather than with a group of couples. The facilitator is able to give more attention to the individual couple than would be possible in a group setting. Issues that are foremost in the couple's relationship may be addressed in more depth in an individual-couple session. The couple may be more focused on their own issues and not get involved in other couples' problems. A disadvantage is that the couple does not have the opportunity to see how other relationships function or to learn from the group (Gleason & Prescott, 1977).

Couples groups also have advantages. Couples groups help to overcome the barriers to relationship enrichment: the myth of naturalism and the intermarital taboo (Mace, 1982). Small groups also encourage people to become active in the learning process. Couples may share their views on marital issues, listen to how the views of others might be similar to or different from their own, and explore as a group a variety of options for working through problems. Perhaps most important, couples find that they are not alone in their struggles. They can appreciate the chance to observe how others handle the same issues they are experiencing. The group helps reduce isolation for couples and often results in the development of new couple friends (Dyer & Dyer, 1999).

Limitations of the group format include the lack of time to address all of the issues that are raised by the couples in the group. Also, if one couple has a problem in a particular area, they may tend to dominate the group in their attempt to resolve the issue. Some people are not comfortable in a group and therefore may be unwilling to disclose in the group situation (Gleason & Prescott, 1977).

What Makes Marriage Preparation Programs Effective?

Based on studies investigating the effectiveness of premarital programs, David Olson (1983) suggests a three-step model for marriage education that would take about 6 to 8 weeks. First, a couple takes some type of premarital inventory and receives feedback on the results of the inventory. Second, the couple participates in a small support group in which they express their feelings and concerns. Third, they are provided with communication and conflict resolution skills to use in dealing with issues in their relationship. A problem with this three-step model is that many times couples do not come for premarital education until a few weeks before the wedding, thereby not allowing time for the entire program. Olson suggests that these couples begin the program prior to marriage and continue 6 months to 1 year after the wedding. Some research has suggested that couples may be more motivated and better able to use the skills if they are trained a few months after their marriage (Bader, Microys, Sinclair, Wilett, & Conway, 1980).

Marriage Enrichment

Marriage enrichment represents a new paradigm in our approach to helping families. It is a positive, dynamic, and preventive philosophy that focuses on the active pursuit of growth and is directed toward "healthy" marriages. Programs in general have emphasized the development of interpersonal skills with which partners can identify, appreciate, and develop the latent strengths they possess within themselves and their relationship to build a satisfying and fulfilling marriage (Dyer & Dyer, 1989).

Marriage enrichment exists today in many secular and faith-based forms. Two of the best known programs are Marriage Encounter and ACME-style marriage enrichment. Marriage Encounter is a faith-based program started by the Catholic Church and now supported by three national organizations: National Marriage Encounter, Worldwide Marriage Encounter, and United Marriage Encounter. ACME-style marriage enrichment is a community-based program sponsored by the Association for Couples in Marriage Enrichment, a nonprofit membership organization. This section focuses on these two types of marriage enrichment.

Father Gabriel Calvo, a Catholic priest, is credited with beginning Marriage Encounter in Barcelona, Spain, in January 1962. Frustrated in his attempts to work with youth in an urban parish, Calvo decided to focus his attention on married couples. He explained his actions in this way:

> I began to realize that . . . I would have to go to the heart of the family—the couple. They are the key to the love revolution the world needs. . . . In many families I could see a characteristic, something special they had that was lacking in other families. I tried to discern what these special qualities were, and I concluded in time that the unique quality was the confidence and trust these couples had in each other. (Calvo, cited in Mace, 1982, p. 121)

A few months after Calvo's first Marriage Encounter groups began and without any knowledge of them, David and Vera Mace stumbled onto an approach to marriage education to which they would dedicate the remainder of their professional lives. In October of 1962, they were invited to meet with a group of eight Quaker couples for a weekend marriage retreat. Mace relates that this was entirely an experiment. He was fully aware of the difficulties of counseling couples with serious marital problems, but his extensive attempts to identify literature on the subject or any individuals who had led programs for couples with working marriages was fruitless. He was fascinated with the potential of finding ways to prevent marital breakdown by working with couples before they became alienated from each other. This retreat led to others, and from these experiences the Maces developed what they called the Quaker Model for marriage enrichment. On their 40th wedding anniversary in 1973, they founded the Association for Couples in Marriage Enrichment, or ACME, as it became known. This nonprofit, nonsectarian organization is the primary promoter of and training source for the Maces' approach to marriage enrichment. It is not clear whether the Maces originated the now generic term "marriage enrichment," but they certainly did much to place it into popular usage.

Although working in two different parts of the world in two different styles, Calvo and the Maces shared two central beliefs: (1) that the husband-wife relationship is the key to a successful family life, and (2) that preventative, educational interventions are more efficient and more effective than treatment delivered when problems arise.

MARRIAGE ENCOUNTER   More than 2 million couples worldwide have now participated in a Marriage Encounter weekend experience, making it the largest marriage education program in the world (Elin, 1999). A Marriage Encounter weekend generally begins on a Friday evening and lasts through Sunday afternoon and includes 10 to 25 couples led by a clergyperson or a couple and two or three volunteer couples. All members of this team have had a previous weekend encounter experience. They have had training in the encounter process and instructions on how to prepare and present their written talks. During the weekend the team gives presentations on 13 specific topics, including discovering oneself, talking to the other, mutual trust, growth in knowledge of each other, growth in understanding of each other, learning to accept each other, learning to help each other, growth in love and union, opening up to each other, and transcendent love (Elin, 1999).

Presentations by the team couples are descriptions of their personal relationship experiences and struggles with the topic at hand. After each presentation, the participating couples are given one or more questions, generally called dialogue questions, on the topic presented. They are asked to spend time as individuals reflecting on and writing about their personal feelings in response to the questions. After a time of personal reflection, spouses come together in private to share their reflections and what they have written. Several low-key religious services are held during the weekend, and the retreat ends with the renewal of marriage vows (Elin, 1999).

No group sharing is done among couples during the entire weekend. The emphasis is on personal reflection and communication between the marital pair. Couples are encouraged to focus on feelings and not on judgments and thoughts. The concentration of approximately 40 hours of time together without interruption is a unique experience for many of the couples.

Although Marriage Encounter began as a program of the Catholic Church, it has now been adopted by many religious organizations. In addition to the three national organizations mentioned previously that support Marriage Encounter, many independent churches and denominations use the program.

ACME-STYLE MARRIAGE ENRICHMENT   The Maces' long experience in marriage counseling and their experimental work with nondistressed couples in small groups led them to the conclusion that marital partners need help long before their marriages have severe problems and serious damage is done to the relationship. Acting on this belief, they formed ACME to give married couples a way to join together in expressing their support for successful marriage. ACME took as a slogan, "To work for better marriages beginning with our own" (Mace & Mace, 1974). Although religious themselves, the Maces purposefully created ACME as a nonsectarian organization based in communities.

ACME supports a wide variety of marriage enrichment activities that include weekend retreats; 2- to 3-hour monthly group meetings; state, local, and international conferences; and 4- and 5-day training events for leader couples. These events differ in structure, setting, and format but must conform to the following parameters (Association for Couples in Marriage Enrichment, 1995):

- Marriage enrichment events are for couples who have a "healthy" marriage; in practice this translates to couples who are not in immediate marital crisis and not seeking couples therapy for marital problems

- The event is led by one or more ACME-trained and certified couples, whose leadership reflects an interacting, participatory style
- The method is basically experiential and dynamic, rather than didactic and intellectual
- Participants have an opportunity for couple interaction in private couple dialogue and within the context of the group
- Use may be made of structured experiential exercises
- Participant couples usually have some voice in determining the agenda for the event

ACME-certified leaders generally follow a five-stage process model in designing marriage enrichment events. The stages are: security and community building, development of individual and couple awareness, development of knowledge and skill, planning for intentional growth, and celebration and closure (Dyer & Dyer, 1989).

ACME-style marriage enrichment differs from Marriage Encounter in several significant ways. Trained leader couples always lead ACME programs. Many ACME-trained leader couples are clergy, but there is no requirement that clergy be involved. Leader couples are considered participating facilitators whose role is to lead a process rather than to provide scripted presentations. As is also true in Marriage Encounter, the couple leaders openly share their marital experiences. However, in ACME style, this is done in a dialogue between the two leaders, with group members listening. Generally, ACME events are much smaller—5 to 12 couples—and a high degree of interaction among couples, as well as interaction between partners, is encouraged.

EVALUATION OF PROGRAMS

Many of the programs designed to prevent breakdowns in relationships have not been created by family scientists or others with a strong interest in systematic program evaluation. Markman et al. (1986) found that the clergy and faith-based organizations were the most extensive providers of marriage preparation programs. Consequently, solid research on the effectiveness of a wide range of marriage and relationship programs is not available.

Several programs developed by practitioner-researchers have been exemplary in providing quality evaluations of the outcomes of their programs. These include the Relationship Enhancement program (Guerney, Brock, & Coufal, 1986), the PREP program (Markman, Floyd, Stanley, & Storaasli, 1988), and the Couple Communication program (Miller & Sherrard, 1999). These three programs have consistently shown effectiveness with premarital and married couples.

One of the most cited studies of marriage and relationship education was a meta-analysis undertaken by Giblin, Sprenkle, and Sheehan (1985). Eighty-five prevention and enrichment programs representing 3,886 couples and families were included in the study. Across all studies, the average participant improvement from pretest to posttest was more than 67% compared with those in the corresponding control group. The Relationship Enhancement program demonstrated the largest effect, followed by Couple Communication programs and Marriage Encounter. Giblin et al. (1985) concluded that programs of the type they studied were effective. Guerney and Maxson (1990) drew similar conclusions in their review of a decade of marriage education literature. Essentially, these studies strongly suggest that skill training is effective in increasing marital satisfaction and reducing the probability of divorce even after the program is over (Cole & Cole, 1999).

Other findings showed that the longer the training lasts, the more emphasis the program puts on the development of skills, and the more practice under competent supervision it allows, the greater chance the program has of producing a positive effect on couples that could be sustained over time (Guerney & Maxson, 1990).

Gottman, Coan, Carrere, and Swanson (1998) have challenged the efficacy of skill-based models of marital education and therapy. They have specifically suggested that the popular communication technique of "active listening" should be abandoned because healthy couples do not use it. They further suggest that it is probably unrealistic to expect couples to use active listening in conflictual situations when faced with negative affect from a partner. These suggestions have created considerable controversy in the field, and Gottman and his associates have been confronted by researchers and practitioners from the fields of therapy and of relationship and marital education. It should be noted that Gottman and colleagues have not said the technique is not effective, just that it is not used by the typical couple. Cole and Cole (1999) are among those who have come to the defense of skill-based programs in therapy and education. They argue that skills such as active listening, using "I-statements," and nondefensive listening and speaking are skills that must be learned and thus may not be used by typical couples who have not been taught to use them. Gottman's challenge is one that can be answered only by replication of his research and by more thorough research on the efficacy of relationship and marital education programs. Research is particularly needed into the long-term effects of educational programs (Berger & DeMaria, 1999; Kelly & Fincham, 1999).

Practitioners of relationship and marital education models should not dismiss the challenge of Gottman and his colleagues too quickly. Basic assumptions about models and theories should be reexamined. Theory must be linked more closely to interventions. Research such as Gottman's into what makes marriages succeed or fail must be taken seriously and incorporated into program development. New programs should build on what has been shown to be effective in existing programs such as Relationship Enhancement, Couple Communication, and PREP. Finally, researchers and practitioners need to work more closely together to create and evaluate relationship and marriage education programs.

SUMMARY

Marriage preparation and marriage education offer hope to a society disenchanted with its ability to establish and maintain close relationships. Although the marriage education/enrichment movement is now more than 40 years old, it is still a relatively new phenomenon in the United States and worldwide. But momentum is gathering as counselors, educators, and ministers begin to bring pressure on schools and legislatures to emphasize marriage preparation courses and counseling. Effectiveness of preventive programs is also being evaluated by serious researchers, and positive results are emerging. Certification for marriage educators is also under consideration by several professional organizations.

Although traditional education can introduce principles, all marriage education experts emphasize the necessity of personal motivation, commitment to intentional work on the relationship, praxis (action with reflection), and reinforcement of skills learned. The short-term program has little hope of success. Fortunately, increasing numbers of couples are being trained as group leaders and mentors for newlyweds. The future is promising.

QUESTIONS/PROBLEMS FOR DISCUSSION AND REVIEW

Class Discussion

1. What could be done by universities, communities, and churches to encourage or motivate more engaged couples to participate in premarital education programs?

2. Why is it important to have trained leadership? Isn't having a satisfactory marriage enough to qualify as a leader couple?

3. Review the myths about marriage that discourage premarital and marriage education. Which do you think is the strongest and why?

Research Problems and Activities

1. Interview 20 engaged couples (males and females separately) about their interest in a premarital education program. If possible, find an ethnically diverse sample. Using the content areas in Box 9.1, assess their level of interest in each area. What do they see as the value of such a program? How do the responses of males and females compare? What about ethnic groups? A second, related, survey might interview engaged couples who have been married before. What differences do you notice in their responses?

2. Review the research on one of the programs mentioned that has undertaken some rigorous evaluation of program results (by Olson, L'Abate, or Gottman, for example). Consider the assumptions and objectives of the

program and how they were carried out. If more than one person works on this activity, choose different programs to assess and then compare differences in assumptions, objectives, and program design.

Case Study Design

1. Develop a premarital or marriage education program for a specific population of couples (incarcerated-partner or drug-rehabilitation-program couples). What would have to be done to alter the design? How would you incorporate and adapt the concepts that have proven to be the most successful in other programs?

2. Invite a leader couple trained in one of the marriage enrichment models to demonstrate their teaching technique in your class, using an interpersonal relationship topic. Your class can role play the couples and small groups, or each class member can bring a friend to participate in this lesson with him or her. Using the praxis model (action with reflection), process the experience in the next class period.

CHAPTER 10

Parenting Education

It's 3:00 A.M. Your 3-week-old son has been crying and fussing since 11:00 P.M. You have fed him, changed him, and rocked him. You are out of ideas and patience. What is it that he needs?

Your day-care provider pulls you aside and informs you that your 3-year-old has been biting the other children. Is this normal? Why is she doing it? What can you do to stop it?

Your 13-year-old has started to come home after his curfew. He has become sullen and uncommunicative. When he does talk to you, it is usually with disrespect or annoyance. The more you push him, the more he pulls away. What can you do to best deal with the situation?

These scenarios occur regularly in households throughout the world. How does a parent best respond to these situations? Is there one best way to respond? Are there books that have all the answers, or do parents just "know" what to do? Can you take a class to learn how to be a good parent?

Although parenting education and support have existed in various forms since the world's first baby was born, parenting education as a profession and field of study is in its adolescence. This chapter looks at the history of parenting education, theories and disciplines influencing the field, and some popular programs and models. We discuss the competencies and qualifications needed to provide effective, quality parenting education and support. Finally, we discuss and consider the future of this emerging profession.

THE HISTORY OF PARENTING EDUCATION

Throughout history society often assumed that parenting came naturally and that women were biologically predetermined to raise children. It was assumed that mothers just knew what to do when it came to discipline, nurturing, toilet training, and so forth. This perception is slowly changing. Today's parents are quicker to acknowledge that they don't always have the answers or that they may not want to raise their children as they were raised. They are less likely to have played a major role in the care of their siblings. Societal changes have made it more difficult to rely on parenting techniques from the past. The rapid pace at which these changes occur leave children facing issues their parents never dreamed of. They have no personal experience to fall back on.

Parents are eager for sources of information and support that will help them in their role. There is increased recognition that, among other things, knowledge of child development can be helpful in determining how to handle a specific behavior, as well as in identifying appropriate behavior and goals.

Early Influences and Organizations

Parenting education in the United States has some of its earliest roots in the colonial period, when church and state shared the goal of influencing parents to raise their children according to religious mandates (Schlossman, 1976). It can be traced back to fields as diverse as medicine, social work, home economics, education, and psychology. G. Stanley Hall was perhaps the first psychologist to bring the study of children to a university setting, but Freud, Watson, Adler, Piaget, Gesell, and others had theories of their own. Hall's focus was on understanding the development of the child for the purpose of discovering how children learn. His methods were considered unconventional, and he eventually lost favor in the academic world, but his ideas were carried out among the women who gathered in 1897 at the first National Congress of Mothers, a nationwide parent-education organization known later as the Parent Teacher Association, or PTA (Schlossman, 1976).

The PTA grew from that first meeting in 1897 to an organization of 60,000 members in 1915 to 6.5 million members in 26,000 local chapters in 1999. The focus of the PTA shifted from early childhood to adolescence and to an emphasis on helping children in trouble or at risk and on reeducating families in modern methods of child care. Eventually, its main objective centered on domestic science and the goal of preparing women in household management and child care, the goal being happier and more stable homes.

The PTA used a number of strategies in reaching families. One involved self-instruction and group discussion. A second included advocacy to the poor through home visiting and the formation of mothers' clubs. The PTA also took on political goals, including lobbying for child labor laws. "Thus to the PTA in the Progressive era, parent education was a lever for changing society by organizing mothers of the nation in common cause" (Schlossman, 1976, p. 451).

A number of other organizations were involved in parent education in various capacities. The Child Study Association of America initiated the National Council of Parent Education in 1925 to coordinate lay and professional groups. This group contributed to the development of instructional materials and sponsored the first university course in parent education at Teachers College, Columbia, Missouri, in 1925. Likewise, the American Home Economics Association (AHEA) began to include parent education in its educational and lobbying interests, also in the mid-1920s. These initial efforts focused on poor families and those considered to be in need (Carter, 1996).

Benjamin Spock's *Baby and Child Care,* first published in 1946, brought the literature of child care and parenting to the middle class. Grassroots parenting groups began to appear and provided parents the opportunity to meet with each other to "compare notes." Still, most parent education followed traditional educational designs, with an "expert" serving as the source of information and answers.

Slowly the focus shifted away from the experts and toward enhancing parents' own knowledge and experience. The Head Start program, launched in the mid-1960s, acknowledged the value and impact of parents in the education of their children (Carter, 1996). By the 1980s community-based parenting education programs were joined by state and federally funded programs and a growing number of for-profit organizations.

In 1995 parent educators began discussing the need to create an organization that could meet the needs of this growing field. The most notable discussions were held at Wheelock College in November of 1995 and at the Family Support America (formerly Family Resource Coalition of America) conference in May of 1996 (Simpson, personal communication). The Parenting Education Network (PEN), later known as the National Parenting Education Network (NPEN), evolved from these discussions. The mission of this organization is to support parenting education practitioners and advance the field of parenting education (Crary, 1996). The development of NPEN represents an important step in the evolution of parenting education as a profession. As discussed in Chapter 2, one step in the development of a profession occurs when those trained in the field establish an association (East, 1980). NPEN is still in its formative stages, but its existence speaks of the recognition of the unique needs and goals of the field of parenting education. The increased interest in this field no doubt comes in response to an increased need for parenting education due to societal changes.

Societal Changes

Societal changes have caused modern-day parents to face challenges unparalleled in previous generations, increasing the need for both formal and informal parenting education. A majority of American adults believe that it is harder to raise children today than it used to be (National Commission on Children, 1991b). The following, written 20 years ago, is even truer today:

> The process of family nuclearization, erosion of community, role differentiation and specialization, geographical distancing of family generations, and the increased entry into the labor force—have created a new reality in which parents no longer benefit from traditional structure in their parenting roles. (Harman & Brim, 1980, p. 14)

Families today are more likely to live away from extended family members, weakening the support network. Changes in health care require some mothers to return home within 12 hours of giving birth, sometimes to an environment that is less than conducive to healthy development. More mothers work outside of the home, either by choice or necessity. The percentage of children living in single-parent families nearly doubled between 1970 and 1995, increasing from 13% to 22%. In 1995, among White children, 25% lived in single-parent families; among African American children, 64% lived in single-parent families; among Hispanics, 36% lived in single-parent families (U.S. Bureau of the Census, 1996). Parents have less time to spend with their children and may rely on them to be more self-sufficient than is developmentally appropriate. "Expecting, indeed demanding, that children grow up fast was one way of avoiding the expenditure of energy that goes along with parenthood" (Elkind, 1987, p. xii).

Technology and retail design also play a role in increasing isolation. Individuals and families spend more time at computers and on the telephone and less time talking face-to-face. Neighborhood grocery and hardware stores have been replaced with strip malls and warehouse retailers, leaving families more isolated and less connected. Neighbors are less likely to know each other and to share information "over the fence" (Carter, 1996).

There are greater influences on children outside of the home, as well. The media is filled with images of sex, violence, and materialism and emphasizes beauty and appearance. Drugs and weapons are more readily available. Increasing numbers of grandparents find themselves raising their grandchildren at a time when they thought they would be retired.

These changes have resulted in dire consequences for our nation's children and families. Incidences of substance abuse, juvenile offenses, teenage pregnancy, adolescent suicide, mental illness, and child abuse have increased, especially in the past 20 years (National Commission on Children, 1991a).

With fewer built-in support networks, parents are more receptive to outside help. The field of parenting education has grown in response to the increased challenges and complexities of modern life.

DEFINITIONS AND ASSUMPTIONS

Definitions

The goals and targets of parenting education are as varied as the approaches used. Some use the term "parent" education; others use "parenting" education to recognize that some people who are not biological or legal parents have a role in the care and raising of children. Nick Carter (1996) defined parenting education as "programs, support services and resources offered to parents and caregivers that are designed to support them or increase their capacity and confidence in raising healthy children" (p. 6). Brock and colleagues describe parenting education as "an organized, programmatic effort to change or enhance the child-rearing knowledge and skills of a family system or a child care system" (Brock, Oertwein, & Coufal, 1993, 88).

The National Parenting Education Network defined parenting education in an Internet discussion in 1995 as:

> a process that involves the expansion of insights, understanding and attitudes and the acquisition of knowledge and skills about the development of both parents and of their children and the relationship between them. Education is most effective, parent educators recognize, if it occurs in an emotionally supportive environment. (Heath, 1995)

Assumptions

The National Extension Parent Education Model (Smith, Cudaback, Goddard, & Myers-Walls, 1998) does not define parenting education specifically but includes nine key assumptions regarding parents and their relationships with their children:

- Parents are the primary socializers of their children.
- Parenting attitudes, knowledge, skills, and behaviors can be positively influenced by parent education efforts.
- Parenting is a learned skill that can be strengthened through study and experience.
- Parent education is more effective when parents are active participants in and contributors to their parent education programs.
- The parent-child relationship is nested within and influenced by multiple social and cultural systems.
- Programs should be responsive to diversity among parents.
- Effective parent education may be accomplished by a variety of methods.

- Both the parent and the child have needs that should be met.
- The goal of parent education is strengthening and educating the parent (or caregiver) so that he or she is better able to facilitate the development of caring, competent, and healthy children.

Carter (1996) includes a similar list of assumptions regarding parenting education. Wandersman (1987) states that "parent education can positively affect the satisfaction and functioning of families by communicating knowledge about human development and relationships that increases their understanding, providing alternative models of parenting that widen their choices, teaching new skills, and facilitating access to community resources" (p. 211).

Parenting education programs therefore cover a number of subjects. Some of the more commonly covered include child development, discipline and limit setting, building self-esteem, health, communication skills, stages of parenthood, parent involvement in education, balancing work and family, family systems, transitions in the family, conflict resolution, advocacy and parent empowerment, parents with specialized needs and concerns, and collaboration and networking.

FORMATS AND SETTINGS

Variations in goals and target audiences are reflected in the settings and approaches used to carry out parenting education.

Formats

Parenting education can be presented in a variety of settings and formats and to a number of different audiences. Harman and Brim (1980) identify three modes of instruction for parenting education: the individual mode, the group mode, and the mass mode. The individual mode is often carried out under the guise of counseling or home visits and is typically focused on interventions for problems. The group mode is a more widely used approach through which instruction is delivered in traditional classroom settings, workshops, seminars, or more informal support groups. The mass mode refers to education carried out through the print media, that is, newsletters, books, and pamphlets, or radio and television programs. Contact through the mass mode is wider reaching but less personal.

Settings

A typology of parenting education program settings identified by Carter (1996) includes eight categories under which he considers all parenting education programs to fall (Box 10.1). In more general terms, parenting education is offered

BOX 10.1

The Universe of Parenting Education

EDUCATION

Literacy Programs
Life Skills Programs
School-Linked
　Services
Parent Involvement
Preschool and Day
　Care
　Head Start
　Day care
　Preschool
Readiness Programs

HEALTH CARE

Hospitals
HMOs
Departments of Public
　Health
Maternal and Child
　Health
Agencies
MDs and Health Care
　Professionals
Private Health Care
　Agencies
　Perinatal programs
　Women's health
　Immunization
　Nutrition
　Childbirth
　　education
　Lactation groups

RESEARCH

Colleges and
　Universities
Centers
Authors and
　Individual
　Researchers

MULTIPLE & COMPLEX NEEDS

Divorce and
　Separation
Incarceration
Teen Pregnancy/
　Parenting
Abuse/Neglect
Antiviolence
Antipoverty
Substance Abuse
Therapy
Family Preservation
Kinship Care
Foster Care
Adoption
Residential Treatment
Child Protective
　Services

SPECIAL NEEDS

Disabilities
Diseases
Impairments
Mental Health/Mental
　Health Resources
Developmental
　Delays
Special Education
Occupational Therapy

ADVOCACY

Public education
Training and
　empowerment
Lobbying

NORMATIVE

Grassroots Programs
Entertainment and
　Play
　Groups
　Museums
　Recreation
　Sports
Skill Development
　Resources and
　　Audiovisual
　Educational classes
Information Services
　Referral
　Libraries
　Newsletters and
　　magazines
　Electronic media
Support Programs
　Group
　One on one
Self-Help Programs
Safety Programs and
　Services
Product Evaluation
　and Discounts
Religious Education

WORK

Employee Assistance
　Support services
　Educational
　　programs
　Training for Manage-
　　ment
Work and Family
　Family leave
　Child care
　Flextime
Welfare-to-Work
　Programs
　Job training
　G.E.D.
　Family services

in a number of different settings, including schools, extension programs, family service agencies, neighborhood resource centers, and community education, religious, and health care settings. In addition, for-profit businesses and corporations have begun to offer brown-bag lunchtime workshops for employees because they recognize the impact personal issues and concerns can have on company productivity. The government is involved in offering parenting education through family support programs provided to family members serving in the armed forces.

JUNIOR AND HIGH SCHOOLS   More and more schools are offering parenting courses. One popular approach in junior high and high school classes involves giving students an egg or a sack of flour to serve as their "baby" for a set amount of time. The egg and flour have recently been replaced with a doll that cries intermittently and can only be cared for by someone with a nonremovable key that is attached to his or her wrist. The intention of this exercise is to give the students a more realistic view of the constancy of parenting. This approach could probably be considered an indirect form of sex education as well, by providing a glimpse into the possible consequences of sexual intercourse!

RELIGIOUS ORGANIZATIONS   Parenting education in religious organizations usually appears in the form of workshops and classes dealing with such topics as "Communicating with Your Adolescent" and "Setting Limits." These classes may or may not involve a religious perspective. Parents may sometimes just feel more comfortable attending parenting classes offered through their religious community rather than an outside organization and may find them to be more accessible.

NEIGHBORHOOD AND FAMILY RESOURCE CENTERS   Neighborhood and family resource centers often offer classes for first-time parents or parents with children of specific ages, such as "Wonderful Ones" or "Terrific Twos." Classes for parents of twins and other multiple births are becoming more common, especially in this time of the increased use of fertility drugs. Neighborhood and family centers often have lending libraries that feature parenting information. In addition to offering information and support to parents, these classes strengthen communities by providing opportunities for neighbors to meet and support each other.

CORPORATIONS AND BUSINESSES   Corporations and businesses are increasingly recognizing that workers who face stress at home are less productive at work. Many employers offer lunchtime brown-bag seminars at which employees can learn communication tips, ways to balance work and family, and other ideas to strengthen family connections. Employers hope that attention to these personal issues will increase productivity and reduce absenteeism. The military has incorporated parenting education into their family support programs. Life within the military involves unique challenges for parents who must sometimes cope with not only spousal separation but also the added stress of living away from extended family and in unfamiliar cities and countries.

HEALTH CARE   Hospitals and clinics are also offering more parenting education programs in the form of prenatal classes, childbirth education, lactation groups, women's health programs, and stress reduction classes. Waiting rooms are often equipped with closed-circuit televisions that carry special parenting education information. As with some businesses, health care organizations recognize the impact of prevention and education on their bottom line.

COURT-ORDERED PROGRAMS   Parenting education, although often offered as a preventative measure, can also be carried out in response to specific problems or issues. Courts can require parents to attend parenting education classes in order to maintain or regain custody of their children. Judges and divorce attorneys in some states encourage and sometimes require parents to take classes to help them understand and minimize the effects of divorce on their children.

These types of programs, though more problem focused, should not be confused with therapy. Parenting education differs from therapy in its emphasis on (1) normative development and the prevention of family problems rather than on individual personality and family dysfunction, (2) techniques that provide support rather than conflict and confrontation, and (3) goals that increase self-confidence and satisfaction rather than restructure personality or family dynamics (Wandersman, 1987).

COMMON THEORIES INFLUENCING PARENTING EDUCATION

Numerous theories and approaches influence parenting education programs. Volumes could be written on the many theories, so our discussion is limited to a summary of some of the main components of the most well-known and utilized human behavior theories and approaches. These include psychoanalytic theory, cognitive-developmental theory, behaviorism, developmental systems theory, temperament theory, Adlerian theory, and humanism. In addition, we will look at an approach that focuses on parenting styles. Although parenting educators may operate predominantly within the context of one main theory—behaviorism or humanism, for example—they may incorporate a variety of approaches and may be open to implementing different theories, depending on the situation. Awareness of a number of theories can help parents and parenting educators better understand children's abilities and behaviors. Theories also provide a framework on which to base responses, as well as a context in which to view the child.

The theories discussed in this chapter differ in the ways in which they view the following questions (Murray, 1992):

Nature versus nurture: What is the influence of biology versus the environment? How much influence can the parent have on the child?

Active versus passive development: Who is in control? Does the environment act on the child or the child on the environment?

Discontinuous versus continuous development: Are stages of development sequential or independent of each other?

Qualitative versus quantitative measurement: How easily can responses be measured?

Developmental direction: Does learning occur in one direction or is it multidirectional?

The "nature versus nurture" argument has been debated for years, but it received increased attention in 1998 when the *The Nurture Assumption* by Judith Harris (1998) was published. Harris argued that parents have almost no influence on their children's development and that peers play a much bigger role. This idea brought cries of protest from psychologists, child development experts, teachers, and parents. Most parenting educators recognize the role of outside influences but would argue that parents play a key role in a child's development.

Psychoanalytic/Psychosocial Theory

Psychological theories that have influenced parenting education include Freud's psychoanalytic theory and Erikson's psychosocial theory. Freud applied his concepts of id, ego, and superego to the development of the child's psyche and viewed the parent as mainly responsible for the child's psychological development (Strong & DeVault, 1998).

Freud influenced Erik Erikson's theory of psychosocial development, but Erikson placed greater emphasis on the influence of society on the development of the child. Erikson's life cycle stages focus on changes in emotional growth and development that have biological, as well as social, influences. Erikson contends that human development over the life span includes a series of tasks (Strong & DeVault, 1998; see Box 10.2). Recognition of these tasks can help in understanding children's behavior.

Cognitive-Developmental Theory

One of the most commonly referenced theories in parenting education is Jean Piaget's cognitive-developmental theory. Piaget determined that children's ability to reason and understand change as they grow older proceeded in a series of sequential stages: sensorimotor (birth to 2 years), preoperational (2 to 6 years), concrete operational (7 to 11 years), and formal operational (12 and older). Piaget also used the terms *assimilation* (making new concepts compatible with existing knowledge) and *accommodation* (adjusting cognition to incorporate new experiences) in describing how children respond to the environment.

BOX 10.2

*Erikson's
Stages of
Development*

Trust vs. Mistrust (Birth to 1 year).
Babies learn to trust others to meet their needs.

Autonomy vs. Shame and Doubt (1 to 3 years).
Children learn either to be self-sufficient or to doubt their own abilities.

Initiative vs. Guilt (3 to 6 years).
Children want to learn and try new things, but if not encouraged, they can experience guilt.

Industry vs. Inferiority (7 to 11 years).
Children learn either to be competent and productive or to feel inferior and unable to do things.

Identity vs. Role Confusion (Adolescence).
Adolescents either establish an identity or are confused over what future roles to play.

Intimacy vs. Isolation (Adulthood).
Young adults seek companionship and love or become isolated from one another.

Generativity vs. Stagnation (Adulthood).
Adults are productive and have meaningful lives or become stagnant and inactive.

Integrity vs. Despair (Adulthood).
Adults make sense out of their lives or despair over goals never reached.

Behaviorism

A number of learning theories have influenced parenting education as well. John B. Watson's and B. F. Skinner's theories of behaviorism argued against emotional or internal drives as motivation for behavior. Instead, they argued that behaviors increase and decrease through reinforcement and rewards. They sought to explain behavior entirely on the basis of what can be observed.

Social Learning Theory

Social learning theory, most often attributed to Albert Bandura, emphasizes the role of thinking or cognition in learning (Bandura, 1977). It considers the interactions of culture, society, and the family, as well as the inner qualities of the individual (Strong & DeVault, 1998). "Social learning theory accepts many of the tenets of behavioral psychology but adds to it the individual's innate ability to think and make choices to change his or her environment" (Schickendanz, Schickendanz, Hansen, & Forsyth, 1993).

Developmental Systems Theory

The developmental systems approach recognizes that children develop within the context of a family system and that influences between the child and the parent are reciprocal. The family in turn is influenced by larger systems that include friends, community, government, and so forth. Bronfenbrenner's ecological model (Bronfenbrenner, 1979) is perhaps the most widely known model that uses a developmental systems approach.

Temperament Theory

Temperament theorists believe that humans are born with certain innate tendencies and characteristics, ways in which they perceive and react to their surroundings (Kagan & Snidman, 1991). Kagan argued that reaction to stimulis by 4-month-old babies could predict certain personality traits evident years later. Babies who responded to high levels of activity and stimulation with distress were more likely to be shy, whereas babies that reacted calmly or positively to the same stimuli were more likely to be outgoing. Although temperamental differences may be rooted in the brain, they can be reinforced through interactions with the environment. A baby who responds positively to lots of activity and stimulation probably encourages his parents to respond with more energy, whereas the parents of a baby who is shy and withdrawn probably respond to their baby's cues by remaining calm and low key. Lerner and Lerner (cited in Brooks, 1994) stress the importance of "goodness of fit" between a child's temperament, those of the parents, and environmental factors. Parents who are aware of and sensitive to their child's temperament are better able to understand and react to their child's behavior. Thus, both nature and nurture are crucial to the outcome of child rearing.

Chess and Thomas (1987), well-known temperament theorists, identified three basic temperaments in babies: difficult, slow to warm up, and easy. Difficult babies had irregular schedules for sleep and bodily functions, were uncomfortable with new situations, were slow to adapt, and tended to have intense emotions. Some slow-to-warm-up babies had regular schedules, whereas others didn't; but all needed extra time to adapt to new situations. Easy babies had regular schedules, reacted positively to new situations, adapted easily to change, were overall positive, and had low mood intensity. Chess and Thomas argued that these temperaments, identifiable very early on in life, were consistent throughout the life span. Understanding a child's temperament can help parents determine the most effective and appropriate way in which to interact with their child.

Adlerian Theory

The theories of Alfred Adler and Rudolf Dreikurs focus on the goal-directed behavior of the child. Adlerian parenting education helps parents understand the

---

BOX 10.3

Concepts and Approaches in the Adlerian Approach to Parenting Education

ADLERIAN THEORY

Mistaken goals
Attention
Power
Retaliation and revenge
Frustration and giving up

METHODS OF TRAINING AND GUIDANCE

Encouragement
Natural consequences
Logical consequences
Maintain order
Avoid conflict
Avoid pampering and overprotection
Family council

---

goal of the child's misbehavior. Adler argued that children have a strong need to belong and will implement mistaken goals in an attempt to be accepted. He identified these mistaken goals as attention, power, retaliation and revenge, and frustration and giving up (Dreikurs, 1964).

Educators using an Adlerian approach encourage appropriate behavior and allow children to accept responsibility for their behavior. They often employ the use of natural and logical consequences. Natural consequences are those that result naturally from a behavior: going outside without a jacket may result in the child being cold. Logical consequences might require involvement from the parent but relate to the behavior. If a child leaves his or her toys out in the living room, the parent may put them away and not allow the child to play with them for a while.

Adler was also very interested in the atmosphere of the family, as well as birth order and position within the family. His methods of training and guidance have become common concepts in parenting education today (Box 10.3).

Humanism

Most often connected with Carl Rogers, humanism centers on the child and the child's conception of self, or self-identity. It contends that development is holistic and moves toward the goal of self-actualization. In order to reach this goal, the child must have love, security, and acceptance. The parent's job is to accept the child as he or she is, trust in the child's ability to solve problems, and provide an environment of acceptance.

Parenting Styles

Although it is not technically a theory of parenting education, Diana Baumrind (1983) identified three basic parenting styles, permissive, authoritative, and authoritarian, which have been widely accepted as a basis for parent education approaches. These styles apply to the interaction and structuring of the relationship between parent and child and have influenced many of the parenting education programs in place today (Brock et al., 1993).

PERMISSIVE STYLE   According to Baumrind, permissive parents generally place few demands upon their children and are highly responsive to their children's needs. They treat their children as though the children's rights are equal to their own and use low coercion. Children in permissive households often have a lot of power within the family.

AUTHORITATIVE STYLE   Parents with a more authoritative style attempt to balance their demands with the needs of the child. They promote individuality by encouraging the child to make his or her own decisions, yet they also set firm rules and enforce them. Authoritative parents tend to discuss behavior with their children rather than punish them, but they will use punishment if the child does not comply with clearly stated expectations.

AUTHORITARIAN STYLE   Authoritarian parents set rigid rules and make strong demands for compliance. Obedience is highly valued. They have low responsiveness to the needs and wants of the child. Children in authoritarian families are seen as having very few rights and therefore have little power in the family.

Most parents will use a variety of styles depending upon the situation. They may be authoritarian when it comes to a situation that they think could be dangerous for their child, such as insisting that he or she is supervised when crossing the street, but more lenient when it comes to allowing the child to decide when to do his or her homework, for example.

Baumrind has expanded her work on parenting styles in the past decade to include a consideration of parenting styles over time. Relationships with adolescent children require more variation in parenting approaches regarding responsiveness and control (Baumrind, 1991). Baumrind's parenting styles provide a framework within which to consider the goals and processes of parenting.

PARENTING PROGRAMS AND MODELS

A number of widely used national parenting education programs are available today. According to Brock et al. (1993), most are based on Baumrind's authoritative parenting style, focus on effective communication, and include principles of behavior modification. Some of the more widely used curriculum programs include Parent Effectiveness Training, (Gordon, 1975), Systematic Training for Effective Parenting (Dinkmeyer & McKay, 1976), and Active Parenting (Popkin, 1987), although there are many more.

Parent Effectiveness Training (PET)

Key elements of the PET program include problem ownership, flexibility, and no-lose conflict resolution. PET instructors are required to participate in a 5½-day training program. Parents who complete a PET program have been found to be more accepting of their children's behavior and to have more egalitarian attitudes (Hammer & Turner, 1990).

Systematic Training for Effective Parenting (STEP)

The STEP program is an Adlerian-based program that focuses on the goals of children's misbehavior, the use of natural and logical consequences, and having family meetings. Parents are guided to look at the goal of a child's misbehavior and determine responses that would result in more positive behaviors and interactions. The STEP program teaches that "emotions in children leading to misbehaviors are often based on faulty interpretations of experiences and events and that, as parents change their behaviors to enable children to have more accurate interpretations, child behaviors will change" (Brock et al., 1993, p. 98). The STEP program is one of the most widely used programs today. The most significant results from STEP classes have generally been positive changes in parent-child interaction, parental attitudes, child behaviors, and parent perceptions of child behavior (American Guidance Service, 1991).

Active Parenting

Active Parenting, developed by Michael Popkin (1987), differs from PET and STEP most notably in its format rather than its content. A series of 40 video-taped vignettes, designed to be used in six 2-hour sessions, provide subject matter for discussion of various parent-child interactions. The program includes discussion of some of the same concepts as featured in STEP and PET: developing responsibility, natural and logical consequences, goals of misbehavior, cooperation, and encouragement.

Certainly there are many more parenting programs, but PET, STEP, and Active Parenting are some of the most widely known and used. The parenting education professional must be aware of the different approaches available and be prepared to match the needs of the parents and the children with appropriate programs. Increasingly, professionals in the field of parenting education are recognizing that the needs of families vary depending upon family composition, ethnicity, culture, economic status, and so forth. Likewise, they are recognizing the inability of any one program to meet such varying needs.

Brock and colleagues (1993) argue that an understanding of family systems theory must be integrated into parenting education programs in order for lasting change to occur. Rather than simply teaching the parents techniques to influence the child's behavior, the whole family might be better served if the child participated in the program as well. This allows both parent and child to practice new skills while also considering sibling and couple relationships. Most packaged parent education programs are geared specifically toward the parent, and few involve the children.

The National Extension Parent Education Model

The National Extension Parent Education Model (NEPEM) (Smith et al., 1998) was developed to help in stimulating and conceptualizing parent education programs at state and county levels. The model includes eight underlying guiding principles. The NEPEM focuses on:

- What parents do to enhance the well-being of their children
- Priority parent practices that are significant across the full range of childhood and adolescence
- Core priorities
- Skills and practices as more important than the arrangement of practices
- Parent skills as having fluid, not rigid, boundaries
- NEPEM as dynamic, not static
- Parent strengths and empowerment
- Parent strengths as sufficiently broad and flexible to be useful in developing programs across the cultural spectrum

NEPEM identifies six categories of skills needed by parents for optimal parenting. They include care for self, understanding (of children, their developmental needs and uniqueness), guidance, nurturance, motivation, and advocacy. This model allows more flexibility to parenting educators by providing a framework on which to base the development of programs based on the needs of their audiences.

A number of other approaches, models, and programs related to parenting education exist throughout the country. Following are some of the more well known.

MELD (FORMERLY MINNESOTA EARLY LEARNING DESIGN) MELD programs bring parents with common needs together into groups that meet over a 2-year period. They provide resources and training for group facilitators.

PARENTS AS TEACHERS (PAT)   This is a program that promotes the development of children from birth to age 3. PAT began in Missouri and now operates at more than 2,000 sites across the country.

HAWAII'S HEALTHY START   This program serves families identified through screening at birth as highly stressed and/or at risk for child abuse.

THE HOME INSTRUCTION PROGRAM FOR PRESCHOOL YOUNGSTERS (HIPPY)   This program seeks to prepare 3- to 5-year-olds for kindergarten and first grade.

PARENTING EDUCATION AS A PROFESSION

The notion of parenting education as a profession and the parent educator as a professional has only recently been considered. Historically, parent education has been carried out within the domains of a number of different disciplines, including medicine, social work, therapy, and education. Typically, parenting education was one of many roles played. For example, parents might ask a pediatrician how best to deal with their toddler's temper tantrums. Although this is not necessarily a medical question, the doctor may be inclined to offer advice. In some situations, parenting advice is given without the benefit of formal training in the area. Seldom is parenting directly addressed in training programs for many of the helping professions.

Many national programs, such as PET or STEP, use paraprofessionals to carry out their particular curriculum. Instructors may have no formal training in child development or parenting but become certified upon completion of a prescribed training program that follows their particular approach or curriculum.

Other parenting programs involve the use of volunteers, usually experienced parents who offer support or facilitation. The Minnesota-based MELD program is a good example. Experienced parents are trained in facilitation techniques and given supporting material on child development and parenting issues. These trained parents then lead parenting groups with new parents. One of the strengths of the MELD model is that it includes parents from the community in leadership roles as group facilitators. These parents often share the same cultural and socioeconomic status as the parents in the rest of the group. This shared background gives the facilitators increased credibility and acceptance.

A relatively small number of professionals have trained specifically in parenting education and consider it to be their primary profession. Degree-granting programs in parenting education are increasing throughout the United States. There is a slowly emerging consensus on the parameters of parenting education and the competencies needed for effective practice. One of the main goals of NPEN, the group that evolved out of discussions among parenting education experts at Wheelock College in 1995, is the establishment of agreed-upon content and competencies for practice in the field of parenting education.

THE ROLE OF THE PARENTING EDUCATOR

What exactly does a parenting educator do? Does his or her role vary depending upon the group or the objective? Myers-Walls (1998) identified three possible role paradigms expected of parent educators. Understanding these varying expectations is necessary in order to identify needed competencies for parenting educators.

The first role paradigm is that of the expert. Parenting educators acting in this role are knowledgeable in certain information and facts and share that knowledge with parents, who see the parent educator as having answers they need and want.

The parenting educator can also take a much less active role. In this situation, the parents are assumed to already have the information and knowledge they need, but the parenting educator can provide a perspective or a setting for discussion and can access appropriate resources. In this role paradigm, the parenting educator operates more as a facilitator to guide group process than as a leader. The parents establish the agenda and goals. This type of approach is especially effective with disadvantaged or oppressed populations, but it takes an especially competent parenting educator who has the ability to know when to participate and when to step back and is familiar with liberation pedagogy. Liberation pedagogy seeks to empower learners and encourages them to challenge and change the world (Shor & Freire, 1986).

A third role paradigm falls between the expert and the facilitator styles. In the collaborator approach, the educator and the parents work together to determine the goals and agenda of the program. The parents are valued for their knowledge, and the parenting educator is recognized for his or her knowledge base, as well as his or her skills in group facilitation.

Because the role of the parenting educator can vary depending upon the audience, the setting, and the goals of the group, a truly competent parenting educator should be capable of moving into whatever role is needed in the particular situation. An educator offering a 1-day workshop may need different skills than one facilitating an ongoing group or writing a newspaper column. Those currently working to define and establish the field of parenting education are faced with the difficulty of trying to move the field forward by defining content and competencies while still supporting the broad diversity of the profession.

COMPETENCIES

Discussion about establishing parenting education as a field and parenting educators as professionals has led to consideration of competencies. What do parent educators need to know in order to effectively practice? What skills should they possess?

An informal discussion among some parenting education experts has occurred over the Internet through a parenting education mailing list started by members of the Parent Education Focus Group of the National Council on Family Relations. In 1997, subscribers to the Talk About Parent Education list held a discussion about competencies needed for effective parenting education. Competencies identified by the Family Resource Coalition (FRC) provided the basis for discussion. The following competencies resulted from the list discussion (Myers-Walls, 1997):

- Interpersonal skills (listening, communicating, empathy, being accepting and nonjudgmental)
- An understanding of family life stages
- Group process skills
- Teaching skills
- Sensitivity to social class, ethnicity, and diversity
- Awareness of one's strengths and biases, knowledge of one's own philosophy, including a willingness and ability to critically examine one's beliefs
- Understanding of human development beyond child development to include a life span perspective and dynamics of intimate adult relationships, including parenting partnerships or community parenting, extended family members, grandparents, married and unmarried heterosexual couples, gay and lesbian couples, and any individual that influences the life of the child and who that child will become
- Good working knowledge of local community support services
- Solid knowledge of life span development, including the importance of nurturing and guidance
- Knowledge and use of effective problem-solving skills and the ability to teach and model this process
- Knowledge of work and family challenges and stresses
- Ethics, professional identity, standards

Minnesota was one of the first states to require parent and family educators to be licensed. Originally, in order to be licensed, parent and family educators had to have completed a specified number of credits in family structures and functions, family dynamics, child development, interpersonal relationships, parenting, and teaching methods (University of Minnesota, 1991). The criteria were recently changed to focus on a competency-based model (Minnesota Department of Children, Families, & Learning, 2000).

There has been increased discussion among parenting education professionals regarding the feasibility of certification or licensure of parenting educators on a national basis. The National Council on Family Relations (NCFR) has a certification program for family life educators that requires knowledge in most of the areas deemed relevant for parenting education. The Certified Family Life Educator (CFLE) designation requires a minimum of a baccalaureate degree in a social science and a minimum of 2 years' experience in family life education. Some argue that professionals practicing in parenting education should have preparation in the broad areas that make up the CFLE criteria. Many parenting educators who are operating as facilitators, paraprofessionals, and volunteers, as well as many that consider themselves to be professional parenting educators, may not be able to meet all of the requirements of the CFLE designation, however. NCFR is considering developing a series of subcertifications of the CFLE designation, including certifications for those practicing specifically in parenting education, marriage education, and other areas. Development of a certification in parent education will no doubt lead to further discussion about the knowledge base and competencies needed for effective practice.

The idea of licensure and/or certification of parenting educators has been met with concern by those who support peer-facilitator models and other grassroots community-based programs. These programs are typically operated through community centers and utilize experienced parents from the surrounding neighborhood. These parents, often trained in facilitation skills but not formally in child development or parenting education, can be especially effective because they often share experience, culture, and economic status with other parents. Establishment of specific academic criteria could prevent many of these parents from practicing as parent educators.

A multitiered or leveling certification process, one that identifies a career track for parenting education, may address these concerns. The Center for Parent Education at the University of North Texas is developing a leveling system for parent educators based on core knowledge and skills (Texas Registry of Parent Educator Resources, 2000).

SUMMARY

In this chapter we've looked at the history of parenting education and some of the societal changes that lead to increased interest and participation. In addition to considering varying definitions and assumptions and the settings in which parenting education often takes place, we reviewed some common theories that have influenced the field. A brief review of some of the more widely used parenting education programs and models was followed by a discussion of the current status of parenting education as a profession, the role of the parenting educator, and competencies needed for effective practice.

This is an exciting time for the field of parenting education. The growing numbers of professionals who consider parenting education to be their primary profession are actively discussing new ideas, approaches, theories, and criteria. Increased recognition of the value and impact of positive parenting on the well-being of individuals and society will no doubt result in continued discussion and growth in this important field.

QUESTIONS/PROBLEMS FOR DISCUSSION AND REVIEW

Class Discussion

1. Can parenting educators be effective if they have never had children themselves?

2. Discuss your thinking about whether parenting education is a profession or a discipline within the profession of education.

3. Should parent educators be required to have at least a baccalaureate degree in order to practice?

4. Which term is better: parent educator or parenting educator? Why?

Research Problems/Activities

1. Where do the theories presented in this chapter (humanism, behaviorism, and so on) fall in relation to Murray's criteria (page 193)?

2. Compare the requirements for the Certified Family Life Educator designation and the competencies needed for parenting educators listed on page 203. How do they differ? Does a parenting educator need to know the same things as a Certified Family Life Educator?

3. What would a community-based parenting program using an Adlerian approach look like if you were to design one for your neighborhood resource center?

4. Apply Doherty's levels of family involvement model (discussed in Chapter 2) to Harman and Brim's three modes of instruction for parenting education: the individual mode, the group mode, and the mass mode.

5. Investigate the availability of parenting education programs in your community. In what settings are they held (health care, community education, extension)? From the descriptions, can you tell what theory of child development they are based on (behaviorism, Adlerian, temperament, and so on)?

Case Study Design

1. Julian and Marie are the parents of 13-year-old Ruby. Ruby refuses to clean her room, and it has become quite a mess. Describe how Julian and Marie would react if they parented using each of the styles described by Baumrind: permissive, authoritative, and authoritarian.

2. How would a parenting educator following a behavioral approach suggest that Julian and Marie deal with Ruby and her room? One following an Adlerian approach?

CHAPTER 11

Adapting Programs for Diverse Settings

ANYWHERE IN AMERICA, an upscale church is sponsoring a family life weekend. The family life minister has her hands full with this one: more than 500 people are registered, representing a wide variety of family types: newlyweds; intact families with children of all ages; stepfamilies with children of all ages and assorted in-laws and former spouses; singles with aging parents, singles with surrogate family, divorced singles, widows; new parents; parents of teens and/or young adults. The varieties and categories overlap and intertwine, and all have special needs. Affluent families are not immune to problems and crises either: divorce, drugs and alcohol abuse, violence, teen pregnancies—even sexual abuse (although no one will talk about it). Often programs about dealing with these stresses have to be presented in disguised form as a way to help those "outside the church," but they need to be dealt with nonetheless. Where to start? How to follow up this one-shot weekend? What will help families to truly learn new coping and communication skills? And can families really learn better ways of coping???

Aleza Brown hopes so. She teaches family life education in an elementary school as part of her job as school counselor. It's elementary, all right. . . . What can you do to help your family? How can you acceptably tell someone you're angry? Are all mothers the same? Are all fathers? It is sort of a ludicrous question when you look at the makeup of the school: 12 different language groups and untold cultural interests are represented. Some of the children are well dressed and well groomed—products of that privileged life in which mother stays home "for the kids" and dad may work 10 to 16 hours a day "for the kids." Other children haven't had it so lucky. Mary's parents have just divorced after an extended battle lasting more than 2 years. And now the custody issue is a battle. George is the oldest son of migrant workers who have spent their lives plucking up crops and themselves from California to Florida. George's father and mother are like many other migrant families. They speak enough English to get by, but they neither read nor write. They want better for George, but they have to keep moving if they are to earn a living the only way they know how. Now that George's father is injured, the fifth grader's chances of finishing high school look extremely dim. Aman's family fled an oppressive political regime in their native country. Although the parents have professional training, they are still struggling to get jobs, learn English, and maintain some of their own cultural heritage. The family has not been welcomed in every context of "melting pot" America. Aman's shyness is understandable.

From a high-rise office building, Sylvia Sanchez of Baker, Simon, and Sanchez, Attorneys at Law, looks down on the school where Aleza Brown teaches and where her daughter Esmerelda goes to school. Sylvia has just had another child. Her husband, Roberto, was from a large family, and they both wanted at least one sibling for Esmerelda. But it makes a law career so hard! She is looking forward to the brown-bag lunch discussions that start today on balancing work and family. A professor from the Department of Family Studies at the local university will be leading the sessions. Sylvia hopes to get some pointers on how to cope better with her schedule, her guilt, her stress, her marriage. She also hopes that the professor won't just talk all the time. Sylvia wants to hear how others in the group have coped with similar situations. That would be so helpful!

The variety of settings in which family life education is offered poses both challenge and opportunity for family life educators. One thing all of the settings have in common is that they tend to relate to people where they live and spend their time, particularly the contexts of school, work, or the religious setting. Each context has its own set of expectations and limitations. If the family life educator does not understand or honor these, he or she will not be successful in accessing and maintaining contact with that particular group. In this chapter, we discuss various contexts and how to work within their expectations and limitations to develop and maintain good programs and good relationships. The final section reviews promising paradigms for the future.

WHAT IS YOUR ROLE?

In any of the settings mentioned previously or in many of the other community settings that call for family life education, a first consideration is your role in the education process. Perhaps you are a staff member with responsibility for planning both short- and long-term family life programs for the agency or institution. Or you may be someone from outside the institution who is called upon to offer a time-limited program on a particular topic. Do you see yourself as the expert, the consultant, or the facilitator?

The expert tends to come loaded with material and handouts and a very set agenda. She or he does most of the talking and offers strong decisive opinions about situations and skills. There is little acknowledgment of the participant's unique situation or culture. The expert has the answers and little personal involvement with the participants.

The consultant recognizes her or his expertise in an area and seeks to apply that knowledge to the particular situations of the participants. Prior planning and a review and assessment of the group's interests and expressed needs are often part of the consultant's preparation for working with the group. Presentation is usually in the form of a minilecture or brief report on results of assessment, followed by feedback and questions from the group. A consultant will value the involvement of the participants and their ownership of the group process.

The facilitator focuses on group dynamics and participant involvement in the education process. He or she draws on the participants' strengths to enhance discussion and resolve issues that surface. Using open-ended questions, reflection, and review of comments made, the facilitator moves the group toward resolution of "problems." The facilitator's own opinions or input are kept to a minimum, although he or she may provide work sheets or case studies to encourage discussion. Although the facilitator is definitely the group "leader," leadership is shared through high levels of interaction with the participants.

One decision about your role may be the situation itself. Are you speaking to a large group in a time-limited format? Or is this an ongoing workshop or seminar with a limited number of participants? Have you been specifically asked to serve as consultant or to assist a group in a carefully defined task? The age group you are working with is also a consideration. Adults are more likely to tolerate—and even appreciate—an "expert" approach. Adolescents and young adults respond much better to a facilitator-leader.

THE RELIGIOUS SETTING

Definition of Family Ministry

Garland and Yankeelov (1998) define *family* in a religious context as

> those persons who commit themselves to God and then to one another to serve as family for one another for the rest of their lives. Family may include biologically and legally related relationships, such as parents and children, and spouses, but it is not necessarily limited to these culturally recognized relationships. (p. 14)

This highlights an important distinction of religious institutions: The members often serve as surrogate or extended family to each other. "It is exceedingly difficult in our culture to reach beyond the bonds of blood and marriage to embrace others as family, yet that is the first responsibility of congregational family ministry" (Garland & Yankeelov, 1998, p. 15). *Family ministry* is defined as "everything that a church and its representatives do which has an impact on the founding, development, and ministry of families" (p. 16).

A second distinction is the homogeneity of the congregation. Members tend to hold the same values and belief stances—whether conservative, moderate, or liberal—and to be of the same socioeconomic level. There is also usually a higher level of intact families than in the general population, and more families exhibit identified family strengths. On the whole, they are less willing to talk candidly about "problem areas" in their family life. Rarely does a congregation have much cultural diversity within its membership, although there are notable exceptions, particularly in urban settings. However, a comprehensive survey and statistical analysis of 16 congregations representing diverse cultural, denominational, and racial perspectives revealed that family functioning and reported family stressors were similar in all groups (Yankeelov & Garland, 1998). Surprisingly, the stressor most often reported was "difficulty on the job for a family member," an area not usually addressed by family ministry programming. Other widely reported stressors were centered within family relationships: tasks and chores left undone, parent-child conflict, disagreement about friends or activities, financial strain, and conflict in another family relationship. When Yankeelov and Garland looked at the reported stressors according to family type, single parents and single senior adults reported more marital conflicts (presumably with ex-spouses or in the marriages of children). Single parents in all samples also reported more financial strain and unsolved problems. The researchers concluded, "With respect to this dimension of family life, as well as others explored in previous sections of this article, denominations have much to gain by perceiving that their families are far more alike than they are different" (p. 45). Garland and Yankeelov (1998) propose a "perspective" approach to family ministry, in contrast to the conventional "programmatic" approach. Such an approach looks at each congregation as unique in its family makeup and challenges. It focuses on equipping rather than telling or directing.

General Characteristics

Understanding some of the general characteristics of religious institutions can lay a foundation for a perspective-taking approach and assist family life educators to relate more effectively to families in a spiritual context.

1. *Congregations tend to be family oriented but age divided.* This characteristic parallels the educational assumption of our society that people should be taught in age-graded classes. However, there is the beginning of a trend, particularly in religious organizations, toward sponsoring multiage programs. Such cross-generational groupings have never died out in many ethnic congregations and faith groups and in smaller congregations. I (Powell) recall being asked to speak at a "mother-daughter" brunch in a rural church in Alabama. I worked hard at identifying parent-adolescent issues to address in my presentation and finding some interactive exercises. Much to my surprise, the brunch was attended by every woman in the church, most of whom weren't mother–teen daughter pairs. I had to do some creative scrambling to re-focus my presentation. I should have checked out the composition of the audience more fully before going!

2. Values and beliefs are of prime importance and form the bond for the congregation. If the family life educator has a religious orientation, this will help a trust relationship to develop quickly. Biblical grounding for your presentation and a personal sharing of faith experience, when appropriate, can also enhance an outsider's credibility. I have found this to be particularly helpful when doing sexuality education seminars. The fact that I am a seminary graduate and the wife of a minister gives me credibility and trustworthiness with the parents and the ministerial staff. Sexuality education, as well as substance abuse prevention, are two areas in which congregations could potentially have a major impact on adolescent decision making and health promotion. Unfortunately, these are issues most congregations have not addressed in a consistent way. A 1995 survey of 527 religious youth workers determined that only 4% of congregations have regular programs to discuss sexuality or substance abuse prevention (Burrill, 1999). Opportunities for clarifying and sharing values and beliefs are crucial. People of faith need to establish their own beliefs about the meaning of sexual expression, then look for opportunities to share these beliefs with young people. "If we don't communicate what we believe about love—about the nature, role and purpose of humanity and how we understand God to be acting in our lives and in the world—who will do it?" (Burrill, 1999, p. 3).

3. Endorsement of your program by the congregation's minister, priest, or rabbi will influence many people to attend. This has certainly been the case when marriage enrichment programs are church sponsored. If the religious leader urges the membership to attend and, in the best case, plans to attend with his or her spouse, the membership will likely follow.

4. The religious family life education program can address values and moral decision making in ways that school programs cannot. On the other hand, some congregations are very uncomfortable with too much candor about controversial issues. In developing sexuality programs for church youth, I ask the congregation's own ministers to address the controversial issues, while I provide a framework of information, a format, and a forum for discussion of the pros and cons of various issues. I have never had trouble with opposition from parents concerned about what I might teach their children, because the congregation's ministers and youth leaders were integrally involved in the program implementation from the start. This brings up another distinctive strength of congregational family life education.

5. Many adult role models are available to assist with small group discussions and interaction. With the exception of community organizations such as the Scouts, this availability of adult mentors is a unique and valuable resource for family life education in the religious context.

"Families genuinely are a cornerstone of human existence, with the power to bless or curse us, as God told Abraham. And because people tend to replicate their family way of being in the work place, in the market place, in school or wherever they are, let us work for blessing" (Wigger, 1998, p. 25). The religious setting has many opportunities to promote and educate for "blessing" the family that will spill over into many other arenas of their lives.

THE WORK SETTING

Composition of the workforce has changed drastically over the past 20 years. It is more racially and ethnically diverse and older (median age is 40) and comprises more women—nearly 50%. The great majority of workers have day-to-day family responsibilities at home. Some 46% have children under 18 who live with them at least half of the time. Seventy-eight percent of married employees have a spouse who is also employed, up 12% from 1977. Single parents make up 20% of the parent population, with 27% of that group being single fathers. All employed fathers report more time spent with their children: 2.3 hours per day, an increase of 30 minutes over 20 years ago. This compares with the constant finding that employed mothers spend 3.2 hours daily with their children. This information is from findings of a National Study of the Changing Workforce conducted in 1997 by the Families and Work Institute (1998). The study also reported that workers are most likely to be satisfied with their jobs, committed to their employers, and productive at work when they have jobs that offer autonomy, meaning, learning opportunities, support from supervisors, and flexible work arrangements that are responsive to individual needs.

A recent study of young adult priorities confirms the interest in family issues of those entering the workforce ("USA Snapshots," 1998). Comparing 1998 responses with those from a similar survey conducted in 1989, the researchers found that 83% of the respondents named a "close-knit family" as their number one priority, a 15% gain since 1989. The second-place priority, job and career, moved down 4 percentage points to 68%, with financial success placing third at 57%. Both studies indicate that employee satisfaction and productivity are more influenced by job quality and workplace support than by pay and benefits, which appear to be generally competitive for the workplace as a whole.

Marketing Your Program

Work-family seminars are one effective way to provide workplace support, but the family life educator will most likely have to "sell" his or her program to company managers. It shouldn't be hard to sell: A 1986 study found that 51% of the companies questioned favored work-family seminars, yet only 13% said they were providing such seminars (Friedman, 1986). On the other hand, it is important to be thoroughly prepared when you approach a business with your idea.

Apgar, Riley, Eaton, and Diskin (1982) give step-by-step assistance in designing programs for the work setting (see Box 11.1). The authors emphasize that it is crucial that your program idea fit the mission of the organization and the goals of the particular department. The more familiar you are with the organization, the better chance you will have of selling your idea to administrators and line staff.

1. Realistically appraise your ability to develop and provide services.
   • Why do you want to develop a FLE program for business?
   • What will this program offer to the employees?
   • What resources do you have to support the start-up phase of the program?
   • Is your agency or sponsoring group willing to make a commitment to provide services?
2. Select your target organization.
   • Do you or your board have members who can assist in making contacts?
   • Which worksites do your clients come from?
   • Are there any potential buyer organizations that are known for their interest in human resources or that have a history of community involvement?
   • Have you or your agency had any previous formal or informal contacts with any organizations?
3. Research the organization.
   • What is the size of the organization?
   • What is the relationship between employees and management?
   • What are the workforce characteristics or specific workforce concerns (alcoholism rate or well-being of retirees, for example)?
   • Are there any related service programs in existence?

Before approaching a business, it is also important to have your proposed seminars carefully designed, complete with learning objectives and methods and evaluation plan. Develop an attractive brochure or notebook with key points and ideas that you can discuss in your meeting and that you can leave with the employer. Present yourself as someone who is capable of providing a quality service. The selling meeting must minimize the business's anxiety about sponsoring this service: Whom will I deal with, is it worth the money, will our problems be helped by this service?

Apgar et al. (1982) refer to the four "Ps" of marketing: program, promotion, price, and place. Regarding price, they advise that you price your services so that you make a profit. A business expects you to include a profit margin. The place, unless the services are out of the ordinary, would be the employer's premises, most often during the lunch hour.

Key Concepts

Apgar et al. (1982) condense the theoretical and practical heart of any adult education program to four key concepts:

1. *Participation.* High involvement by employees in articulating needs to be addressed and an interactive program design.

4. Schedule a meeting.
   - Identify the persons within the organization who are responsible for such programs.
   - Arrange a meeting, bringing a descriptive brochure that you can leave with them.
   - Help the organization's representatives to identify what some of the needs are that these programs might address.
   - Be clear about what you and your agency can and cannot provide.
   - Describe other existing agency programs so they can get a sense of where the seminar service fits in with the total service delivery of your agency.
5. Follow up on the contact.
   - Send a letter referring to the visit and suggesting what the next steps are.
   - Keep in touch personally.
   - Identify whether additional persons should be involved.

Note. From *Life Education in the Workplace,* by K. Apgar, D. P. Riley, J. T. Eaton, & S. Diskin, 1982, New York: Alliance for Children and Families. Copyright 1982 by Alliance for Children and Families, reprinted by permission of Manticore Publishers.

2. *Powerful ideas.* Address a few key concepts that you can communicate well.

3. *Parsimony.* Sessions should not be overloaded. Remember that you usually have less than an hour per session. Select the most important ideas, skills, or attitudes that you wish to convey in a participatory fashion.

4. *Practicality.* Adults enroll in programs that address issues of immediate, rather than future, concerns.

The Working Family Resource Center of St. Paul, Minnesota, a collaborative effort with the public school system, outlines some options for work-family seminars in a brochure that they present to company managers (Working Family Resource Center, 1999). Under the major headings of "Work/Family Balance," "Child Development," "Self-Esteem," "Personal Development," "Communication," and "Consumer," they list several appealing seminar titles. For example, under "Personal Development" are listed "Living Positively in a Negative World" and "Seven Habits of Happy and Effective People." The Resource Center also offers parent education, individual consultations, work/family specialist consultations, a resource library, and a newsletter that employer-subscribers can distribute to their employees. "The Center's role is to provide information, stimulate thought and facilitate discussion in order to encourage individuals to improve their personal and family life. Programming covers work/family issues throughout the life cycle" (Working Family Resource Center, 1999).

The growing interest of both employees and employers in quality-of-life issues and how they affect the work environment is good news to family life educators. Well-designed and well-presented programs should get a warm reception from businesses who want to be seen as family-friendly.

THE SCHOOL SETTING

The Value of Relationship Skills Training

Schools also are increasingly interested in relationship issues. A course in relationship development is now required for all high school students in Minneapolis, Minnesota, for example. Other cities and states are incorporating values education and conflict management courses as well. Probably the hardest thing we ever have to do in life is develop and maintain close relationships, yet we have the least formal education in how to do this successfully.

"With the increasing rate of violence between people, the high rate of divorce and family problems, we need to be more proactive and help prevent relationship problems," says David Olson, codeveloper and author, with John DeFrain and Amy K. Olson, of a new relationship development program for use in schools and community settings (Olson, 1999). "We need to add the *fourth R* for 'Relationships' to the three 'R's taught in schools. Relationship skills are something that people can use every day."

Family life educators who are employed by public schools have an opportunity to share new knowledge and skills training with more students and families than in any other setting. Additionally, community agencies and public schools are forming collaborations that address high-risk children and their families. One successful example is a program called Families and Schools Together (FAST), developed in 1990 by family scientist Lynn McDonald and the Family Service America organization (now Alliance for Children and Families). A school-based, collaborative, family-focused program, FAST is designed to increase the self-esteem and improve the school performance of at-risk elementary school children by supporting the natural strength of the family unit (Families and Schools Together, 1999). The program involves a well-defined collaboration between parents, the school, a local mental health agency, and a local substance abuse prevention provider.

Participation by the whole family in 8 weeks of carefully orchestrated, research-based fun activities is the heart of the program. This is followed by 2 years of monthly family self-help support group meetings. The program has been highly successful, with more than 200 programs established in 24 states since 1990.

According to Laura Pinsoneault, the national training coordinator of FAST, family life educators can "plug in" through the mental health agency role, or other community partners can be added. The program can also be sponsored primarily by a domestic violence agency or a community resource center rather than by a school district.

Working with Schools

Pinsoneault (1999, personal communication) also offers suggestions on how to work with schools in establishing collaborative programs of any kind. (1) Co-operation is greatest when the school decides that they want the program. They buy into it and don't have to be persuaded. Often, observing an effective pro-gram in action will be the turning point. Linking with principals who are al-ready involved is also helpful. (2) Exercise care in choosing a school partner. Make sure the principal fully understands the extent of the school's involve-ment and the needed time commitment. The principal and the teachers need to be fully committed to the concept. An in-service meeting that explains the program's goals and outcomes can be very helpful, because it gives the teachers opportunities to ask questions and hear and see firsthand what is being consid-ered. (3) The family life educator must convey a spirit of cooperation and com-petency. This enhances the administration-teacher comfort level, and the school representatives become more supportive. (4) If there are resisters, get them involved as soon as possible. Encourage them to talk with students and parents who are "graduating" from the program to see what effect it had on their family life. (5) A final suggestion is to develop reasonable goals. Sexuality education—and indeed all family life education programs—is often held to much higher standards than other school programs. Few other school courses are expected to demonstrate behavior change (as opposed to knowledge in-crease) in order to be deemed successful.

> Many family life education programs embody the assumption that learning is equivalent to behavior change and knowledge acquisition. The "personally lived" nature of most family life education content suggests, however, that considerations of the learners' prior experiences should be central in program conceptualization. (Thomas, Schvaneveldt, & Young, 1993, p. 115)

All learners do not start at the same point nor do they assimilate or accommo-date experiences and information in the same way. Family life educators must stress this point to program sponsors and funders who may expect universal vis-ible behavior change results.

Gaining community support and involvement is also the key to establish-ing comprehensive sexuality education programs in local schools. Many com-munities have developed community advisory committees, which may be ap-pointed by the school board or may consist of interested citizens who convince the school board of the need for a sexuality education program. Such a com-mittee will be most effective if its members represent the broad spectrum of diversity and interests of the community. A community-wide educational forum can provide an opportunity to caution people about the risks of inaccurate information on sexual health issues. Experts in the fields of research, public health, and medicine (including doctors, family planning providers, nurses, professors, HIV/AIDS prevention educators, and teachers) can educate parents and school board members on the value of comprehensive sexual health education. SIECUS (1998) also advises advocates to work in coalitions and to remember that the target audience is not the opposition minority. Although they are often more vocal, the opposition rarely reflects the majority opinion. SIECUS also advises considering help from national organizations, contacting other community leaders, and involving local religious leaders.

LOOKING TO THE FUTURE

Family support programs, another collaborative community approach, continue to gain momentum as a model paradigm for engaging the family and providing needed resources for successful family functioning. They began in the 1970s as spontaneous shoestring organizations of parents who wanted information, friendships, and support in raising their children. Currently, some family support programs have evolved into large complex systems funded by a variety of public sources, complete with target populations, eligibility standards, and outcome measures (Goetz, 1992, p. viii). The settings in which family support programs operate vary widely, as do the types of services and resources they offer to families. But all programs are geared toward a common goal: increasing the ability of families to successfully nurture their children. In addition, policy makers and other national groups such as the Boys' and Girls' Clubs of America have begun infusing family support principles into the services that they provide to children and families. Believing that families often struggle with multiple difficulties, the family resource center provides a variety of services under one roof, from literacy and GED classes to health clinics and child care.

The Center for Family Life (CFL) in Sunset Park, Brooklyn, New York, is an example of such an approach. Located in a low-income, ethnically diverse neighborhood in which 30% of the population is under 18, the center aims to sustain children and youth in their own homes by enhancing the capacity of parents in a variety of ways. The center is open 15 hours a day, and around-the-clock emergency service is available from the live-in project director and the director of clinical services.

> CFL's philosophy is that (1) child well-being and family strengths are closely interrelated and (2) are themselves outcomes of a large number of factors within the family and within the community; and therefore, that (3) social services—including personal social services to families and children—are important, particularly in economically depressed neighborhoods. (Goetz, 1992, p. 3)

Such a holistic approach in the context of a multiservice center is proving to be very effective. Goetz (1992) stresses the concept of parent empowerment as the key:

A central challenge to the family resource field is to maintain and enhance this empowerment theme as the principles of family support are translated ever more widely into use in arenas which have not traditionally viewed parents as partners or even as worthy participants in their children's lives. Institutions such as schools or child welfare systems which are reaching out to involve parents in new ways are learning to alter their own expectations and assumptions about parents, and to create many avenues of communicating and facilitating the new partnership they hope to build. (p. x)

Resources for family life educators also continue to expand. Instant access to Web sites on life management topics is opening up innumerable information channels. For those who want hard copies of ready-to-use materials, Family Information Services, established in 1989, mails monthly professional resource materials and tapes to its subscribers. Materials include information and updates on contemporary family issues, program designs, transparency and handout masters, and interviews with researchers and practitioners on their latest work. Increasingly, program designers are utilizing videotapes to illustrate concepts and present case studies that form the basis for discussion by a local family life educator/facilitator. For a well-trained facilitator, the packaged program can be easily adapted to fit the needs of the particular audience and setting. Videotaped subjects are frequently representative of the diversity in our society, and issues also vary by cultural context. Professional organizations and certification are also more available and responsive to community educators, yet this is still an area of challenge. As family scientists and educators enter the twenty-first century, there is growing awareness that cooperation and collaboration with families and professionals at all levels of involvement are the keys to success. Family life educators are no longer seen as the "source of all knowledge," but as valuable resources and catalysts for family development and strength.

Family Support America (formerly Family Resource Coalition of America) has articulated its organizational vision in a way that can apply to all who work with families. We conclude our discussion with their shining hope:

We envision an America in which:

All children, youth and families can get the resources they need, right in their own neighborhoods, to be strong and healthy. Classes and support groups, after-school programs, emergency assistance, counseling, or job training: whatever families need, they find it.

All communities reinforce the efforts of families to raise responsible, productive, confident, joyous children. Neighbors watch out for each other across racial, ethnic, religious, and economic lines. Diversity is a cause for celebration, not discrimination.

All institutions that serve children and families (including schools, human services, health and mental health care providers, and private agencies) work together. They embrace family support principles and put those principles into practice.

All levels of government make family and youth needs (including economic security, adequate housing, and the viability and safety of every community) a priority.

All workplaces have family-friendly policies and practices.

For the good of all families in all circumstances, the future is full of promise.

QUESTIONS/PROBLEMS FOR DISCUSSION AND REVIEW

Class Discussion

1. In program design, how do you determine which role to assume as a family life educator (expert, consultant, facilitator)? What are the advantages and disadvantages of each role in terms of teaching effectiveness?

2. Look at the general characteristics of religious congregations and compare them with your own experience for similarities and differences. What could account for the differences? If you do not have a strong religious background, how could you establish trust and validity with a congregational group?

3. Which institution do you think it would be harder to convince that a family life education program would be of benefit: church, business, or school? Give the reasons for your answer.

4. Future directions of family life education are moving toward more comprehensive services, more collaboration, and more input from target group participants. What additional preparation do you think family life educators need in order to be well equipped for their role(s) in this new paradigm?

Research Problems/Activities

Choose a specific example of one of the three areas (church, business, school). Interview the head of that organization about her or his interest in family life education programs and ask permission to conduct a survey of representative persons in the organization to ascertain their interest in family life education programs. Design the survey and review the results with your class. What characteristics of the particular group might have skewed the survey results? How would you change the survey so that you can get more specific results and more generalizable data?

Case Study Design

Design the presentation of a workplace program for a specific organization with which you are familiar. Perhaps it is the place where your parents work, or it could be the university you attend. Use the planning steps in Box 11.1 to develop your plan.

APPENDIX A

Framework for Life Span Family Life Education

This framework expands on definitions of family life education by specifying major content for broad, life span family life education programs. It reflects current conceptual development and empirical knowledge in each topic area and gives attention to relevant knowledge, attitudes, and skills. Communicating, decision making, and problem solving have not been treated as separate concepts but should be incorporated into each topic area. It is assumed that this framework incorporates education that is multicultural, gender fair, and aware of special needs.

AREAS ADDRESSED IN FLE PROGRAMS FOR STAGES OF

I. Childhood   II. Adolescence   III. Adulthood   IV. Later Adulthood

A. Families in Society

B. Internal Dynamics of Families

C. Human Growth and Development

D. Human Sexuality

E. Interpersonal Relationships

F. Family Resource Management

G. Parent Education and Guidance

H. Family Law and Public Policy

I. Ethics

Note. From "Framework for Life-Span Family Life Education" (rev. ed.), by the National Council on Family Relations, 1997, Minneapolis, MN: Author. Copyright 1997 by the National Council on Family Relations, 3989 Central Ave. NE, Suite 550, Minneapolis, MN 55421. Reprinted by permission.

I. Childhood

A. Families in Society
  - Jobs, money, and the family
  - Programs that support individuals and families
  - Importance of families, neighborhood, and the community
  - Families and schools working together
  - Differing spiritual beliefs and practices

B. Internal Dynamics of Families
  - Family members as individuals
  - Individuality and importance of all family members
  - Getting along in the family
  - Expressing feelings in families
  - Personal family history
  - Family similarities and differences
  - Impact of change on families
  - Responsibilities, rights, interdependence of family members
  - Family rules
  - Families as sources of protection, guidance, affection, support
  - Families as possible sources of anger and violence
  - Family problems

C. Human Growth and Development
  - Emotional and social development
  - Responsibility for keeping healthy—nutrition, personal hygiene
  - Uniqueness of each person
  - Similarities and differences in individual development
  - Understanding people with special needs
  - Perceptions about older people—adolescents, adults, elderly
  - Social and environmental conditions affecting growth and development

D. Human Sexuality
  - Physical and sexual development
  - Body privacy and protection against sexual abuse
  - Uniqueness of each person
  - Similarities and differences in individual sexual development
  - Aspects of human reproduction—prenatal development, birth, puberty
  - Children's perceptions about sexuality
  - Social and environmental conditions affecting sexuality

E. Interpersonal Relationships
  - Respecting self and others
  - Sharing feelings constructively
  - Expressing emotions
  - Developing, maintaining, and ending relationships

- Building self-esteem and self-confidence
- Identifying and enhancing personal strengths
- Communicating with others
- Learning from and teaching others
- Sharing friends, possessions, time
- Acting with consideration for self and others
- Handling problems with others

F. Family Resource Management
  - Taking care of possessions
  - Helping with family tasks
  - Learning about time and schedules
  - Learning to choose
  - Earning, spending, and saving money
  - Understanding space and privacy
  - Developing talents and abilities
  - Selecting and consuming—food, clothing, recreation
  - Using and saving human and nonhuman resources
  - Influences on consumer decisions—values, costs, media, peers

G. Parent Education and Guidance
  - Safety for children
  - Responsibilities of parents
  - Different types of caregivers
  - Parents who live away from children
  - Meeting children's needs at different stages of development
  - Differing parenting styles and behaviors
  - Responsibilities of children
  - Sources of help for parents—family, neighborhood, community
  - Problems of family violence, abuse, neglect

H. Family Law and Public Policy
  - Understanding and respecting the law
  - Laws and policies affecting families
  - Children's legal rights
  - Public policy as it affects families with children, including taxes, civil rights, social security, economic support laws, regulations

I. Ethics
  - Taking responsibility for actions
  - Consequences of actions for self and others
  - Discovering spirituality
  - Respect for all persons
  - Gaining new rights and responsibilities with age
  - Rights of all persons

II. Adolescence

A. Families in Society
- Families and the workplace
- Reciprocal influences of the economy and families
- School as preparation for the future
- Education throughout the life span
- Functioning in the school system
- Individual and family responsibility in the community
- Influence of religion and spirituality on families
- Support for families with special needs and problems
- Reciprocal influences of technology and families
- Population issues and resource allocation
- Role of family in society
- Supportive networks—family, peers, religious institutions, community

B. Internal Dynamics of Families
- Becoming an adult within the family
- Changes in family composition—births, divorce, death
- Managing and expressing feelings in families
- Coping with internal change and stress in the family
- Interaction of friends and family
- Personal and family decision making
- Communicating in families
- Interaction between family members
- Different needs and expectations of family members
- Family rules—overt and covert
- Intergenerational relationships
- Influence of family background
- Family history, traditions, and celebrations
- Families as sources of protection, guidance, affection, support
- Families as possible sources of anger and violence
- Family differences—membership, economic level, role performance, values

C. Human Growth and Development
- Accepting individual differences in development
- Responsibility for personal health—nutrition, personal hygiene, exercise
- Understanding the basis for choosing a family lifestyle—values, heritage, religious beliefs
- Effects of chemical substances on physical health and development
- Types of development—physical, cognitive, affective, moral, personality, social, sexual
- Interaction among types of development
- Patterns of development over the life span—conception to death
- Stereotypes and realities about adulthood and aging
- Developmental disabilities
- Social and environmental conditions affecting growth and development

D. Human Sexuality
  - Physical and sexual development
  - Interaction among types of development
  - Body privacy and protection against sexual abuse
  - Communicating about sexuality—personal values, beliefs, shared decision making
  - Choices, consequences, responsibility of sexual behavior
  - Prevention and transmission of sexually transmitted diseases
  - Human reproduction and conception
  - Normality of sexual feelings and sexual responses
  - Stereotypes and realities about human sexuality
  - Varying family and societal beliefs about sexuality

E. Interpersonal Relationships
  - Respecting self and others
  - Changing and developing one's thoughts, attitudes, values
  - Dealing with success and failure
  - Accepting responsibility for one's actions
  - Assessing and developing personal abilities and talents
  - Communicating information, thoughts, and feelings
  - Managing and expressing emotions
  - Initiating, maintaining, and ending friendships
  - Building self-esteem and self-confidence in self and others
  - Assessing compatibility in interpersonal relationships
  - Acting with consideration for self and others
  - Understanding the needs and motivations involved in dating
  - Factors influencing mate selection—social, cultural, personal
  - Understanding the dimensions of love and commitment
  - Exploring the responsibilities of marriage

F. Family Resource Management
  - Allocating time for work, school, leisure
  - Negotiating privacy and independence
  - Selection of resources to meet personal needs—food, clothing, recreation
  - Using personal resources
  - Earning, spending, and saving money
  - Responsibility for decisions
  - Developing leisure interests
  - Values as a basis for choices
  - Choosing long- and short-term goals
  - Exploring career choices
  - Assessment of and changes in personal and family resources
  - Influences on consumer decisions—values, costs, media, peers

G. Parent Education and Guidance
  - Parent-child communication
  - Meeting children's needs at different stages of development

- Responding to individual differences in children
- Rewards and demands of parenthood
- Understanding marital and parenting roles
- Factors to consider in deciding if and when to become a parent
- Child-rearing practices
- Teaching life skills to children—self-sufficiency, safety, decision making
- Family conflict and conflict resolution
- Problems of family violence, abuse, neglect
- Sources of help for parents—family, neighborhood, community
- Varied parenting situations—single parenting, stepparenting, adoption, caretaking of disabled children
- Influences on parenting styles—ethnic, racial, gender, social, cultural

H. Family Law and Public Policy
- Respecting civil rights of all people
- Understanding legal definitions and laws affecting families
- Individual and family legal protection, rights, and responsibilities
- Laws relating to marriage, divorce, family support, child custody, child protection and rights, family planning
- Family conflict and legal protection of family members
- Families and the justice system
- Impact of laws and policies on families
- Public policy as it affects families with adolescent children, including taxes, civil rights, social security, economic support laws, regulations

I. Ethics
- Developing a personal ethical code
- Exploring personal spirituality
- Personal autonomy and social responsibility
- Interrelationship of rights and responsibilities
- Ethical principles as one kind of value
- Ethical values as a guide to human social conduct
- Complexity and difficulty of ethical choices and decisions
- Ethical implications of social and technological change

III. Adulthood

A. Families in Society
- Family participation in the education of children
- Utilizing the education system
- Influence of religion and spirituality on families
- Supportive networks—family, peers, religious institutions, community
- Understanding and obtaining community support services
- Lifelong learning
- Population issues and resource allocation
- Reciprocal influences of technology and families

- Economic fluctuations and their impact on families
- Interrelationship of families, work, and society
- Individual and family responsibility in the community
- Role of the family in society

B. Internal Dynamics of Families
- Individual development in the family
- Individual and family roles
- Intimate relationships in the family
- Sources of stress and coping with stress
- Lifestyle choices
- Changing needs and expectations of family members
- Intergenerational dynamics through the life span
- Responsibilities, rights, interdependence of family members
- Family transitions—marriage, birth, divorce, remarriage, death
- Family history, traditions, and celebrations
- Factors affecting marital and family relationships
- Giving and receiving affection
- Power and authority in the family
- Effects of family on self-concepts of its members
- Family rules—overt and covert
- Families as sources of protection, guidance, affection, support
- Differences in families—membership, economic level, role performance, values
- Families as possible sources of anger and violence
- Varying influences on family interaction patterns—ethnic, racial, gender, social, cultural

C. Human Growth and Development
- Factors influencing individual differences in development
- Types of development: physical, cognitive, affective, moral, personality, social, sexual
- Interaction among types of development
- Responsibility for personal and family health
- Promoting development in self and others
- Patterns of development over the life span—conception to death
- Myths and realities of adulthood and aging
- Adjusting to disabilities
- Social and environmental conditions affecting growth and development

D. Human Sexuality
- Responsible sexual behavior—choices, consequences, shared decision making
- Normality of sexual feelings and sexual responses
- Communicating about sexuality—personal values, beliefs, shared decision making
- Prevention and transmission of sexually transmitted diseases

- Contraception, infertility, genetics
- Prevention of sexual abuse
- Varying societal beliefs about sexuality

E. Interpersonal Relationships
  - Establishing personal autonomy
  - Building self-esteem and self-confidence in self and others
  - Achieving constructive personal changes
  - Communicating effectively
  - Managing and expressing emotions
  - Developing, maintaining, and ending relationships
  - Exercising initiative in relationships
  - Recognizing factors associated with quality relationships
  - Taking responsibility and making commitments in relationships
  - Evaluating choices and alternatives in relationships
  - Acting in accordance with personal beliefs with consideration for others' best interest
  - Understanding the effects of self-perceptions on relationships
  - Varying influences on roles and relationships—ethnic, racial, gender, social, cultural
  - Types of intimate relationships
  - Creating & maintaining a family of one's own
  - Changes in the marital relationship over time
  - Dealing with crises

F. Family Resource Management
  - Expendability of human energy
  - Developing personal resources
  - Development of personal resources through career choices
  - Values as a basis for choices
  - Developing leisure interests
  - Varying needs of family members for privacy and independence
  - Using resources to meet basic needs of family—food, clothing, shelter
  - Differing views about uses of family resources
  - Establishing long- and short-term goals
  - Financial planning
  - Resource consumption and conservation—material and nonmaterial
  - Balancing work and family roles
  - Influences on consumer decisions—values, costs, media, peers
  - Retirement planning

G. Parent Education and Guidance
  - Factors to consider in deciding if and when to become a parent
  - Preparation for birth and parenthood
  - Changing parental responsibilities as children become independent
  - Parent-child communication
  - Child-rearing practices, guidance, and parenting strategies

- Changing parent-child relationships over the life span
- Importance of parental communication regarding child-rearing practices
- Providing a safe environment for children
- Teaching life skills to children—self-sufficiency, safety, decision making
- Rewards and demands of parenthood
- Varied parenting situations—single parenting, stepparenting, adoption, caretaking of disabled child, elderly parent
- Sources of help for parents—family, neighborhood, community
- Problems of family violence, abuse, neglect
- Influences on parenting styles—ethnic, racial, gender, social, cultural

H. Family Law and Public Policy
- Transmitting values regarding education, justice, and the law
- Understanding and affecting laws and policies
- Laws relating to marriage, divorce, family support, child custody, child protection and rights, family planning
- Family conflict and legal protection of family member
- Public policy as it affects families, including taxes, civil rights, social security, economic support laws, regulations

I. Ethics
- Establishing an ethical philosophy of life
- Acting in accordance with personal beliefs with consideration for others
- Continued growth in personal spirituality
- Personal autonomy and social responsibility
- Interrelationship of rights and responsibilities
- Ethical principles as one kind of value
- Ethical values as a guide to human social conduct
- Complexity and difficulty of ethical choices and decisions
- Assisting in the formation of ethical concepts and behavior in others
- Ethical implications of social and technological change

IV. Later Adulthood

A. Families in Society
- Influence of religion and spirituality on families
- Supporting the education system
- Supportive networks—family, peers, religious institutions, community
- Understanding and obtaining community support services
- Lifelong learning
- Population issues and resource allocation—health care, transportation, housing
- Reciprocal influences of technology and aging families
- Social issues—age discrimination, elder abuse, caregiving
- Role of the family in society
- Economic fluctuations and their impact on aging families

B. Internal Dynamics of Families
- Individual development in the family
- Individual and family roles
- Intimate relationships in the family
- Sources of stress and coping with stress, diseases, disabilities
- Lifestyle choices and changes—retirement planning, retirement
- Changing needs and expectations of family members
- Intergenerational dynamics through the life span
- Responsibilities, rights, interdependence of family members and productivity
- Family transitions—marriage, divorce, remarriage, retirement of mate, death
- Family history, traditions, and celebrations
- Factors affecting marital and family relationships
- Giving and receiving affection
- Effects of family on self-concepts of its members
- Family rules—overt and covert
- Families as sources of protection, guidance, affection, support
- Differences in families—membership, economic level, role performance, values
- Families as possible sources of anger and violence
- Varying influences on family interaction patterns—ethnic, racial, gender, social, cultural
- Changes in power and authority in the family
- Understanding the effects of self-perceptions on relationships

C. Human Growth and Development
- Factors influencing individual differences in development
- Types of development: physical, cognitive, affective, moral, personality, social, sexual
- Interaction among types of development
- Patterns of development over the life span—conception to death
- Myths and realities of aging
- Adjusting to disabilities
- Social and environmental conditions affecting growth and development
- Adapting to and coping with physical changes in later adulthood
- Responsibility for personal health and safety
- Grieving and adjusting to loss

D. Human Sexuality
- Human sexual response and aging
- Normality of sexual feelings and sexual responses
- Communicating about sexuality—personal values, beliefs, shared decision making
- Body privacy and prevention of sexual abuse

- Sexuality education about later adulthood
- Sexual expression and intimacy in later adulthood
- Awareness of sexuality needs in adult living situations
- Varying societal beliefs, myths, and realities about sexuality and aging

E. Interpersonal Relationships
- Continuing personal autonomy
- Building self-esteem and self-confidence in self and others
- Communicating effectively
- Managing and expressing emotions
- Exercising initiative in relationships
- Recognizing factors associated with quality relationships
- Taking responsibility and making commitments in relationships
- Evaluating choices and alternatives in relationships
- Acting in accordance with personal beliefs with consideration for others' best interest
- Varying influences on roles and relationships—ethnic, racial, gender, social, cultural
- Maintaining relationships with one's own family
- Changes in the marital relationship over time
- Dealing with crisis and loss

F. Family Resource Management
- Values as a basis for choices
- Establishing a plan for the distribution of resources and management if incompetent—will, living will
- Using personal resources
- Expanding leisure interests
- Balancing life patterns of retirees with work roles of children
- Varying needs of family members for privacy and independence
- Using resources to meet basic needs of family—food, clothing, shelter
- Differing views about uses of family resources
- Establishing long- and short-term goals
- Managing financial resources in retirement
- Resource consumption and conservation—material and nonmaterial
- Influences on consumer decisions—values, costs, media, peers

G. Parent Education and Guidance
- Changing parent-child relationships in later life—negotiating adult relationships with adult children
- Demands and rewards of grandparenthood, including the possibility of rearing and caring for grandchildren
- Importance of parental communication regarding differences in parenting styles and values between parents and grandparents
- Grandparent-child communication
- Sources of help for grandparents—family, neighborhood, community
- Family conflict and conflict resolution

- Problems of family violence, elder abuse, neglect
- Adapting to the complexities of varied parenting situations—single parenting, stepparenting, caretaking of disabled children, return of adult children to the household

H. Family Law and Public Policy
- Transmitting values regarding education, justice, and the law
- Understanding and affecting laws and policies
- Protecting the civil rights of all people
- Laws relating to marriage, divorce, family support, protection and rights of vulnerable individuals, property, wills, estate planning, and living wills
- Family conflict and legal protection of family member
- Public policy as it affects families, including taxes, civil rights, social security, economic support laws, regulations

I. Ethics
- Acting in accordance with personal beliefs with consideration for others
- Continued growth in personal spirituality
- Personal autonomy and social responsibility
- Interrelationship of rights and responsibilities
- Ethical principles as one kind of value
- Ethical values as a guide to human social conduct
- Complexity and difficulty of ethical choices and decisions—quality-of-life issues, end-of-life issues
- Protection from exploitation
- Ethical implications of social and technological change
- Assisting in the formation of ethical concepts and behavior in others

Family Life Education Substance Areas for the Certified Family Life Educator Designation

1. Families in Society

An understanding of families and their relationships to other institutions, such as the educational, governmental, religious, and occupational institutions in society.

> Structures and functions; cultural variations (family heritage, social class, geography, ethnicity, race, and religion); dating, courtship, marital choice; kinship; cross-cultural and minority (understanding of lifestyles of minority families and the lifestyles of families in various societies around the world); changing gender roles (role expectations and behaviors of courtship partners, marital partners, parents and children, siblings, and extended kin); demographic trends; historical issues; work-family relationships; societal relations (reciprocal influence of the major social institutions and families).

2. Internal Dynamics of Families

An understanding of family strengths and weaknesses and how family members relate to each other.

> Internal social processes (including cooperation and conflict); communication (patterns and problems in husband-wife relationships and in parent-child relationships, including stress and conflict management); conflict management; normal family stresses (transition periods in the family life cycle, three-generation households, caring for the elderly, and dual careers); family crises (divorce, remarriage, death, economic uncertainty and hardship, violence, substance abuse); special needs in families (including adoptive, foster, migrant, low income, military, and blended families, as well as those with disabled members).

Note. From College and University Curriculum Guidelines in *Family Life Education Curriculum Guidelines* (pp. 12–14), edited by D. Bredehoft and D. Cassidy, 1995, Minneapolis, Minnesota: National Council on Family Relations. Copyright 1995 by National Council on Family Relations. Reprinted with permission.

3. Human Growth and Development over the Life Span

An understanding of the developmental changes of individuals in families throughout the life span. Based on knowledge of physical, emotional, cognitive, social, moral, and personality aspects.

> Prenatal; infancy; early and middle childhood; adolescence; adulthood; aging.

4. Human Sexuality

An understanding of the physiological, psychological, and social aspects of sexual development throughout the life span, so as to achieve healthy sexual adjustment.

> Reproductive physiology; biological determinants; aspects of sexual involvement; sexual behaviors; sexual values and decision making; family planning; sexual response; sexual dysfunction; influence on relationships.

5. Interpersonal Relationships

An understanding of the development and maintenance of interpersonal relationships.

> Self and others; communication skills (listening, empathy, self-disclosure, decision making, problem solving, and conflict resolution); intimacy, love, romance; relating to others (respect, sincerity, and responsibility).

6. Family Resource Management

An understanding of the decisions individuals and families make about developing and allocating resources, including time, money, material assets, energy, friends, neighbors, and space, to meet their goals.

> Goal setting and decision making; development and allocation of resources; social environment influences; life cycle and family structure influences; consumer issues and decisions.

7. Parent Education and Guidance

An understanding of how parents teach, guide, and influence children and adolescents.

> Parenting rights and responsibilities; parenting practices/processes; parent-child relationships; variation in parenting solutions; changing parenting roles over the life cycle.

8. Family Law and Public Policy

An understanding of the legal definition of the family and laws that affect the status of the family.

> Family and the law (relating to marriage, divorce, family support, child custody, child protection and rights, and family planning); family and social services; family and education; family and the economy; family and religion; policy and the family (public policy as it affects the family, including taxes, civil rights, social security, economic support laws, and regulations.)

9. Ethics

An understanding of the character and quality of human social conduct, and the ability to critically examine ethical questions and issues.

> Formation of values; diversity of values in pluralistic society; examining ideologies; social consequences of value choices; ethics and technological changes, ethics of professional practice.

10. Family Life Education Methodology

An understanding of the general philosophy and broad principles of family life education in conjunction with the ability to plan, implement, and evaluate such educational programs.

> Planning and implementing; evaluation (materials, student progress, and program effectiveness); education techniques; sensitivity to others (to enhance educational effectiveness); sensitivity to community concerns and values (understanding of the public relations process).

A P P E N D I X C

Example of Permission Form to Do Needs Assessment

(Date)

Dear parents,

Smartkids Middle School has asked me to assist them in developing and conducting an "encouragement" program for girls in grades 6, 7, and 8. Many girls at this age struggle with their new identities as pubertal changes occur. Often academic scores in the sciences and math drop dramatically. Socially, many young women become vulnerable to peer—and boyfriend—pressures. Eating disorders and attempted suicides become an increasing problem. This program would encourage the development of positive and strong images for young women through the use of role models and peer support. It is designed as an after-school, optional program that will be held once a week for the coming school year.

I am a Certified Family Life Educator (CFLE) and a family support counselor at Community Services, Inc., where I have worked for the past three years. I have a master's degree in Human Development Counseling from the University of Ivytwine, and I have designed youth programs for school, community, and church organizations for more than 15 years.

In order to get to know the students better, and to design a program that truly meets their needs, I would like to meet with several "focus groups" of teens at Smartkids over the next two weeks. The permission slip below indicates that you agree for your daughter to participate in a focus group (if randomly selected). Participation is strictly voluntary and will be used anonymously. Please return the signed permission form by Friday to Ms. Joan Brown, Principal of Smartkids Middle School.

If you have other questions about the focus groups or the program, please feel free to call me at 222-2222. Thank you for your support of this new endeavor.

Sincerely,

Mary Jones, BA, MA, CFLE

- -

PERMISSION TO PARTICIPATE

My daughter _____ has my permission to participate in a focus group conducted by Ms. Mary Jones of Community Services, Inc., at Smartkids Middle School. I understand that all participation is voluntary and all information will be used anonymously.

Signed,

_____   _____

                                                                                                (Relation—mother, father, guardian)

The National Coalition to Support Sexuality Education: Goals and Membership

Date: _____

Coalition members are committed to the mission of assuring that comprehensive sexuality education is provided for all children and youth in the United States. Their goals are to:

- Advocate for sexuality education policies and programs at the national and state level

- Develop strategies for implementing sexuality education initiatives at the local, state, and national level

- Assist national organizations concerned with youth to establish policies and programs on sexuality education

- Provide an opportunity for networking, resource sharing, and collaborating among national organizations supporting sexuality education

- Develop strategies to address the activities of those who oppose providing children with comprehensive sexuality education

- Host seminars on key issues in sexuality education

- Identify the latest research, data analysis, and program evaluation materials in the field of sexuality education

- Strive to improve the cultural competency of materials and messages within the field of sexuality education

MEMBERSHIP, AS OF 2000

Advocates for Youth

AIDS Action Council

Alan Guttmacher Institute

American Academy of Child and Adolescent Psychiatry

American Academy of Pediatrics

American Association for Health Education

American Association for Marriage and Family Therapy

American Association of Family and Consumer Sciences

American Association on Mental Retardation

American Association of School Administrators

American Association of Sex Educators, Counselors and Therapists

American Civil Liberties Union, Reproductive Freedom Project

American College of Nurses and Midwives

American College of Obstetricians and Gynecologists

American Counseling Association

American Jewish Congress

American Library Association

American Medical Association

American Medical Women's Association

American Nurses Association

American Orthopsychiatric Association

American Psychiatric Association

American Psychological Association

American Public Health Association

American School Health Association

Association of Reproductive Health Professionals

Association for Sexuality Education and Training

Association of State and Territorial Directors of Public Health Education

Association of State and Territorial Health Officials

ASTRAEA National Lesbian Action Foundation

AVSC International

Balm in Gilead

Blacks Educating Blacks About Sexual Health Issues

Boston Women's Health Book Collective

Catholics for a Free Choice

Center for Law and Social Policy

Center for Policy Alternatives

Center for Reproductive Health Policy Research

Center for Reproductive Law and Policy

Center for Sexuality and Religion

Center for Women Policy Studies

Child Welfare League of America

Children's Defense Fund

Coalition on Sexuality and Disability, Inc.

Education Development Center, Inc.

ETR Associates

Federation of Behavioral, Psychological and Cognitive Sciences

Feminist Majority Foundation

Gay and Lesbian Medical Association

Girls, Incorporated

Hetrick-Martin Institute

Human Rights Campaign

The Institute for Advanced Study of Human Sexuality Alumni Association

Jewish Women International

The Kinsey Institute for Research in Sex, Gender and Reproduction

The Latina Roundtable on Health and Reproductive Rights

Midwest School Social Work Council

Mothers' Voices

National Abortion Federation

National Abortion and Reproductive Rights Action League

National Alliance of State and Territorial AIDS Directors

National Asian Women's Health Organization

National Association of Counties

National Association of County and City Health Officials

National Association for Equal Opportunity in Higher Education

National Association of People with AIDS

National Association of School Psychologists

National Black Women's Health Project

National Center for Health Education

National Coalition of Advocates for Students

National Coalition of STD Directors

National Committee for Public Education and Religious Liberty

National Council on Family Relations

National Council of La Raza

National Council of Negro Women

National Council of State Consultants for School Social Work Services

National Education Association Health Information Network

National Family Planning and Reproductive Health Association

National Gay and Lesbian Task Force

National Information Center for Children and Youth with Disabilities

National Latina Health Organization

National Latina/o Lesbian and Gay Organization (LLEGO)

National League for Nursing

National Lesbian and Gay Health Association

National Medical Association

National Mental Health Association

National Minority AIDS Council

National Native American AIDS Prevention Center

National Network for Youth

National Organization on Adolescent Pregnancy, Parenting and Prevention

National Resource Center for Youth Services

National School Boards Association

National Urban League

National Women's Health Network

National Women's Law Center

Network for Family Life Education

Office of Family Ministries and Human Sexuality, National Council of Churches

Parents, Families and Friends of Lesbians and Gays

People for the American Way

Planned Parenthood Federation of America

Population Communications International

Presbyterians Affirming Reproductive Options

Religious Coalition for Reproductive Choice

Sexuality Information and Education Council of the United States

Society for Adolescent Medicine

Society for Developmental and Behavioral Pediatrics

Society for Public Health Education

Society for the Scientific Study of Sexuality

Unitarian Universalist Association

United Church Board for Homeland Ministries

United States Conference of Mayors

University of Pennsylvania, Graduate School of Education

YAI/National Institute for People with Disabilities

The Young Women's Project

YWCA of the U.S.A.

Zero Population Growth, Inc.

Note. From "Fact Sheet: The National Coalition to Support Sexuality Education," SIECUS, 1997, *SIECUS Report, 25*. Copyright 1997 by the Sexuality Information and Education Council of the United States. Reprinted with permission of the Sexuality Information and Education Council of the United States.

APPENDIX E

Selected Web Sites for Sexuality Information

AIDS Virtual Library: *www.planetq.com/aidsvi/index.html*

Alan Guttmacher Institute: *www.agi-usa.org*

American Journal of Public Health: *www.apha.org*

Association of Voluntary and Safe Contraception: *www.avsc.org./avsc*

Body Health: A Multimedia AIDS and HIV Information Resource: *www.thebody.com*

CDC Division of STD Prevention: *www.cdc.gov/hiv/pubs/facts.htm*

CDC National AIDS Clearinghouse: *www.cdcnac.org*

Center for AIDS Prevention Studies: *www.caps.ucsf.edu/capsweb*

Centers for Disease Control and Prevention: *www.cdc.gov*

Coalition for Positive Sexuality: *www.positive.org*

Contraceptive Contemplation: *www.tripod.com/living/contraceptive/index.html*

Does Sex Education Work?: *www.caps.ucsf.edu/sexedtext.html*

Free Med-Line: National Library of Medicine: *www.nlm.nih.gov/databases/freemedl.html*

Menstruation Education (Planned Parenthood): *www.ppfa.org/ppfa/ period-main.html*

National Abortion Rights League: *www.naral.org*

National Gay and Lesbian Task Force: *www.ngltf.org*

National Right to Life: *www.nrlc.org*

Natural Family Planning: *www.missionnet.com*

Northeastern Centre Against Sexual Assault: *www.northern.casa.org.au*

Planned Parenthood Federation of America: *www.plannedparenthood.org*

Rape, Abuse, and Incest National Network (RAINN): *feminist.com/rainn.htm*

Ruth Westheimer's (Dr. Ruth's) Home Page: *www.drruth.com*

Sexual Health Advocate Peer Education: *www.muhealth.org/~student health/health_ed.shtml*

Sexuality in Later Life: *www.nih.gov/nia/health/pubpub/sexual.htm*

Sexually Transmitted Diseases: *www.niaid.nih.gov/factsheets/stdinfo.htm*

Teen Pregnancy: *www.teenpregnancy.org*

Teen Pregnancy Prevention Research: *www.pserie.psu.edu/hss/psych/bibweb.htm*

Women and AIDS: *www.thebody.com/whatis/women.html*

REFERENCES

Ahlburg, D. A., & DeVita, C. J. (1992). New realities of the American family [Special issue]. *Population Bulletin, 47*(2).

Alan Guttmacher Institute. (1994). *Sex and America's teenagers*. New York: Author.

Alan Guttmacher Institute. (1996). *Facts in brief: Teen sex and pregnancy*. New York: Author.

Allen, K. R., & Baber, K. M. (1992). Starting a revolution in family life education: A feminist vision. *Family Relations, 41*(4), 378–384.

Allgeier, E. R. (1984). The personal perils of sex researchers: Vern Bullough and William Masters. *SIECUS Report, 12*(4), 16–19.

American Guidance Service. (1991). *STEP research studies*. Circle Pines, MN: American Guidance Service.

Andrews, M. P., Bubolz, M. M., & Paolucci, B. (1980). An ecological approach to the study of the family. *Marriage and Family Review, 3*(1–2), 29–49.

Annie E. Casey Foundation. (1998). *When teens have sex: Issues and trends. KIDS COUNT Special Report.* Baltimore: Author.

Apgar, K., Riley, D. P., Eaton, J. T., & Diskin, S. (1982). *Life education in the workplace*. New York: Family Service Association of America.

Arcus, M. E. (1986). Should family life education be required for high school students? An examination of the issues. *Family Relations, 35*, 347–356.

Arcus, M. E., Schvaneveldt, J. D., & Moss, J. J. (1993). The nature of family life education. In M. E. Arcus, J. D. Schvaneveldt, & J. J. Moss (Eds.), *Handbook of family life education* (Vol. 1, pp. 1–25). Newbury Park, CA: Sage.

Arcus, M. E., & Thomas, J. (1993). The nature and practice of family life education. In M. E. Arcus, J. D. Schvaneveldt, & J. J. Moss (Eds.), *Handbook of family life education* (Vol. 2, pp. 1–32). Newbury Park, CA: Sage.

Arlin, P. K. (1984). Adolescent and adult thought: A structural interpretation. In M. L. Commons, F. A. Richards, & C. Armon (Eds.), *Beyond formal operations: Late adolescent and adult cognitive development* (pp. 258–271). New York: Praeger.

Association for Couples in Marriage Enrichment. (1995). *Standards for the training and certification of leader couples for marriage enrichment*. Winston-Salem, NC: Author.

Aulette, J. R. (1994). *Changing families*. Belmont, CA: Wadsworth.

Avery, C. E. (1962). Inside family life education. *The Family Life Coordinator, 11*(2), 27–39.

Avery, C. E., & Lee, M. R. (1964). Family life education: Its philosophy and purpose. *The Family Life Coordinator, 13*(2), 27–37.

Bader, E., Microys, G., Sinclair, C., Wilett, E., & Conway, B. (1980). Do marriage preparation programs really work? A Canadian experiment. *Journal of Marital and Family Therapy, 6*, 171–179.

Bahr, K. S. (1990). Student responses to genogram and family chronology. *Family Relations, 39*(3), 243–249.

Bahrick, H. P. (1984). Semantic memory content in permastore: Fifty years of memory for Spanish learned in school. *Journal of Experimental Psychology: General, 113*, 1–35.

Baldwin, K. E. (1949). *The AHEA saga*. Washington, DC: American Home Economics Association.

Bales, R., & Cohen, S. (1979). *SYMLOG: A system for multiple level observation of groups*. New York: The Free Press.

Bales, R. F. (1950). *Interaction process analysis: A method for the study of small groups*. Reading, MA: Addison-Wesley.

Bandura, A. (1977). *Social learning theory*. Englewood Cliffs, NJ: Prentice-Hall.

Barbe, W. B. (1985). *Growing up learning.* Washington, DC: Acropolis Books.

Barozzi, R. L., & Engel, J. W. (1985). A survey of attitudes about family life education. *Social Casework, 66,* 106–110.

Bartley, P., & Loxton, C. (1991). *Plains women in the American West.* Cambridge, England: Cambridge University Press.

Baumrind, D. (1983). Rejoinder to Lewis's reinterpretation of parental firm control effects: Are authoritative families really harmonious? *Psychological Bulletin, 94,* 132–142.

Baumrind, D. (1991). Parenting styles and adolescent development. In R. M. Lerner, A. C. Petersen, & J. Brooks-Gunn (Eds.), *Encyclopedia of adolescence* (Vol. 2, pp. 746–758). New York: Garland.

Bearinger, L. H. (1990). Study group report on the impact of television on adolescent views of sexuality. *Journal of Adolescent Health Care, 11*(1), 71–75.

Beebe, S. A., & Masterson, T. (1990). *Communicating in small groups: Principles and practices.* Glenview, IL: Scott, Foresman and Little, Brown.

Beecher, C. E. (1858). *A treatise on domestic economy* (3rd ed.). New York: Harper & Brothers.

Berger, R., & DeMaria, R. (1999). Epilogue: The future of preventive interventions with couples. In R. Berger & M. T. Hannah (Eds.), *Preventive approaches in couples therapy* (pp. 391–428). Philadelphia, PA: Brunner/Mazel.

Berger, R., & Hannah, M. T. (1999). Introduction. In R. Berger & M. T. Hannah (Eds.), *Preventive approaches in couples therapy* (pp. 1–24). Philadelphia, PA: Brunner/Mazel.

Berne, E. (1963). *The structure and dynamics of organizations and groups.* New York: Grove Press.

Bertalanffy, L. V. (1950). An outline of general system theory. *British Journal of the Philosophy of Science, 1,* 134–165.

Bertcher, H. J., & Maple, F. F. (1996). *Creating groups* (2nd ed.). Thousand Oaks, CA: Sage.

Bion, W. R. (1961). *Experience in groups.* New York: Basic Books.

Bogenschneider, K. (1996). An ecological risk/protective theory for building prevention programs, policies, and community capacity to support youth. *Family Relations, 45,* 127–138.

Botwinick, J. (1967). *Cognitive processes in maturity and old age.* New York: Springer.

Bowman, T. (1990a, September). Group methods for dealing with grief and loss. Reflections from a group leader's notebook (Material and Methods section), 43–45. *Family Information Services Professional Resource Materials.* Minneapolis, MN: Family Information Services.

Bowman, T. (1990b, November). Striving for congruency: Matching intentions, words and methods. Reflections from a group leader's notebook (Material and Methods section), 67–69. *Family Information Services Professional Resource Materials.* Minneapolis, MN: Family Information Services.

Bowman, T. (1991a, March). The importance of rituals and traditions for group life. Reflections from a group leader's notebook (Material and Methods section), 15–17. *Family Information Services Professional Resource Materials.* Minneapolis, MN: Family Information Services.

Bowman, T. (1991b, November). Sharing the wisdom. Reflections from a group leader's notebook (Material and Methods section), 58–59. *Family Information Services Professional Resource Materials.* Minneapolis, MN: Family Information Services.

Bowman, T. (1993, March). Encouraging full participation. Reflections from a group leader's notebook (Material and Methods section), 58–59. *Family Information Services Professional Resource Materials.* Minneapolis, MN: Family Information Services.

Bowman, T. (1994a, January). Matchmaking: The variety of needs and learning styles. Reflections from a group leader's notebook (Material and Methods section), 1–4. *Family Information Services Professional Resource Materials.* Minneapolis, MN: Family Information Services.

Bowman, T. (1994b, May). Bad hair days and the group leader. Reflections from a group leader's notebook (Material and Methods section), 27–29. *Family Information Services Professional Resource Materials.* Minneapolis, MN: Family Information Services.

Bowman, T. (1995a, January). Dealing with surprises in groups: The pinch model. Reflections from a group leader's notebook (Material and Methods section), 1–3. *Family Information Services Professional Resource Materials.* Minneapolis, MN: Family Information Services.

Bowman, T. (1995b, March). Dancing together: Experiential group processes. Reflections from a group leader's notebook (Material and Methods section), 17–18. *Family Information Services Professional Resource Materials*. Minneapolis, MN: Family Information Services.

Bowman, T. (1995c, September). Bifocals: An asset for group leaders. Reflections from a group leader's notebook (Material and Methods section), 44–46. *Family Information Services Professional Resource Materials*. Minneapolis, MN: Family Information Services.

Bowman, T. (1995d, November). Beginning and ending with effective closure. Reflections from a group leader's notebook (Material and Methods section), 60–61. *Family Information Services Professional Resource Materials*. Minneapolis, MN: Family Information Services.

Bredehoft, D., & Cassidy, D. (Eds.). (1995). *College and university curriculum guidelines in Family Life Education Curriculum Guidelines* (2nd ed., pp. 12–14). Minneapolis, MN: National Council on Family Relations.

Bridgeman, R. P. (1930). Ten years' progress in parent education. *Annals of the American Academy of Political and Social Science, 151*, 32–45.

Brim, O. (1959). *Education for child rearing*. New York: Russell Sage Foundation.

Briscoe, D. (2000, February 10). Millions of Americans going hungry [Press release]. Washington, DC: Associated Press.

Brock, G. (1993). Ethical guidelines for the practice of family life education. *Family Relations, 42*(2), 124–127.

Brock, G. W., Oertwein, M., & Coufal, J. D. (1993). Parent education theory, research, and practice. In M. E. Arcus, J. D. Schvaneveldt, & J. J Moss (Eds.), *Handbook of family life education* (Vol. 2). Newbury Park, CA: Sage.

Bronfenbrenner, U. (1979). *The ecology of human development*. Cambridge, MA: Harvard University Press.

Brooks, J. (1994). *Parenting in the 90s*. Mountain View, CA: Mayfield.

Brown, J. (1995). *Sex and the mass media*. Menlo Park, CA: Kaiser Family Foundation.

Brown, L. M., & Gilligan, C. (1992). *Meeting at the crossroads: Women's psychology and girls' development*. Cambridge, MA: Harvard University Press.

Bubolz, M. M., & Sontag, M. S. (1993). Human ecology theory. In P. G. Boss, W. J. Doherty, R. LaRossa, S. K. Steinmetz, & W. R. Schumm (Eds.), *Sourcebook of family theories and methods: A contextual approach* (pp. 419–448). New York: Plenum.

Burgess, E., Locke, H. J., & Thomas, M. M. (1971). *The family* (4th ed.). New York: Van Nostrand Reinhold.

Burgess, E. W. (1926). The family as a unit of interacting personalities. *The Family, 7*, 3–9.

Burr, W. R., Day, R. D., & Bahr, K. S. (1993). *Family science*. Belmont, CA: Brooks/Cole.

Burrill, M. (1999). *The role of religious congregations in fostering adolescent sexual health* [On-line]. Available: Religious Coalition for Reproductive Choice. http://www.rcrc.org. (March 2000).

Carrera, M. A. (1995). Preventing adolescent pregnancy: In hot pursuit. *SIECUS Report, 23*(6), 16–19.

Carter, N. (1996). *See how we grow: A report on the status of parenting education in the U.S.* Philadelphia, PA: Pew Charitable Trusts.

Chess, S., & Thomas, A. (1987). Babies are different from the start: Temperament and its significance. *Know your child*. New York: Basic Books.

Child Trends. (1996). *Facts at a glance*. Washington, DC: Author.

Clark, J. E., Lanphear, A. K., & Riddick, C. C. (1987). The effects of videogame playing on the response selection processing of elderly adults. *Journal of Gerontology, 42*, 82–85.

Cole, C. L., & Cole, A. L. (1999). Marriage enrichment and prevention really works: Interpersonal competence training to maintain and enhance relationships. *Family Relations, 48*, 273–275.

Cole, S. (1979). Age and scientific performance. *American Journal of Sociology, 84*, 958–977.

Coles, R. (1997). *The moral intelligence of children*. New York: Random House.

Columbia School of Public Health. (1996). *One in four: America's youngest poor*. New York: Author.

Cooke, B. (1991, March). Family program evaluation basics. *Family Information Services Professional Resource Materials*, 10–14. Minneapolis, MN: Family Information Services.

Crain, W. (2000). *Theories of development: Concepts and applications* (4th ed.). Englewood Cliffs, NJ: Prentice-Hall.

Crary, E. (1996). *Parenting education network*. Boston, MA: Wheelock College.

Cromwell, B. E., & Thomas, V. L. (1976). Developing resources for family potential: A family action model. *The Family Coordinator, 25*, 13–20.

Czaplewski, M. J., & Jorgensen, S. R. (1993). The professionalization of family life education. In M. E. Arcus, J. D. Schvaneveldt, & J. J. Moss (Eds.), *Handbook of family life education* (Vol. 1, pp. 51–75). Newbury Park, CA: Sage.

Dail, P. W. (1984). Constructing a philosophy of family life education: Educating the educators. *Family Perspective, 18*(4), 145–149.

Daley, D. (1996). Fact sheet on sexuality education. *SIECUS Report, 24*(6).

Darling, C. A. (1987). Family life education. In M. B. Sussman & S. K. Steinmetz (Eds.), *Handbook of marriage and the family* (pp. 815–833). New York: Plenum.

Darling, C. A., & Cassidy, D. (1998). Professional development of students: Understanding the process of becoming a Certified Family Life Educator. *Family Science Review, 11,* 106–118.

Datan, N., Rodeheaver, D., & Hughes, F. (1987). Adult development and aging. *Annual Review of Psychology, 38,* 153–180.

de la Vega, E. (1990). Considerations for reaching the Latino population with sexuality and HIV/AIDS information and education. *SIECUS Report, 18*(3), 1–8.

Derman-Sparks, L. (1989). *Anti-bias curriculum: Tools for empowering young children.* Washington, DC: National Association for the Education of Young Children, ABC Task Force.

Dickinson, H. E. (1950). *The origin and development of the aims of family life education in American secondary schools.* Unpublished doctoral dissertation, George Peabody College for Teachers, Nashville, TN.

Dinkmeyer, D., & McKay, G. (1976). *Systematic training for effective parenting: Parent's handbook.* Circle Pines, MN: American Guidance Service.

Doherty, W. J. (1995). Boundaries between parent and family education and family therapy: The levels of family involvement model. *Family Relations, 44*(4), 353–358.

Doyle, R. E. (1992). *Essential skills and strategies in the helping process.* Pacific Grove, CA: Brooks/Cole.

Dreikurs, R. (1964). *Children: The challenge.* New York: New York Books.

Duvall, E. M. (1950). *Family living.* New York: Macmillan.

Duvall, E. M. (1957). *Family development.* Philadelphia: Lippincott.

Duvall, E. M. (1977). *Marriage and family development* (5th ed.). New York: Lippincott.

Duvall, E. M., & Hill, R. (1945). *When you marry.* New York: Heath.

Duvall, E. M., & Miller, B. C. (1985). *Marriage and family development* (6th ed.). New York: Harper & Row.

Dyer, P. M., & Dyer, G. H. (1989). *Marriage enrichment process, methods, and techniques.* Winston-Salem, NC: Association for Couples in Marriage Enrichment.

Dyer, P. M., & Dyer, G. H. (1999). Marriage enrichment, A.C.M.E.-style. In R. Berger & M. T. Hannah (Eds.), *Preventive approaches in couples therapy.* Philadelphia: Brunner/Mazel.

Early Childhood Family Education Demonstration Site Coordinators. (1997). *Manual for implementing Levels 3 and 4 family involvement in early childhood education.* St. Paul, MN: Minnesota Department of Children, Families, and Learning.

East, M. (1980). *Home economics: Past, present and future.* Boston: Allyn & Bacon.

Elin, R. J. (1999). Marriage encounter: A positive preventive enrichment program. In R. Berger & M. T. Hannah (Eds.), *Preventive approaches in couples therapy* (pp. 55–71). Philadelphia: Brunner/Mazel.

Elkind, D. (1987). *Miseducation: Preschoolers at risk.* New York: Knopf.

Engel, J. W., Saracino, M., & Bergen, M. B. (1993). Sexuality education. In M. E. Arcus, J. D. Schvaneveldt, & J. J. Moss (Eds.), *Handbook of family life education* (Vol. 2). Newbury Park, CA: Sage.

Families and Schools Together (1999). Supporting the natural strength of families: A proven approach to success with at-risk kids. In *Circles of support for stronger families* (pp. 1–2). Milwaukee, WI: Alliance for Children & Families.

Family Service Association of America. (1976). *Overview of findings of the FSAA Task Force on family life education, development, and enrichment.* New York: Author.

Felton, R. L. (1919). *Country life in Georgia in the days of my youth.* Atlanta: Index Printing.

Figueroa, D., & Hanock-Jasie, L. (1999, June 2). *Public support for sexuality education reaches highest level* [On-line]. Available: http://www.siecus.org/media/press/press0005.html (June 24, 1999).

Finkelhor, D. (1984). The prevention of child sexual abuse: An overview of needs and problems. *SIECUS Report, 13*(1), 1–5.

Fisher, B. A. (1975). Communication study in systems perspective. In B. Rubin & J. Y. Kim (Eds.), *General systems theory and human communication.* Rochelle Park, NJ: Hayden Press.

Fisher, B. L., & Kerckhoff, R. K. (1981). Family life education: Generating cohesion out of chaos. *Family Relations, 30,* 505–509.

Fletcher, M. A. (1999, July 2). For better or worse, marriage hits a low. *The Washington Post,* p. A01.

Fohlin, M. B. (1971). Selection and training of teachers for life education programs. *The Family Coordinator, 20,* 231–240.

Forrest, J. D., & Silverman, J. (1989). What public school teachers teach about preventing pregnancy, AIDS and sexually transmitted diseases. *Family Planning Perspectives, 21*(2), 65–72.

Frank, L. K. (1962). The beginnings of child development and family life education in the twentieth century. *Merrill-Palmer Quarterly of Behavior and Development, 8,* 207–227.

Franklin, B. (2000, February). America's poorest people have no place to go. *The Washington Spectator, 26*(3), 1–3.

Freeman, N. K. (1997, September). Using NAEYC's Code of Ethics: Mama and daddy taught me right from wrong. Isn't that enough? *Young Children, 52*(6), 64–67.

Freire, P. (1970). *Cultural action for freedom* (Monograph Series No. 1). Cambridge, MA: Harvard Educational Review.

Fresh look at population (1998, December). *Kiplinger Washington Letter, 75*(52), 1–4.

Friedman, Z. P. (1986, January). Work-family seminars: Help for the home front. *American Way,* 30–33.

Frost, J. J., & Forrest, J. D. (1995). Understanding the impact of effective teenage pregnancy prevention programs. *Family Planning Perspectives, 25*(5), 188–196.

Gambrell, A., & Haffner, D. (1993). *Unfinished business: A SIECUS assessment of state sexuality education programs.* New York: Sex Information and Education Council of the U.S.

Garland, D. R., & Yankeelov, P. A. (1998). The church census: A congregational assessment tool for family ministry. *Family Ministry, 12*(3), 11–22.

Gibb, J. R. (1961). Defensive communication. *Journal of Communication, 2,* 141–148.

Giblin, P., Sprenkle, D. H., & Sheehan, R. (1985). Enrichment outcome research: A meta-analysis of premarital, marital and family interventions. *Journal of Marital and Family Therapy, 11,* 257–271.

Gilgun, J. F., & Gordon, S. (1985). Sex education and the prevention of child sexual abuse. *Journal of Sex Education and Therapy, 11*(1), 46–52.

Gilligan, C., Taylor, J., & Ward, J. (Eds.). (1988). *Mapping the moral domain.* Cambridge, MA: Harvard University Press.

Gleason, J., & Prescott, M. (1977). Group techniques for premarital preparation. *Family Coordinator, 26,* 277–280.

Glenn, N. D. (1991). The recent trend in marital success in the United States. *Journal of Marriage and the Family, 53,* 261–270.

Goetz, K. (Ed.). (1992). *Programs to strengthen families: A resource guide.* Chicago: Family Resource Coalition.

Gordon, T. (1975). *Parent effectiveness training.* Bergenfield, NJ: Penguin.

Gottman, J. M., Coan, J., Carrere, S., & Swanson, C. (1998). Predicting marital happiness and stability from newlywed interactions. *Journal of Marriage and Family, 60,* 5–22.

Gottman, J. M., & Gottman, J. S. (1999). The Marriage Survival Kit: A research-based marital therapy. In R. Berger & M. T. Hannah (Eds.), *Preventive approaches in couples therapy* (pp. 304–330). Philadelphia: Brunner/Mazel.

Graham, L., & Harris-Hart, M. (1988). Meeting the challenge of child sexual abuse. *Journal of School Health, 58*(7), 292–294.

Graham, L., & Harris-Hart, M. (1989). *Child sexual abuse prevention programs.* Ottawa, Ontario, Canada: National Clearinghouse on Family Violence, Health and Welfare.

Gregorc, A. F. (1982). *An adult's guide to style.* Columbia, CT: Author. (Available from Learning Styles Unlimited, Inc., 1911 S.W. Campus Drive, Suite 370, Federal Way, WA 98023)

Griggs, M. B. (1981). Criteria for the evaluation of family life education materials. *Family Relations, 30*(4), 549–555.

Gross, P. (1985). *On family life education: For family life educators* (2nd ed., rev.). Montreal, Quebec,

Canada: Concordia University Centre for Human Relations and Community Studies.

Gross, P. (1993). *On family life education: For family life educators* (3rd ed., rev.). Montreal, Quebec, Canada: Concordia University Centre for Human Relations and Community Studies.

Groves, E. R., & Groves, G. H. (1947). *The contemporary American family.* Chicago: Lippincott.

Grunseit, A., & Kippax, S. (1993). Effects of sex education on young people's sexual behaviour. Unpublished manuscript, World Health Organization.

Guerney, B. G., Jr. (1977). *Relationship enhancement: Skill training programs for therapy, problem prevention, and enrichment.* San Francisco: Jossey-Bass.

Guerney, B. G., Jr., Brock, G., & Coufal, J. (1986). Integrating marital therapy and enrichment: The relationship enhancement approach. In N. S. Jacobson & A. S. Gurman (Eds.), *Clinical handbook of marital therapy* (pp. 151–172). New York: Guilford Press.

Guerney, B. G., & Maxson, P. (1990). Marital and family enrichment research: A decade review and look ahead. *Journal of Marriage and the Family, 52,* 1127–1137.

Haffner, D. (1990). Moving toward a healthy paradigm of teen development: Helping young people develop into sexually healthy adults. *SIECUS Report, 18*(4), 12–14.

Haffner, D. (1995). Facing facts: Sexual health for America's adolescents. The report of the National Commission on Adolescent Sexual Health. *SIECUS Report, 23*(6), 2–8.

Haffner, D. W., & Goldfarb, E. S. (1997). But does it work? Improving evaluations of sexuality education. *SIECUS Report, 25*(6), 2–15.

Haffner, D. W., & Kelly, M. (1987). Adolescent sexuality in the media. *SIECUS Report, 15*(4), 9–12.

Hamner, T. J., & Turner, P. H. (1990). *Parenting in contemporary society* (2nd ed.). Englewood Cliffs, NJ: Prentice-Hall.

Harman, D., & Brim, O. G., Jr. (1980). *Learning to be parents: Principles, programs, and methods.* Beverly Hills, CA: Sage.

Harris, J. R. (1998). *The nurture assumption: Why children turn out the way they do.* New York: Free Press.

Harris, L. (1986). *American teens speak.* New York: Planned Parenthood Federation of America.

Harris, L. (1988). *America speaks: Americans' opinion on teenage pregnancy, sex education and birth control.*

New York: Planned Parenthood Federation of America.

Heath, H. (1995, March 25). "Defining parenting education." [On-line]. *National Parenting Educators Network Listserv.* Available: npen-l@postoffice. cso.uiuc.edu.

Heighway, S. (1989). Promoting healthy sexual development for adolescents with developmental disabilities or chronic illnesses. *SIECUS Report, 18*(1), 4–5.

Herold, E. S., Kopf, K. E., & deCarlo, M. (1974). Family life education: Student perspectives. *Canadian Journal of Public Health, 65,* 365–368.

HHS Poverty Guidelines, 64 Fed. Reg. 13428 (1999).

Hildreth, G. J., & Sugawara, A. I. (1993). Ethnicity and diversity in family life education. In M. E. Arcus, J. D. Schvaneveldt, & J. J. Moss (Eds.), *Handbook of family life education* (Vol. 1, pp. 162–188). Newbury Park, CA: Sage.

Hill, R., & Rodgers, R. H. (1964). The developmental approach. In H. Christensen (Ed.), *Handbook of marriage and the family.* Chicago: Rand McNally.

Hof, L., & Miller, W. R. (1981). *Marriage enrichment: Philosophy, process, and program.* Bowie, MD: Robert J. Brady.

Homans, G. (1958). Social behavior as exchange. *American Journal of Sociology, 63,* 597–606.

Homans, G. C. (1961). *Social behavior: Its elementary forms.* New York: Harcourt Brace.

Howard, R. (1981). *A social history of American sociology, 1865–1940.* Westport, CT: Greenwood.

Howe, R. L. (1963). *The miracle of dialogue.* New York: Seabury Press.

Hughes, R., Jr. (1999). Program clarification: What are we really trying to do? *Human Development and Family Life Bulletin, 5*(1), 6–7. http://www.hec. ohiostate.edu/famlife/bulletin/volume.5/ bull51xxhtml.

Irwin, D. B., & Simons, J. A. (1994). *Lifespan developmental psychology.* Madison, WI: Brown & Benchmark.

Jacobs, F. H. (1988). The five-tiered approach to evaluation: Context and implementation. In H. B. Weiss & F. H. Jacobs (Eds.), *Evaluating family programs* (pp. 37–68). New York: Aldine DeGruyter.

Jaffeson, R. C. (1998, May). Continuing education credit. *Certification Communications, 53.*

Jemmott, J. B., III, Jemmott, L. S., & Fong, G. T. (1998). Abstinence and safer sex HIV risk-reduction interventions for African American adolescents:

A randomized controlled trial. *Journal of the American Medical Association, 279,* 1529–1536.

Joint Committee on Standards for Educational Evaluation. (1981). *Standards for evaluation of educational programs, projects, and materials.* New York: McGraw-Hill.

Kagan, J., & Snidman, N. (1991). Temperamental factors in human development. *American Psychologist, 46*(8), 856–862.

Kaiser Family Foundation (1998). *National survey of teens: Teens talk about dating, intimacy, and their sexual experiences.* Menlo Park, CA: Author.

Kastenbaum, R. J. (1984). When aging begins: A lifespan developmental approach. *Research on Aging, 6,* 105–117.

Kelly, A. B., & Fincham, F. D. (1999). Preventing marital distress: What does research offer? In R. Berger & M. T. Hannah (Eds.), *Preventive approaches in couples therapy* (pp. 361–390). Philadelphia: Brunner/Mazel.

Kelly, C., Huston, T., & Cate, R. (1985). Premarital relationship correlates of the erosion of satisfaction in marriage. *Journal of Social and Personal Relationships, 2,* 167–178.

Kerckhoff, R. K. (1964). Family life education in America. In H. T. Christiansen (Ed.), *Handbook of marriage and the family* (pp. 881–911). Chicago: Rand McNally.

Kids Count Special Report. (1998). *When teens have sex: Issues and trends.* Baltimore: Annie E. Casey Foundation.

Kilpatrick, A. C., & Holland, T. P. (1995). *Working with families: An integrative model by level of functioning.* Boston: Allyn & Bacon.

Kirby, D. (1994). Sex education in the schools. In J. A. Garrison, M. D. Smith, & D. J. Besharov (Eds.), *Sexuality and American school policy.* Menlo Park, CA: Kaiser Family Foundation.

Kirby, D. (1997). *No easy answers: Research findings on programs to reduce teen pregnancy* [Summary]. Washington, DC: National Campaign to Reduce Teen Pregnancy.

Kirby, D., Short, L., Collins, J., Rugg, D., Kolbe, L., Howard, M., Miller, B., Sonenstein, F., & Zabin, L. S. (1994). School-based programs to reduce sexual risk behaviors: A review of effectiveness. *Public Health Reports, 109*(3), 339–360.

Kirkendall, L. A. (1973). Education for marriage and family life. In A. Ellis & A. Abarbanel (Eds.), *The encyclopedia of sexual behavior* (2nd ed.). New York: Hawthorne.

Kirkendall, L. A. (1984). The journey toward SIECUS: 1964, a personal odyssey. *SIECUS Report, 12*(4), 1–4.

Knowles, M. (1989). *The making of an adult educator.* San Francisco: Jossey-Bass.

Kohlberg, L. (1984). *Psychology of moral development.* New York: Harper & Row.

Kolb, D. A. (1984). *Experiential learning: Experience as the source of learning and development.* Englewood Cliffs, NJ: Prentice-Hall.

Krivacska, J. J. (1991). Child sexual abuse prevention programs: The need for childhood sexuality education. *SIECUS Report, 19*(6), 1–7.

Krueger, M. M. (1991). The omnipresent need: Professional training for sexuality education teachers. *SIECUS Report, 19*(4), 1–5.

L'Abate, L. (1981). Skill training programs for couples and families. In A. S. Gurman & D. P. Kniskern (Eds.), *Handbook of family therapy* (pp. 631–661). New York: Brunner/Mazel.

L'Abate, L. (1983). Prevention as a profession: Toward a new conceptual frame of reference. In D. R. Mace (Ed.), *Prevention in family services: Approaches to family therapy and counseling* (pp. 46–52). Beverly Hills, CA: Sage.

L'Abate, L. (1986). *Systematic family therapy.* New York: Brunner/Mazel.

L'Abate, L. (1999). Structured enrichment and distance writing for couples. In R. Berger & M. T. Hannah (Eds.), *Preventive approaches in couples therapy* (pp. 106–124). Philadelphia: Brunner/Mazel.

Labouvie-Vief, G. (1986). Modes of knowledge and the organization of development. In M. L. Commons, L. Kohlberg, F. Richards, & J. Stinnott (Eds.), *Beyond formal operations: Models and methods in the study of adult and adolescent thought.* New York: Praeger.

Lapsley, D. G. (1989). Continuity and discontinuity in adolescent social cognitive development. In R. Montemayor, G. Adams, & T. Gullota (Eds.), *Advances in adolescence research* (Vol. 2). Orlando, FL: Academic Press.

Lee, D. A., & Fong, K. (1990). HIV/AIDS and the Asian and Pacific Islander community. *SIECUS Report, 18*(3), 16–19.

Lee, M. R. (1963). How do experts define "family life education"? *The Family Life Coordinator, 12*(3–4), 105–106.

Leiberman, M. E., Yalom, I. D., & Miles, M. B. (1973). *Encounter groups: First facts.* New York: Basic Books.

Leveat, R. F. (Ed.). (1986). *Psychoeducational approaches to family therapy and counseling.* New York: Springer-Verlag.

Levin, E. (1975). Development of a family life education program in a community social service agency. *The Family Coordinator, 24,* 343–349.

Lewin, K., Lippitt, R., & White, R. (1939). Patterns of aggressive behavior in experimentally created "social climates." *Journal of Social Psychology, 10,* 271–299.

Lewis, J. M., Beavers, W. R., Gossett, J. T., & Phillips, V. A. (1976). *No single thread: Psychological health in family systems.* New York: Brunner/Mazel.

Lewis-Rowley, M., Brasher, R. E., Moss, J. J., Duncan, S. F., & Stiles, R. J. (1993). The evolution of education for family life. In M. E. Arcus, J. D. Schvaneveldt, & J. J. Moss (Eds.), *Handbook of family life education* (Vol. 1, pp. 26–50). Newbury Park: Sage.

Littell, J. H. (1986). *Building strong foundations: Evaluation strategies for family resource programs.* Chicago: Family Resource Coalition.

Mace, D. (1970). *The Christian response to the sexual revolution.* Nashville: Abingdon Press.

Mace, D. (1981). The long, long trail from information-giving to behavioral change. *Family Relations, 30,* 599–606.

Mace, D. (1982). *Close companions: The marriage enrichment handbook.* New York: Continuum Publishing.

Mace, D. R. (Ed.). (1983). *Prevention in family services: Approaches to family wellness.* Beverly Hills, CA: Sage.

Mace, D. R., & Mace, V. (1974). *We can have better marriages.* Nashville, TN: Abingdon.

Mace, D. R., & Mace, V. (1975). Marriage enrichment: Wave of the future? *The Family Coordinator, 24,* 171–173.

Mace, D. R., & Mace, V. (1976). Marriage enrichment: A preventive group approach for couples. In D. H. L. Olson (Ed.), *Treating relationships* (pp. 321–338). Lake Mills, IA: Graphic.

Markey, B., & Micheletto, M. (1997). *FOCCUS facilitator manual* (2nd ed.). Omaha, NE: Archdiocese of Omaha, Family Life Office.

Markman, H. J. (1979). The application of a behavioral model of marriage in predicting relationship satisfaction of couples planning marriage. *Journal of Consulting and Clinical Psychology, 47,* 743–749.

Markman, H. J. (1981). Predicting marital distress: A 5-year follow-up. *Journal of Consulting and Clinical Psychology, 49,* 173–196.

Markman, H. J., Floyd, F. J., Stanley, S. M., & Lewis, H. (1986). Prevention. In H. Jacobson & A. Gruman (Eds.), *Clinical handbook of marital therapy* (pp. 173–196). New York: Guilford Press.

Markman, H. J., Floyd, F. J., Stanley, S. M., & Storaasli, R. D. (1988). Prevention of marital distress: A longitudinal investigation. *Journal of Consulting and Clinical Psychology, 56,* 210–217.

Markman, H., Stanley, S., & Blumberg, S. L. (1994). *Fighting for your marriage.* San Francisco: Jossey-Bass.

Maslow, A. (1959). Creativity in self-actualizing people. In H. H. Anderson (Ed.), *Creativity and its cultivation.* New York: Harper & Row.

Mattessich, P., & Hill, R. (1987). Life cycle and family development. In M. B. Sussman & S. K. Steinmetz (Eds.), *Handbook of marriage and the family.* New York: Plenum Press.

McAdoo, J. L. (1993). Decision making and marital satisfaction in African American families. In H. P. McAdoo (Ed.), *Family ethnicity: Strength in diversity.* Newbury Park, CA: Sage.

McConnell, E. (1970, September). The history of home economics. *Forecast for Home Economics, 86–87,* 134.

McGilly, K., & Siegler, R. S. (1989). How children choose among serial recall strategies. *Child Development, 60,* 172–182.

Mead, M. (1985). Is sex necessary? *SIECUS Report, 13*(3), 5–6. (Reprinted from *SIECUS Newsletter,* February 1969)

Medina, C. (1987). Latino culture and sex education. *SIECUS Report, 15*(3), 1–4.

Miles, M. B. (1981). *Learning to work in groups.* New York: Columbia University, Teacher's College Press.

Miller, B. C. (1998). *Families matter: A research synthesis of family influences on adolescent pregnancy.* Washington, DC: National Campaign to Prevent Teen Pregnancy.

Miller, J. P., & Seller, W. (1990). *Curriculum perspectives and practices.* New York: Longman.

Miller, S. L., Miller, P. A., Nunnally, E. W., & Wackman, D. B. (1992). *Couple communication instructor manual.* Denver, CO: Interpersonal Communication Programs.

Miller, S. L., Nunnally, E. W., & Wackman, D. B. (1975). *Alive and aware.* Minneapolis, MN: Interpersonal Communications.

Miller, S., & Sherrard, P. A. D. (1999). Couple Communication: A system for equipping partners to talk, listen, and resolve conflicts effectively. In R. Berger & M. T. Hannah (Eds.), *Preventive approaches in couples therapy* (pp. 125–148). Philadelphia: Brunner/Mazel.

Minnesota Council on Family Relations. (1997). *Ethical thinking and practice for parent and family educators.* Minneapolis, MN: Ethics Committee, Parent and Family Education Section.

Minnesota Department of Children, Families, and Learning. (2000). *Minnesota State Board of Teaching adopted permanent rules relating to teaching licensing of parent and family educators* [On-line]. Available: http://cfl.state.mn.us/teachbrd/8710_3100.html.

Moore, K. A. (1995). *Adolescent pregnancy prevention programs: Interventions and evaluations.* Washington, DC: Child Trends.

Moreno, J. L. (1953). *Who shall survive?* (Rev. ed.). Beacon, NY: Beacon Press.

Moss, J. J., & King, K. F. (1970). Involving students for productive learning in marriage and family living classes. *The Family Coordinator, 19,* 78–82.

Mudd, E., Freeman, C., & Rose, E. (1941). Premarital counseling in the Philadelphia marriage counsel. *Mental Hygiene, 25*(1), 98–119.

Murray, T. R. (1992). *Comparing theories of child development* (3rd ed.). Belmont, CA: Wadsworth.

Myers-Walls, J. (1997, November 25). "Competencies." [On-line]. *Talk About Parent Education.* Available: pareduc@extension.unm.edu.

Myers-Walls, J. (1998). *What is your parent education approach?* Lafayette, IN: Purdue University Cooperative Extension Service.

Napier, R. W., & Gershenfeld, M. K. (1983). *Making groups work: A guide for group leaders.* Boston: Houghton Mifflin.

National Campaign to Prevent Teen Pregnancy Report. (1998). *Snapshots from the front line: 2. Lessons from programs that involve parents and other adults in preventing teen pregnancy.* Washington, DC: National Campaign Publications.

National Center for Health Statistics. (1996). *Advance report of final divorce statistics, 1989 and 1990.* Hyattsville, MD: Author.

National Center for Health Statistics. (1998). *Teen births in the United States: State trends, 1991–1996, an update.* Washington, DC: U.S. Department of Health and Human Services, Centers for Disease Control and Prevention.

National Commission on Children. (1991a). *Beyond rhetoric: A new American agenda for children and their families.* Washington, DC: Author.

National Commission on Children. (1991b). *Speaking of kids: A national survey of children and parents.* Washington, DC: Author.

National Commission on Family Life Education. (1968). Family life education programs: Principles, plans, procedures. A framework for family life educators. *The Family Coordinator, 17,* 211–214.

National Council on Family Relations. (1995a). *Ethical principles and guidelines.* Minneapolis, MN: Author.

National Council on Family Relations. (1995b). *Family life education curriculum guidelines.* Minneapolis, MN: Author.

National Council on Family Relations (1997a). *Framework for life-span family life education* (Rev. ed.). Minneapolis, MN: Author.

National Council on Family Relations. (1997b). *Standards and criteria for the certification of family life educators, college/university curriculum guidelines, and content guidelines for family life education: A framework for planning programs over the life span* (Rev. ed.). St. Paul, MN: Author.

National Council on Family Relations. (1999). *Tools for ethical thinking and practice in family life education.* Minneapolis, MN: Author.

National Marriage Project (1999). *The state of our unions, 1999.* New Brunswick, NJ: Author.

National Native American AIDS Prevention Center. (1990). *We owe it to ourselves and to our children.* Oakland, CA: Author.

Office of Technology Assessment. (1986). Indian health care (Publication No. OTA-H-290). Washington, DC: U.S. Government Printing Office.

Olson, D. H. (1999). *Building relationships: Developing skills for life* [On-line]. Available: http://www.life innovation.com.

Olson, D. H. (Ed.). (1976). *Treating relationships.* Lake Mills, IA: Graphic.

Olson, D. H. (1983). How effective is marriage preparation? In D. R. Mace (Ed.), *Prevention in family services* (pp. 196–216). Beverly Hills, CA: Sage.

Olson, D. H. (1998). *PREPARE/ENRICH counselor's manual.* Minneapolis, MN: Life Innovations.

Olson, D. H., Dyer, P. M., & Dyer, G. H. (1998). *Growing together: Leader's manual.* Minneapolis, MN: Life Innovations.

Olson, D. H., & Olson, A. K. (1999). PREPARE/ENRICH program: Version 2000. In R. Berger & M. T. Hannah (Eds.), *Preventive approaches in couples therapy.* Philadelphia: Brunner/Mazel.

Overton, W. F., & Byrnes, J. P. (1991). Cognitive development. In R. M. Lerner, A. C. Petersen, & J. Brooks-Gunn (Eds.), *Encyclopedia of adolescence* (Vol.1). New York: Garland.

Palm, G. (1998, Spring). Ethical thinking and practice for family professionals. *Views,* 14–17.

Parker, F. J. (1980). *Home economics: An introduction to a dynamic profession.* New York: Macmillan.

Parrott, L., III, & Parrott, L. (1999). Preparing couples for marriage: The SYMBIS model. In R. Berger & M. T. Hannah (Eds.), *Preventive approaches in couples therapy* (pp. 237–254). Philadelphia: Brunner/Mazel.

Patton, M. Q. (1982). *Practical evaluation.* Beverly Hills, CA: Sage.

Peters, R. S. (1967). *The concept of education.* London: Routledge & Kegan Paul.

Peterson, D. A. (1985). A history of education for older learners. In D. B. Lumsden (Ed.), *The older adult as learner.* Washington, DC: Hemisphere.

Phinney, J. S. (1990). Ethnic identity in adolescents and adults: Review of research. *Psychological Bulletin, 108,* 499–514.

Ponzetti, J. (1995). An examination of certification in family science and home economics. *Family Science Review, 8*(1–2), 41–47.

Popkin, M. (1987). *Active parenting: Teaching courage, cooperation, and responsibility.* New York: Harper Collins.

Powell, J. (1969). *Why am I afraid to tell you who I am?* Niles, IL: Argus Communications.

Powell, L., & Jorgensen, S. (1985). Evaluation of a sex-education program for church youth. *Family Relations, 34*(4), 475–482.

Quigley, E. (1974). *Introduction to home economics* (2nd ed.). New York: Macmillan.

Quindlen, A. (1993). *Thinking out loud.* New York: Random House.

Rasmussen, W. D. (1989). *Taking the university to the people.* Ames: Iowa University Press.

Remafedi, G. (1992). Demography of sexual orientation in adolescents. *Pediatrics, 89,* 714–721.

Rettig, K. D. (1988, November*). A framework for integrating family relations and family resource management.* Paper presented at the workshop on Theory Construction and Research Methodology, National Council on Family Relations, Philadelphia.

Rodgers, R. H., & White, J. M. (1993). Family development theory. In P. G. Boss, W. J. Doherty, R. LaRossa, W. R. Schumm, & S. K. Steinmetz (Eds.). *Sourcebook of family theories and methods: A contextual approach* (pp. 225–254). New York: Plenum Press.

Rodman, H. (1970). *Teaching about families: Textbook evaluations and recommendations for secondary schools.* Cambridge, MA: Doyle.

Rodriquez, M., Young, R., Renfro, S., Asencio, M., & Haffner, D. (1996). Teaching our teachers to teach: A SIECUS study on training and preparation for HIV/AIDS prevention and sexuality education. *SIECUS Report, 24*(2), 15–23.

Ross, S., & Kantor, L. M. (1995). Trends in opposition to comprehensive sexuality education in public schools: 1994–1995 school year. *SIECUS Report, 23*(6), 9–15.

Rowell, R. M. (1990). Native Americans, stereotypes, and HIV/AIDS: Our continuing struggle for survival. *SIECUS Report, 18*(3), 9–15.

Rudrauff, A. (1999). Student-centered sex education. *Human Development and Family Life Bulletin, 4*(4), 4.

Ryerson, E. (1984). Sexual abuse and self-protection education for developmentally disabled youth: A priority need. *SIECUS Report, 13*(1), 6–7.

Saluter, A. F. (1994). *Marital status and living arrangements: March 1993* (Bureau of Census Current Population Reports, Series P20-478). Washington, DC: Government Printing Office.

Samuels, H. (1995). Sexology, sexosophy, and African-American sexuality. *SIECUS Report, 23*(3), 3–5.

Santrock, J. W. (1992). *Life-span development* (4th ed., rev.). Dubuque, IA: Brown.

Satir, V. (1972). *Peoplemaking.* Palo Alto, CA: Science and Behavior Books.

Satir, V. (1988). *The new peoplemaking.* Mountain View, CA: Science and Behavior Books.

Schaie, K. W. (1977/1978). Toward a stage theory of adult cognitive development. *International Journal of Aging and Human Development, 8*(2), 129–138.

Schaie, K. W. (1991). Developmental designs revisited. In S. H. Cohen & H. W. Reese (Eds.), *Life-span developmental psychology: Methodological innovation.* Hillsdale, NJ: Erlbaum.

Schickendanz, J., Schickendanz, D., Hansen, K., & Forsyth, P. (1993). *Understanding children.* Mountain View, CA: Mayfield.

Schlossman, S. L. (1976, August). Before home start: Notes toward a history of parent education in America, 1897–1929. *Harvard Educational Review, 46*(3), 436–467.

Schneider, D. M. (1980). *American kinship: A cultural account* (2nd ed.). Englewood Cliffs, NJ: Prentice-Hall.

Schultz, B. G. (1989). *Communicating in the small group: Theory and practice.* New York: Harper & Row.

Schultz, J. B. (1994, Summer). Family life education: Implications for home economics teachers education. *Journal of Home Economics, 30*–36.

Scott-Jones, D., & Peebles-Wilson, W. (1986). Sex equity in parenting and parent education. *Theory into Practice, 25*(4), 235–242.

Selverstone, R. (1989). Where are we now in the sexual revolution? *SIECUS Report, 17*(4), 7–12.

Settles, M. (1998). *Sexuality education and a needs assessment* [On-line]. Available: http://www.klingenstein. org/Additional_Resources/projects/settles.htm.

Shaw, M. E. (1981). *Group dynamics: The psychology of small group behavior* (3rd ed.). New York: McGraw-Hill.

Sheek, B. W. (1984). *A nation for families.* Washington, DC: American Home Economics Association.

Sherwood, J. J., & Scherer, J. J. (1975). A model for couples: How two can grow together. In S. Miller (Ed.), *Marriages and families: Enrichment through communication.* Beverly Hills, CA: Sage.

Shor, I., & Freire, P. (1986). *A pedagogy for liberation: Dialogues on transforming education.* South Hadley, MA: Bergin & Garvey.

SIECUS. (1998a). *SIECUS community action kit: Suggestions for community organizing* [On-line]. Available: http://www.SIECUS.org/pubs/kits/kits/0001.html.

SIECUS. (1998b). Fact sheet: Gay, lesbian, and bisexual adolescents. *SIECUS Report, 26*(4).

SIECUS. (1994). Teens talk about sex: Adolescent sexuality in the 90's. *SIECUS Report, 22*(5), 16–17.

SIECUS. (1997a). Fact sheet: Sexually transmitted diseases in the United States. *SIECUS Report, 25*(3).

SIECUS. (1997b). Fact sheet: The National Coalition to Support Sexuality Education. *SIECUS Report, 25*(4), 17–18.

SIECUS. (1997c). Fact sheet: Guidelines for comprehensive sexuality education, kindergarten–12th grade. *SIECUS Report, 25*(6).

Silliman, B., & Schumm, W. R. (1995). Client interests in premarital counseling: A further analysis. *Journal of Sex and Marital Therapy, 21*(1), 43.

Simonton, D. K. (1977). Creativity, age and stress. *Journal of Personality and Social Psychology, 35,* 791–804.

Simpson, G., & Yinger, J. (1985). *Racial and cultural minorities.* New York: Plenum Press.

Smith, C. A., Cudaback, D., Goddard, H. W., & Myers-Walls, J. A. (1998). *National Extension Parent Education Model: Of critical parenting practices* [On-line]. Available: http://www.cyfernet.mes.umn. edu/parenting_practices/preface.html.

Smith, I. (1999, September 13). Misjudged threat: The word about AIDS still needs to get out, especially among African Americans. *Time,* 88.

Smith, W. M., Jr. (1968). Family life education: Who needs it? *The Family Coordinator, 17,* 55–61.

Somerville, R. M. (1967). The relationship between family life education and sex education. *Journal of Marriage and the Family, 29,* 374–389.

Somerville, R. M. (1971). Family life education and sex education in the turbulent sixties. *Journal of Marriage and the Family, 33,* 11–35.

Special report: A conference stressing marital education over marital therapy. (1999, July). *Psychotherapy Finances, 1*(7), 6–10.

Sprafkin, J. N., & Silverman, L. T. (1981, Winter). Update: Physically intimate and sexual behavior on prime-time television, 1978–1979. *Journal of Communication.*

Stahmann, R., & Hiebert, W. (1987). *Premarital counseling: The professional's handbook* (2nd ed.). Lexington, MA: Lexington.

Stahmann, R., & Salts, C. (1993). Educating for marriage and intimate relationships. In M. E. Arcus, J. D. Schvaneveldt, & J. J. Moss (Eds.), *Handbook of family life education* (Vol. 2, pp. 33–61). Newbury Park, CA: Sage.

Stanley, S. M., Blumberg, S. L., & Markman, H. J. (1999). Helping couples fight for their marriages: The PREP approach. In R. Berger & M. T. Hannah (Eds.), *Preventive approaches in couples therapy.* Philadelphia: Brunner/Mazel, pp. 279–303.

Stern, E. E. (1969). Family life education: Some rationales and contents. *The Family Coordinator, 18,* 39–43.

Sternberg, R. J. (1988). Mental self-government: A theory of intellectual styles and their development. *Human Development, 31,* 197–224.

Strong, B., & DeVault, C. (1998). *The marriage and family experience: Intimate relationships in a changing society.* Belmont, CA: Wadsworth.

Taylor, R. (1994). Minority families in America: An introduction. In R. L. Taylor (Ed.), *Minority families in the United States: A multicultural perspective* (pp. 1–16). Englewood Cliffs, NJ: Prentice-Hall.

Telljohann, S. K., & Price, J. H. (1993). A qualitative examination of adolescent homosexual's life experiences: Ramifications for secondary school personnel. *Journal of Homosexuality, 26*(1), 48.

Tennant, J. (1989). Family life education: Identity, objectives, and future directions. *McGill Journal of Education, 24,* 127–142.

Texas Registry of Parent Educator Resources. (2000). *Core knowledge for parents and professionals who work with families.* Denton, TX: University of North Texas Center for Parent Education.

Thibaut, J. W., & Kelley, H. H. (1959). *The social psychology of groups.* New York: Wiley.

Thomas, J. (1988, November). *Theoretical perspectives of curriculum in family life education: Implications for practice.* Paper presented at the annual meeting of the National Council on Family Relations, Philadelphia.

Thomas, J., & Arcus, M. (1992). Family life education: An analysis of the concept. *Family Relations, 41,* 3–8.

Thomas, J., Schvaneveldt, J. D., & Young, M. H. (1993). Programs in family life education: Development, implementation, and evaluation. In M. E. Arcus, J. D. Schvaneveldt, & J. J. Moss (Eds.), *Handbook of family life education* (Vol. 1). Newbury Park, CA: Sage.

Torstendahl, R., & Burrage, M. (1990). *The formation of professions: Knowledge, state and strategy.* London: Sage.

Tuckman, B. W. (1965). Developmental sequences in small groups. *Psychological Bulletin, 63,* 384–399.

United Way of America (1996). *Measuring program outcomes: A practical approach.* Alexandria, VA: Author.

University of Minnesota (1991). *Family education/ parent education licensure.* Department of Work, Family and Community Education.

USA snapshots: Young adult priorities. (1998, April 13). *USA Today.*

U.S. Bureau of the Census. (1996). *Statistical abstract of the United States* (116th ed.). Washington, DC: U.S. Government Printing Office.

U.S. Bureau of the Census. (1999). Selected characteristics of all persons [On-line]. Available: http://www.gov:80/population/socdemo/ancestry/All_persons.txt

Vanier Institute of the Family. (1971). *Report of family life education survey: Part 2. Family life education in the schools.* Ottawa: Author.

Vella, J. (1994). *Learning to listen, learning to teach: The power of dialogue in educating adults.* San Francisco: Jossey-Bass.

Vincent, C. E. (1973). *Sexual and marital health.* New York: McGraw-Hill.

Wandersman, L. P. (1987). New directions for parent education. In S. L. Kagan & E. F. Zigler (Eds.), *America's family support programs.* New Haven, CT: Yale University Press.

Weigley, E. S. (1976). The professionalization of home economics. *Home Economics Research Journal, 4*(4), 253–259.

Weiss, H. B., & Jacobs, F. H. (1988). *Evaluating family programs.* New York: Aldine DeGruyter.

Wertheimer, R., & Moore, K. (1998). Childbearing by teens: Links to welfare reform. *New federalism issues and options for states* (Series No. A-24). Washington, DC: The Urban Institute.

Whatley, A. E. (1973). Graduate students' perceptions of needed personal characteristics for family life educators. *The Family Coordinator, 22,* 193–198.

Wigger, J. B. (1998). Entangled in mystery: History and hopes for the Center for Congregations and Family Ministries. *Journal of Family Ministry, 12*(2), 13–28.

Williams, J. (1707). *The redeemed captive returning to Zion.* Boston: The Brick Shop.

Winton, C. A. (1995). *Frameworks for studying families.* Guilford, CT: Dushkin.

Wood, J. T. (1977). Leading in purposive discussions: A study of adaptive behavior. *Communication Monographs, 44,* 152–165.

Working Family Resource Center. (1999). Available: http://www.spps.org/wfrc/wfrc.html.

Yankeelov, P. A., & Garland, D. R. (1998). The families in our congregations: Initial research findings. *Family Ministry, 12*(3), 23–45.

Youcha, G. (1995). *Minding the children: Childcare in America from colonial times to the present.* New York: Scribner.

Ziglar, E. F., & Gilman, E. P. (1990). An agenda for the 1990's: Supporting families. In D. Blankenhorn, S. Bayme, & J. B. Elshtain (Eds.), *Rebuilding the nest: A new commitment to the American family* (pp. 237–250). Milwaukee, WI: Family Service America.

Zimmerman, S. L. (1995). *Understanding family policy: Theories and applications* (2nd ed.). Thousand Oaks, CA: Sage.

INDEX